GLOBALIZATIONS
AND
EDUCATION

Collected Essays on
Class, Race, Gender, and the State

GLOBALIZATIONS AND EDUCATION

Collected Essays on Class, Race, Gender, and the State

Carlos Alberto Torres

Foreword by Michael W. Apple
Afterword by Pedro Demo

Teachers College, Columbia University
New York and London

The chapters in this book have been reprinted from the following sources by permission of the original publishers:

Chapter 1: Torres, C. A. (1999). Critical theory and political sociology of education: Arguments. In T. J. Popkewitz & L. Fendler (Eds.), *Critical theories in education: Changing terrains of knowledge and politics* (pp. 87–115). New York: Routledge.

Chapter 2: Torres, C. A., & A. Puiggrós. (1997). The state and public education in Latin America. In C. A. Torres & A. Puiggrós (Eds.), *Latin American education: Comparative perspectives* (pp. 1–28). Boulder, CO: Westview Press.

Chapter 3: Torres, C. A. (1998). Democracy, education, and multiculturalism: Dilemmas of citizenship in a global world. *Comparative Education Review, 42*(4), 421–447.

Chapter 4: Torres, C. A. (2002). Globalization, education, and citizenship: Solidarity versus markets? *American Educational Research Journal, 39*(2), 363–378.

Chapter 5: Torres, C. A. (1994). Education and the archeology of consciousness: Hegel and Freire. *Educational Theory, 44*(4), 429–445.

Chapter 6: Torres, C. A. (1992). From *The pedagogy of the oppressed* to *A luta continua*: The political pedagogy of Paulo Freire. In P. McLaren & P. Leonard (Eds.), *Paulo Freire: A critical encounter* (pp. 119–145). London: Routledge.

Published by Teachers College Press, 1234 Amsterdam Avenue, New York, NY 10027

Copyright © 2009 by Teachers College, Columbia University

Library of Congress Cataloging-in-Publication Data

Torres, Carlos Alberto.
    Globalizations and education : collected essays on class, race, gender, and the state / Carlos Alberto Torres ; foreword by Michael W. Apple ; afterword by Pedro Demo.
       p. cm.
    Includes bibliographical references and index.
    ISBN 978-0-8077-4937-1 (pbk : alk. paper)
    ISBN 978-0-8077-4938-8 (hc : alk. paper)
       1. Education—Social aspects. 2. Education and globalization. 3. Education and state. 4. Critical pedagogy. I. Title.
    LC191.T578   2009
    306.43′2—dc22   2008042651

ISBN 978-0-8077-4937-1 (paper)
ISBN 978-0-8077-4938-8 (cloth)

Printed on acid-free paper
Manufactured in the United States of America

16   15   14   13   12   11   10   09   8   7   6   5   4   3   2   1

Contents

Foreword by Michael W. Apple   ix

    Education and Power   ix

    Globalization, Postcolonialism, and Education   xi

    Freire and Critical Education: A Personal Vignette   xiii

    The Critical Sociologist   xvi

    A Political Conclusion   xviii

**Introduction: The Scholarship of Class, Race,
Gender and the State in Education:
A Life Journey in the Political Sociology of Education**   1

    Why a Political Sociology of Education?   2

    Theories of the State and Education   8

    Paulo Freire's Political Philosophy of Education   14

    Education, Democracy, and Multiculturalism:
        Dilemmas of Citizenship in a Global World   18

    Teachers Unions and the State: Alternatives to Neoliberalism   20

    The Comparative Studies of Globalization and Education   25

    Epilogue   28

**1. Critical Theory and Political Sociology of Education:
Arguments**   33

    Critical Theory: Definitions   34

    A Political Sociology of Education:
        A Critical Modernist Perspective   40

    A Historical-Structural Perspective:
        The Dialectics of Policy Formation   41

Theories of the State and Educational Policy Formation   43

The Critique of Instrumental Reason   44

The Politicity of Education   48

Postmodernism and Multicentered Notions of Power   50

Weltanschauung and the Seduction of
    Ideology in Educational Policy Formation   51

Critical Theory, Critical Intellectuals, and a Political
    Sociology of Education: In the Guise of a Conclusion   56

2. **The State and Public Education in Latin America**   **63**
    WITH ADRIANA PUIGGRÓS

The State in Latin America:
    From the Oligarchical State to Neoliberalism   64

The Pedagogical Subject   73

Conclusion: Rethinking/Unthinking
    Latin American Education in Comparative Perspective   80

3. **Democracy, Education, and Multiculturalism:**
    Dilemmas of Citizenship in a Global World   **86**

The Theoretical Problem   86

Citizenship and Education   88

Democracy and Education   97

Democracy and Multiculturalism   99

Key Democratic Issues for a
    Democratic Multicultural Citizenship   101

Canon, Culture, and Democratic Multicultural Citizenship:
    Conclusions   104

4. **Globalization, Education, and Citizenship:**
    Solidarity Versus Markets?   **114**

The Phenomenon of Globalization   115

Citizenship: Sovereignty, Markets, and Human Rights   117

Citizens and Markets   117

Organized Solidarity and
    Human Rights Against the Markets?   121

Education in a Global Era: Questions and Queries   126

5. Education and the Archeology of Consciousness:
   Freire and Hegel   131

   The Dialectic of the Master and the Slave   134

   The Dialectic of the Pedagogy of the Oppressed   140

   Hegel on Freire: An Interdialectic Comparison   144

6. From *The Pedagogy of the Oppressed* to *A Luta Continua*:
   The Political Pedagogy of Paulo Freire   152

   The Latin American Background   152

   Paulo Freire's Political Philosophy   157

   The African Background   161

   The Last Freire: Brazil, 1980–91   170

   Are There Any Dark Clouds in the Sky? Final Remarks   172

Afterword by Pedro Demo   178

   Critical Vision   179

   Liberating Vision   181

   Multicultural Vision   183

   To Conclude   185

References   187

Index   209

About the Author   220

DEDICATION

My gratitude to my graduate students, who over the years inspired, challenged, and supported my work. They helped me to identify, redefine, and refine arguments, seeking new avenues in the quest for knowledge and praxis. A great deal of my own learning is owed to their friendship, energy, and inquisitive minds.

My friend and former student, Dr. Liliana Esther Olmos, deserves a very special mention. Her tireless, enthusiastic, and talented work as my Teaching Assistant, Research Assistant, and co-author over many years has been invaluable to me and to the UCLA–Paulo Freire Institute, where she has served as Program Officer.

I dedicate this book to my children, Carlos Alberto, Pablo Sebastián, Laura Silvina, and Ian, true sources of inspiration and love.

—Carlos Alberto Torres

Foreword

Michael W. Apple

EDUCATION AND POWER

I have known Carlos Alberto Torres for over 2 decades. He has been many things to me: interviewer, translator, political comrade, teacher, and friend. Over the course of our careers, Carlos and I have been dealing with very similar questions. We have both been deeply concerned about the relationship between culture and power, about the relationship among the economic, political, and cultural spheres (see Apple & Weis, 1983), about the multiple and contradictory dynamics of power and social movements that make education such a site of conflict and struggle, and about what all this means for educational work. Both of us are trying to answer a question that was put so clearly by George Counts (1932) when he asked "Dare the School Build a New Social Order?"

Counts was a person of his time and the ways he both asked and answered this question were a bit naive. But the tradition of radically interrogating schools and other pedagogic sites, of asking who benefits from their dominant forms of curricula, teaching, evaluation, and policy, of arguing about what they might do differently, and of asking searching questions of what would have to change in order for this to happen—all of this is what has worked through us. We stand on the shoulders of many others who have taken such issues seriously; and in a time of neoliberal attacks with their ensuing loss of collective memory, both of us hope to have contributed to the recovery of the collective memory of this tradition and to pushing it farther along conceptually, historically, empirically, and practically. Whereas I have focused much of my attention on formal institutions of schooling and on social movements that influence them, Carlos has devoted his attention to a variety of issues, with a special focus on nonformal and adult education.

Of course, no author does this by himself. This is a collective enterprise. And no one who takes these questions seriously can answer them fully or without contradictions or even wrong turns or mistakes. As a collective project, it is one in which we not only stand on the shoulders of those whose work we draw upon critically but also one in which thoughtful criticism of our work is essential to progress. Compelling arguments cannot be built unless they are subjected to the light of others' thoughtful analyses of the strengths and limits of our claims. Carlos Alberto Torres has been a key figure in these discussions and debates.

One of the guiding questions within the field of education is a deceptively simple one: What knowledge is of most worth? Over the past 4 decades, an extensive tradition has grown around a restatement of that question. Rather than "*What* knowledge is of most worth?" the question has become "*Whose* knowledge is of most worth?" (Apple, 1993, 1996, 2004). There are dangers associated with such a move, of course, including impulses toward reductionism and essentialism. However, the transformation of the question has led to immense progress in our understanding of the cultural politics of education in general and of the relations among educational policies, curricula, teaching, evaluation, and differential power. Indeed, some of the most significant work on the intimate connections between culture and power has come out of the area of the sociology of school knowledge and critical educational studies in general.

In the process of making the conceptual, historical, and empirical gains associated with this move, there has been an accompanying internationalization of the issues involved. Thus issues of the cultural assemblages associated with empire and previous and current imperial projects have become more visible. There has been an increasing recognition that critical educational studies must turn to issues of the global, of the colonial imagination, and to postcolonial approaches in order to come to grips with the complex and at times contradictory synchronic and diachronic relations between knowledge and power, between the state and education, and between civil society and the political imaginary.

For example, under the influences of a variety of critical works on the history of literacy and on the politics of popular culture (Raymond Williams's work was crucial historically here; see Williams, 1961, 1977; Apple, 2004), as in a number of other fields, it became ever clearer to those of us in education that the very notion of the canon of "official knowledge" had much of its history in a conscious attempt to "civilize" both the working class and the "natives" of an expanding empire (Apple, 1993). The very idea of teaching the "other" was a significant change, of course. For many years in Europe and Latin America, for example, the fear of working-class and "peasant" literacy was very visible. This will be more than a little familiar to those with an interest in the history of the relationship among books, literacy, and popular movements. Books themselves, and one's ability to read them, have been inherently caught up in cultural politics. Take the case of Voltaire, that leader of the Enlightenment who so wanted to become a member of the nobility. For him, the Enlightenment should begin with the "grands." Only when it had captured the hearts and minds of society's commanding heights could it concern itself with the masses below. But, for Voltaire and many of his followers, one caution should be taken very seriously: One should take care to prevent the masses from learning to read (Darnton, 1982, p. 130). This of course was reinscribed in often murderous ways in the prohibitions against teaching enslaved peoples how to read (although there is new historical evidence that documents that many enslaved people who were brought to the Americas were Moslem and may already have been literate in Arabic).

Such changes in how education and literacy were thought about did not simply happen accidentally. They were (and are) the result of struggles over who has the right to be called a person, over what it means to be educated, over what counts as official or legitimate knowledge, and over who has the authority to speak to these issues (Apple, 1993). And these struggles need to be thought about using a range of critical tools, among them analyses based on theories of the state, of globalization, of the postcolonial, and so much more. But none of this is or will be easy. In fact, our work may be filled with contradictions. Take, for instance, the recent (and largely justifiable) attention being given to issues of globalization and postcolonialism in critical education, issues to which Carlos Alberto Torres has significantly contributed.

GLOBALIZATION, POSTCOLONIALISM, AND EDUCATION

At the outset, let me be honest: I no longer have any idea what the words *globalization* and *postcolonial* mean. They have become "sliding signifiers," concepts with such a multiplicity of meanings that their actual meaning in any given context can only be determined by their use. As Wittgenstein (1963) and others reminded us, language can be employed to do an impressive array of things. It can be used to describe, illuminate, control, legitimate, mobilize, and many other things. For example, the language of postcolonialism(s)—the plural is important—has many uses. However, all too often it has become something of a "ceremonial slogan," a word that is publicly offered so that the reader may recognize that the author is au courant in the latest linguistic forms. When used in this way, its employment by an author is largely part of the conversion strategies so well captured by Bourdieu in *Distinction* (1984) and *Homo Academicus* (1988). Linguistic and cultural capital are performed publicly to gain mobility within the social field of the academy. In my most cynical moments, I worry that this is at times all too dominant within the largely White academy.

But, of course, the postcolonial experience(s)—and again, the plural is important—and the theories of globalization that have been dialectically related to them are also powerful ways of critically engaging with the politics of empire and with the ways in which culture, economy, and politics all interact globally and locally in complex and overdetermined ways. Indeed, the very notions of postcolonialism and globalization "can be thought of as a site of dialogic encounter that pushes us to examine center/periphery relations and conditions with specificity, wherever we may find them" (Dimitriadis & McCarthy, 2001, p. 7). It is to Carlos Alberto Torres's credit that his work provides important assistance to all of us in understanding what this means.

As they have influenced critical educational scholarship, some of the core politics behind postcolonial positions are summarized well by Dimitriadis and McCarthy (2001) when they state that "the work of the postcolonial imagination subverts extant power relations, questions authority, and destabilizes received traditions of identity" (p. 10; see also Bhabha, 1994; Spivak, 1988). Many of the chapters included in this book provide exemplary instances of this point.

Educators interested in globalization, in neoliberal depredations, and in postcolonial positions have largely taken them to mean one or more of the following: They imply a conscious process of repositioning, of "turning the world upside down" (Young, 2003, p. 2). They mean that the world is seen relationally—as being made up of relations of dominance and subordination and of movements, cultures, and identities that seek to interrupt these relations. They also mean that if you are someone who has been excluded by the "West's" dominant voices geographically, economically, politically, and/or culturally or you are inside the West but not really part of it, then "postcolonialism offers you a way of seeing things differently, a language and a politics in which your interests come first, not last" (Young, 2003, p. 2). Some of the best work in the field of education mirrors Robert Young's more general claim that postcolonialism and the global sensitivities that accompany it speak to a politics and a "philosophy of activism" that involve contesting these disparities. It extends the anticolonial struggles that have such a long history and asserts ways of acting that challenge "Western" ways of interpreting the world (p. 4). This is best stated by Young (2003) in the following statements:

> Above all, postcolonialism seeks to intervene, to force its alternative knowledges into the power structures of the west as well as the non–west. It seeks to change the way people think, the way they behave, to produce a more just and equitable relation between different people of the world. (p. 7)

Postcolonialism . . . is a general name for those insurgent knowledges that come from the subaltern, the dispossessed, and seek to change the terms under which we all live. (p. 20)

Of course, what Young says about postcolonialism is equally true about theories of globalization. The essays collected in this book document one person's consistent attempt to understand what these positions actually mean intellectually and politically.

Of course, as Carlos knows, in the Americas and elsewhere the positions inspired by, say, postcolonialism are not actually especially new in education. Even before the impressive and influential work of the great Brazilian educator, Paulo Freire (1970b), subaltern groups had developed counterhegemonic perspectives and an extensive set of ways of interrupting colonial dominance in education and in cultural struggles in general (see, e.g., Jules, 1991; Lewis, 1993, 2000; Livingston, 2003; Wong, 2002). But the fact that theories of globalization and postcolonialism are now becoming more popular in critical educational studies is partly due to the fact that the field itself in the United States and throughout Latin America has a very long tradition of engaging in analyses of hegemonic cultural form and content and in developing oppositional educational movements, policies, and practices (see, e.g., Apple, 2004, 2006a; Apple & Buras, 2006), a tradition that Carlos has tracked and has helped build. But, as Carlos shows in such a clear and very detailed manner, the place that Freire has as both an activist in and theorist of these movements is unparalleled.

Reading Torres on Freire is more than a reminder of the past. It points to the continuing significance of Freire and Freirean–inspired work for large numbers of people throughout the world. While some have rightly or wrongly challenged the Freirean tradition and argued against a number of its tendencies (see, e.g., Au & Apple, 2007), the tradition out of which he came, that he developed throughout his life, and that continues to evolve is immensely resilient and powerful. Like Carlos, I, too, had a history of interacting with Paulo Freire. This is one of the reasons that Carlos's reflections about Paulo and about his work seem so thoughtful to me. I hope that you will forgive me if I add a personal example of my own here, one that ratifies the respect Carlos has for the man and his ideas.

FREIRE AND CRITICAL EDUCATION: A PERSONAL VIGNETTE

After delayed flights, I finally arrived in São Paulo. The word *exhausted* didn't come close to describing how I felt. But a shower and some rest weren't on the agenda. We hadn't seen each other for a while, and Paulo was waiting for me to continue our ongoing discussions about what was happening in São Paulo now that he was Secretary of Education there. It may surprise some people to know that, unlike Carlos Alberto Torres, I was not influenced greatly by Paulo Freire, at least not originally. I came out of a radical laborist and antiracist tradition in the United States that had developed its own critical pedagogic forms and methods of interruption of dominance. I had immense respect for him, however, even before I began going to Brazil in the mid–1980s to work with teachers unions and the Worker's Party. Perhaps it was the fact that my roots were in a different, but still very similar, set of radical traditions that made our public discussions so vibrant and, certainly for me, as with Carlos, compelling.

There were some areas where Freire and I disagreed. Indeed, I can remember the look of surprise on people's faces during one of our public dialogues when I supportively yet critically challenged some of his positions. And I can all too vividly remember the time when I had just gotten off those delayed flights and he and I quickly went to our scheduled joint seminar before a large group that had been waiting for us to arrive. The group was made up of the militants and progressive educators he had brought to work with him at the Ministry of Education offices in São Paulo. During the joint seminar, I worried out loud about some of the tactics that were being used to convince teachers to follow some of the ministry's policies. While I agreed with the ministry's agenda and was a very strong supporter of Paulo's nearly Herculean efforts, I said that—as a former president of a teachers union and as someone who had worked with teachers in Brazil for a number of years—there was a risk that the tactics being employed could backfire. He looked directly at me and said that he and I clearly disagreed about this.

The audience was silent, waiting—for distress, for "point scoring," for a break in our friendship? Instead what happened was one of the most detailed and intense discussions I have ever had in my life. For nearly 3 hours, we ranged over an entire terrain: theories about epistemologies; the realities of teachers' lives; the realities of life in favelas; the politics of race and gender that needed to be dealt with seriously alongside class; the international and Brazilian economy; rightist media attacks on critical education in Brazil and on him personally; the strategies needed to interrupt dominance in the society and in the daily lives of schools; his criticisms of my criticisms of their strategies; my suggestions for better tactics; and the list could on and on.

This wasn't a performance in masculinities, as so many public debates are. This was something that demonstrated to me once again why, like Carlos, I respected Paulo so much. There was no sense of "winning" or "losing" here. As the chapters in the book you are about to read demonstrate, Paulo was fully engaged, wanting to think publicly, enjoying both the richness of our dialogue and our willingness (stimulated constantly by him) to enter into a field that required that we bring in *all* that we knew and believed. For him, and for me and Carlos, education required the best of our intellectual and emotional resources. I'm not certain we ultimately resolved our disagreements. I know that I was taken with his passion and his willingness to listen carefully to my worries, worries based on my previous experiences with political/educational mobilization in other nations.

I also know that he took these issues very seriously (see, e.g., Apple, 1999). Perhaps a measure of this can be seen when, after that 3-hour dialogue that seemed to go by in a flash, he had to leave for another meeting that had been delayed because of our discussion. As he and I said our good-byes, he asked the audience to stay. He then asked me if I could stay for as long as it took so that the audience and I could continue the discussion at a more practical level. What could be done to deal with the concerns I had? Were there ways in which the people from the ministry and from the communities that were in the audience might lessen the risk of alienating teachers and some community members? What strategies might be used to create alliances over larger issues, even when there might be some disagreements over specific tactics and policies?

It is a measure of Paulo's ability as a leader and as a model of how critical dialogue could go on, that another 2 hours went by with truly honest and serious discussion that led to creative solutions to a number of problems that were raised as people reflected on their experiences in favelas and in the ministry. This to me is the mark of a truly great teacher. Even when he wasn't there, his emphasis on honestly confronting the realities we faced, on carefully listening, on using one's lived experiences to think critically about that reality and how it might be changed—all of this remained a powerful presence.

This was not the only time Paulo and I engaged with each other. We had a number of such discussions in front of large audiences. Indeed, in preparation for writing the introduction to this book and after reading the chapters that Carlos Alberto Torres has included about Freire, I took out the tape of one of our public interactions to listen to it. It reminded me that what I've said here can't quite convey the personal presence and humility Paulo had. Nor can it convey how he brought out the best in me and others. One of the markers of greatness is how one deals with disagreement. And here, once again, Paulo demonstrated how special he was, thus giving us one more reason that Paulo—friend, teacher, comrade—is still missed. It also makes clear why Carlos Alberto Torres justifiably devotes so much attention to him in this book.

THE CRITICAL SOCIOLOGIST

But Carlos is not simply a follower of Freire, to say the least. He is a critical political sociologist of education, with his own major contributions
and affiliations. And a critical sociology is always grounded in two key
questions: (1) Sociology for whom? and (2) Sociology for what? (Burawoy,
2005). The first asks us to think about repositioning ourselves so that we
see the world through the eyes of the dispossessed. The second asks us
to connect our work to the complex issues surrounding a society's moral
compass, its means and ends.

For many people, their original impulses toward critical scholarship in
education were fueled by a passion for social justice, economic equality,
human rights, sustainable environments, an education that is worthy of its
name—in short a better world. Yet this is increasingly difficult to maintain
in the situation in which so many of us find ourselves. Ideologically and
politically, much has changed. The early years of the twenty-first century
have brought us unfettered capitalism that fuels market tyrannies and
massive inequalities on a truly global scale (Davis, 2006). "Democracy"
is resurgent at the same time, but it all too often becomes a thin veil for
the interests of the globally and locally powerful and for disenfranchisement, mendacity, and national and international violence (Burawoy, 2005,
p. 260). The rhetoric of freedom and equality may have intensified, but
there is unassailable evidence that there is ever-deepening domination
and inequality and that earlier gains in education, economic security, civil
rights, and more are either being washed away or are under severe threat.
The religion of the market (and it does function like a religion, since it does
not seem to be amenable to empirical critiques) coupled with very different visions of what the state can and should do can be summarized in one
word—*neoliberalism* (Burawoy, 2005). Carlos is crystal clear about what
this has meant for Latin America and elsewhere.

At the same time, in the social field of power called the "academy"—
with its own hierarchies and disciplinary (and disciplining) techniques,
the pursuit of academic credentials, bureaucratic and institutional rank-
ings, tenure files, indeed, the entire panoply of normalizing pressures surrounding institutions and careers—all of this seeks to ensure that we all
think and act "correctly." Yet the original impulse is never quite entirely
vanquished (Burawoy, 2005). The spirit that animates critical work can
never be totally subjected to rationalizing logics and processes. Try as the
powerful might, it will not be extinguished—and it certainly remains alive
in this book.

What Michael Burawoy (2005) has called "organic public sociology"
provides key elements here. In this view the critical sociologist works

in close connection with a visible, thick, active, local, and often counter–
public. . . . with a labor movement, neighborhood association, communities
of faith, immigrant rights groups, human rights organizations. Between the
public sociologist and a public is a dialogue, a process of mutual education.
. . . The project of such [organic] public sociologies is to make visible the
invisible, to make the private public, to validate these organic connections
as part of our sociological life. (p. 265)

Grounded in a Habermasian vision of reciprocity and communicative
action (Habermas, 1984), dialogic relations between the critical sociologist
and varied publics then become one of the central ways in which one's
work is validated and makes an impact. This Habermasian vision, coupled
with a clear sense of being an organic public sociologist, is what seems to
guide Carlos's work as a critical scholar and critical educator.

This act of becoming (and this is a project, for one is never finished, always becoming) a critical scholar is a complex one. Because of this, let me
extend my earlier remarks about the role of critical research in education.
In general, there are five tasks in which critical analysis (and the critical
analyst) in education must engage (Apple, 2006b):

1. It must "bear witness to negativity." That is, one of its primary
   functions is to illuminate the ways in which educational policy
   and practice are connected to the relations of exploitation and
   domination—and to struggles again such relations—in the
   larger society.
2. In engaging in such critical analyses, it also must point to
   contradictions and to spaces of possible action. Thus its aim
   is to critically examine current realities with a conceptual-
   political framework that emphasizes the spaces in which
   counterhegemonic actions can be or are now going on.
3. At times, this also requires a redefinition of what counts as
   "research." Here I mean acting as "secretaries" to those groups
   of people and social movements who are now engaged in
   challenging existing relations of unequal power or in what
   elsewhere has been called "nonreformist reforms" (Apple,
   1995, 2003; Apple & Beane, 2007).
4. In the process, critical work has the task of keeping traditions
   of radical work alive. In the face of organized attacks on the
   "collective memories" of difference and struggle, attacks that
   make it increasingly difficult to retain academic and social
   legitimacy for multiple critical approaches that have proven
   so valuable in countering dominant narratives and relations,
   it is absolutely crucial that these traditions be kept alive,

renewed, and, when necessary, criticized for their conceptual, empirical, historical, and political silences or limitations. This includes not only keeping theoretical, empirical, historical, and political traditions alive but, very importantly, extending and (supportively) criticizing them. And it also involves keeping alive the dreams, utopian visions, and "nonreformist reforms" that are so much a part of these radical traditions (Jacoby, 2005; Teitelbaum, 1993).

5. Finally, critical educators must *act* in concert with the progressive social movements their work supports or in movements against the rightist assumptions and policies they critically analyze. Thus scholarship in critical education or critical pedagogy does imply becoming an "organic intellectual" in the Gramscian sense of that term (Gramsci, 1971). One must participate in and give one's expertise to movements surrounding struggles over what Nancy Fraser (1997) has called a "politics of redistribution" and a "politics of recognition." This implies that the role of the "unattached intelligentsia" (Mannheim, 1936), someone who "lives on the balcony" (Bakhtin, 1968), is not an appropriate model. As Bourdieu (2003, p. 11) reminds us, for example, our intellectual efforts are crucial, but they "cannot stand aside, neutral and indifferent, from the struggles in which the future of the world is at stake."

These five tasks are demanding and no one person can engage equally well in all of them simultaneously. The chapters collected in this book, as well as his extensive other work, represent Carlos Alberto Torres's continuing attempt to come to grips with the complex intellectual, personal, and political tensions and activities that respond to the demands of this role.

A POLITICAL CONCLUSION

In light of this point about the importance of connections to movements, let me end my introductory remarks with another personal story, this one about something more specific that both Carlos and I experienced. A number of years ago, we were in Buenos Aires together. I was giving a series of lectures there and Carlos had graciously agreed to act as my translator. It was a highly charged situation politically, economically, and ideologically.

And there was a good deal of politics, tension, and anticipation surrounding what everyone knew would be the issues upon which I was going to focus.

An added element made this situation even more tense. The public universities in Buenos Aires were on strike over yet another round of neoliberal attacks on higher education. The government was imposing ever larger fees on students. We all knew that the ultimate effects of such fees would be the educational disenfranchisement of large numbers of poor and working-class students. Universities would become even more the bastions of those who could afford to go to them. There was to be a large demonstration against the government. Carlos and I were honored by an invitation to march with the students and faculty to the square in front of the Argentinian Congress. We were very near the front when government-sponsored provocateurs engaged in violence. Predictably, the police attacked with tear gas and clubs. This wasn't the first time I had been gassed, nor was it the last. Yet anyone who is truly honest about this knows that each time it brings forth that unromantic emotion called fear. The task is to face reality and what can happen squarely in the face, to not let the worry rule, and to go forward collectively.

Throughout that night, with the mobilization, the march, the attack, and its aftermath in the days that followed, it was clear from Carlos's own actions that he was also deeply committed to causes with which we both agreed. I learned much about Carlos as we together acted in concert with those whose very lives were being radically changed by neoliberal attacks on the gains in education that had taken decades to win. This too is one of the reasons I respect his work as a well-known critical scholar. It is another reason that makes this book of essays definitely worth reading.

The Scholarship of Class, Race, Gender and the State in Education

A Life Journey in the Political Sociology of Education

This book provides the reader with a selection from my collected works, synthesizing my research and learning over 3 decades in the development of a political sociology of education. For critical theorists, research cannot be separated from political struggle; hence scholarship and activism are inevitably part and parcel of our life journey. Paulo Freire argued that politics and education cannot be easily separated. The same applies to scholarship and political struggle which cannot be easily dissociated, not even for purely didactic purposes. We conduct research and teaching to change the world, not simply to observe as the detached scientist what happens around us or to manipulate knowledge as social *alquimia* or as social engineering. Critical scholars do not share with technocrats the illusion that manipulating knowledge, using technocratic means and the stern application of instrumental rationality, will solve most if not all the problems of education.

The primary contribution of my scholarly work has been the development of a political sociology of education, trying to understand how education (particularly nonformal education, adult education, and popular education) contributes to social change, national development, and the betterment of individuals and families. In doing so, I have tried to reconciled the scholarship of discovery with the scholarship of integration and the scholarship of intervention, always guided by a research agenda which has been historically an exploration, at a theoretical level, of issues and questions in the scholarship of race, class, gender, and the state in education (see Torres, 1991b).

During the past 3 decades my work has been guided by the following question: How, in the field of nonformal education and schooling, are educational policies related to the overall process of political legitimation and capital accumulation developed by the capitalist states, in Latin America and internationally?

My conceptual and empirical analysis has focused in particular on three issues:

- Understanding through a political sociology of education why a given educational policy is created, planned, constructed, and implemented; who the most relevant actors are in its formulation and operationalization; and what historical-structural, systemic, symbolic, and organizational processes are involved from its origins to the implementation and evaluation of the policy.
- Understanding and analyzing the specific characteristics of the *dependent state* in Latin America insofar as they apply to educational policy formation; that is to say, how the nature and legitimacy needs of the dependent state conditions the nature of policy formation in nonformal education settings.[1]
- Identifying and analyzing what alternatives, if any, have been developed in Latin America from perspectives other than compensatory legitimation—for example, alternatives to state policy making in nonformal education. From a critical theory perspective, this issue relates to the work of Brazilian educator and philosopher Paulo Freire, his proposal for a "pedagogy of the oppressed" as emancipatory education, and his contribution to critical pedagogy.

While I discuss each of these bodies of work separately in the next sections, they are conceptually and historically linked.

WHY A POLITICAL SOCIOLOGY OF EDUCATION?

The first focus of my work is the development of a political sociology of education. Though a political sociology of education has intimate connections with a sociology of education in the conventional sense (with questions of equity, efficiency, equality, mobility, and so on), its center of attention is an emphasis on questions of power, influence, and authority, and its goal is to explain the process of decision making and educational planning at several levels.

Through a political sociology of education, I seek to explain public policy formation in education by bringing together analyses of the decision-making process with problems in policy implementation and evaluation of policy results. In addition, I seek to explore innovations in adult education as a way to enhance conventional policy making and implementation in Latin America. This theoretical work in the political sociology of education includes a book with Raymond Morrow entitled *Social Theory and Education: A Critique of Theories of Social and Cultural Reproduction* (Morrow & Torres, 1995). The research reported in this book and in a variety of articles and chapters is a comprehensive survey, critique, and expansion of the literature published in Western Europe, Canada, the United States, Australia, New Zealand, and Latin America on sociology of education and social reproduction in the last three decades (e.g., see Carnoy & Torres, 1992; Gadotti & Torres, 1992; Torres, 1990b, 1995b, 1999).

Using the notion of a political sociology of education with a focus on the relationships among education, power, and the state, my research agenda offers a conceptual and synthetic review of the notion of social and cultural reproduction in education and advances new directions for theoretical and empirical research in the sociology of education. Theories of social and cultural reproduction rest on the argument that schools primarily reproduce the functions required by the economic system. Thus, rather than providing a tool for changing society by reducing inequalities, schools reproduce and legitimate the social order. After a careful synthesis, analysis, and criticisms of several sociological theories, including functionalism, structuralism, system theories, and Marxism, my colleagues and I have advanced an agenda for research and policy, including discussions of the interactions among class, gender, race, and social reproduction in the context of the postmodernist critique. Let me explain in detail why I consider this research agenda so important in the context of contemporary sociological debates on schooling.

In the last few years, Morrow and I have attempted a reconstruction of theories of social and cultural reproduction in education from closed structuralist models based on economic and class determination to relatively open ones based on parallel determinations stemming from class, gender, and race. It is argued that this shift in reproduction theories took place largely within the context of critical modernist theory, even though more recently in response to postmodernist critiques. The original formulation of reproduction theories is based on the *correspondence principle*—that is, the assumption of a strong structural link (isomorphism) between economic and educational structures. We argue that despite the criticism of economy-based models in sociology of education and political economy of education, the general notion of social and cultural reproduction has remained a central assumption of critical sociologies of schooling. To be sure, this has required fundamental revisions of social and cultural reproduction theories involving both the incorporation of concepts of agency and resistance, along with the diversification of the causal nexus of power to include nonclass forms of exclusion and domination. As well, the metatheoretical status of such theorizing has shifted from a functionalist structuralism to that of a more fallibilistic, historically specific, and comparative structural method.

Two broad shifts can be identified as contributing to the reorientation of debates in these domains and in social theory generally. The first shift—visible by the end of 1970s—involved primarily immanent forms of self-criticism and was initially associated with theories of social and cultural reproduction in relation to theories of social inequality and stratification and theories of the state. The outcome was a move away from the correspondence principle. Subsequent developments in theories of educational reproduction, however, have also expanded the points of reference of the forms of social relations reproduced that are the target of social criticism, especially to gender and race as autonomous principles of structuration of social action and domination.

The second shift (often interrelated with the first) involved a broader intellectual phenomenon associated with the notion of postmodernism (and the related, further radicalization of the methodological problematic of poststructuralism): a calling into question of aspects of all modernist conceptions of social theory, knowledge, and cultural change, not simply those associated with classical functionalism. The consequence has been a critique that provides fundamental challenge for the modernist impulses (i.e., enlightenment critique) behind the overall project of theoretical representation shared by all forms of reproduction theory (i.e., whether associated with the conflict or functionalist traditions, or whether voiced in the name of class, race, or gender).

Our argument builds on a systematic criticism of social theory resting on a metatheoretical framework, and is built on three related claims with respect to these theoretical transformations (see Morrow & Torres, 1994). First, though the actual term "reproduction" has often tended to slip out of sight, we suggest that the basic problematic of social and cultural reproduction remains a central preoccupation of critical theories of the relationships between schooling and society. Second, a new model, the *parallelist strategies*—social action as the product of parallel determinations of social action stemming from class, gender, and race—while highly sensitive to history, agency, and social practices, still employs structuralist methodological strategies, thus remaining within the realm of theories of social and cultural reproduction. However, the parallelist models have effectively encouraged the exploration of the independent effects of class, gender, and race, and other forms of domination in the context of schooling. Third, despite their analytical progress, the parallelist models have failed to address adequately three fundamental issues: (a) Each of these forms of domination has a significantly different systemic character with crucial consequences for their conceptualization as forms of domination; (b) the analysis of the interplay of these "variables" has been obscured by the language of "relative autonomy" left over from structuralist Marxism;[2] and (c) even though the explanatory objectives of parallelist reproduction theory are necessarily more modest and historically contingent than envisioned by classic structuralist reproduction theories, this still involves avoidance of the postmodernist tendency to endlessly fragment and pluralize conflicts and differences as if there were no systematic links among them.

These new, emerging perspectives in sociology of education have been clearly documented in a book that I edited with Ted Mitchell (Torres & Mitchell, 1998), and three elements stand out. First is the emergence of the new epistemological approaches, which sharply differ from positivism and empiricism. Second, the new sociology of education is pressed to confront the dilemmas posed by the dichotomy of modernism and postmodernism, or poststructuralist forms of theoretical representation, and its implications for the scholarship of class, race, and gender. Finally, these new theoretical developments pose new risks and challenges for educational research, and particularly for the future of public education in the United States and elsewhere.

Several lessons are drawn from the studies presented in this book. First, at the level of the empirical argumentation, it is unclear that the picture that several right-wing and some left-wing critics of public education paint of the all-embracing crisis of schooling is entirely adequate. The research has shown convincing empirical evidence that there is plenty of knowledge acquisition and creative work going on in the schools. Hence schools appear as segmented, with excellent schools working side by side with schools doing very poorly in scholastic terms. This segmentation is both inter- and intra-schools. Similarly, there is evidence that while resistance to cultural knowledge may prevail in several schools settings, this process of resistance is not simply a process of rejecting mainstream forms of knowledge. Resistance processes help to constitute people's identities, helping them in many ways to negotiate the complexity of capitalist society, beyond the contributions of reading, writing, and arithmetic. Alas, this production of knowledge takes place in a contested terrain. Thus educational policies and practices emerge as a convoluted mixture where students' and teachers' resistance, emancipatory practices, bureaucratic behavior, and the ideological norms all intersect in different ways, at different times, and for different purposes. It is unclear then, whether the picture that standard criticism of schooling (e.g., no learning, wastage of resources, and so on) accurately describes what goes on in schools and classrooms in America, and elsewhere for that matter.

Second, if there are empirical questions about knowledge acquisition, citizenship training, and human capital formation in schools, then at least what can be said about the arguments is that they rest on a set of generalizations that can be questioned in a democratic conversation about schooling. Although realizing the importance of processes of discrimination and cultural and social reproduction, I want to reassert the centrality of politics in education, considering many of the criticisms to public schools as perhaps too catastrophic.

Third, at a political and practical level, it is clear that scholars and activists struggling to defend public education from the attacks of traditionalists, the New Right, advocates of fundamentalist education, vouchers advocates, anti-multiculturalist forces, and so on, find plenty of room for social reform, social transformation, and the implementation of innovative models of teaching and learning as described in recent contributions to the reform of public education.

Another important direction of my research has been my analysis of adult education as compensatory legitimization (Arnove & Torres, 1996; Torres, 1989b, 1996; Torres, Pannu, & Kazim Bacchus, 1993; Torres & Schugurensky, 1993, 1994, 1995). I have argued for the last decade or so that adult education policy is usually oriented to prepare people for the secondary labor markets, where job stability is limited, income low and fragmented, social benefits scarce or nonexistent, and the supply of barely qualified labor very abundant. Likewise, I have shown that adult education has been usually co-opted by the state and employed as an instrument of social legitimation and the extension of state authority more than as a tool for self-reliance of individuals and communities in the poor segments of the Latin American and Third World societies.

In this comparative and cross-cultural research, I analyzed the role and purposes of adult education policy by discussing six rationales for policy making. These rationales, when transformed into policy, may take the form of constitutional prescriptions, investment in human capital, political socialization, compensatory legitimation, international pressures, and social movements. Drawing from critical theory and research in adult education in Canada and developing countries, I concluded that despite the rhetoric underlying a particular policy narrative, the dominant logic among policy makers in adult education is instrumental rationality, and the dominant *weltanschauung* in adult education policy planning is technocratic thinking. Discussing the notion of instrumental rationality as developed by Weber—that is, the rule of impersonal economic forces and bureaucratic administration—I have documented how the ideology of the welfare state has resulted in a depoliticization of policy makers' views regarding the social world. While the notion of power is clearly expressed in the narratives of adult education policy makers, they have no conceptual expressions of emancipatory action or heuristic analyses of social action.[3] Let us take policy makers' language as an example. The language of policy makers tends to be technically aseptic and noncontroversial, borrowing conceptual categories from systems theories, human capital theories, and functionalist or neofunctionalist paradigms. Key dimensions in policy formation, such as social class differences, gender, and ethnic or racial discrimination, remain subdued in the narratives of policy makers. This is so because the sharper the conceptual categorization of a phenomenon, the more difficult it becomes to set policy that will accommodate multiple interests and incompatible goals within any organization.

With these concerns in mind, and using a political economy of adult education, I studied literacy training, adult basic education, and skill-upgrading programs in Alberta, Canada, in Mexico, and in Cuba, Nicaragua, Granada, and Tanzania. These societies were selected for comparison not only because they represent distinct political and economic experiences but also because all of them have developed innovative and quality programs in adult education. Through a comparison of state-sponsored programs, and an analysis of opinions, aspirations, and expectations of policy makers, teachers, and adult learners, Daniel Schugurensky and I identified three different models of adult education policy: a "therapeutical model" in Canada, a "recruitment model" in Mexico, and a "forced modernization" model in Tanzania.

Our analytical and empirical research shows that in the Canadian therapeutical model the state is a benefactor, and the problem of poverty and illiteracy are see seen either as the result of temporary economic dislocations that may be adjusted through market mechanisms or as the result of individual deficits in skills or attitudes that may be addressed through instructional means. The role of the experts is to determine the nature of the training given to the individuals, who should be integrated into the job market as soon as possible. Teachers are professionals and enjoy great autonomy in the programs. In the Mexican recruitment model the emphasis is on a constant and active attraction of large numbers of learners to adult education programs. The rationale seems to be the incorporation of a disenfranchised clientele into the dominant political model. Teachers are mainly volunteers and follow textbooks designed by central agencies. In this model, the main concern is not the quality of learning but the recruitment and massive control of large numbers of people who otherwise could remain outside the corporatist channels of political participation. Finally, in Tanzania's forced modernization model the emphasis is placed on capital accumulation through the implementation of modern agricultural techniques and, therefore, on increasing Tanzania's integration into the world market economy. Such a model is resisted both by women who produce for home consumption and by young males whose main interest in attending adult education programs is to get employment in urban areas and leave the rural enclaves.

The three models show common traits that are surprising considering the diversity of living conditions, state structures, and political philosophies in each society. First, all three models are nonparticipative, where social and political issues and issues that may bring conflict into the operation of adult education services are ignored or perceived exclusively as problems that may be fixed through technical measures. Second, in all three societies, adult education is a clear instrument of the state contributing to capital accumulation and political legitimation practices, neglecting any emancipatory practices that may empower learners or communities. Third, in all three models, literacy training is irrelevant and marginal, isolated from productive work and skill upgrading programs. Fourth, in the absence of participatory organizational structures and practices, a top-down decision-making system prevails. Despite the operation of three different models of adult education oriented by fairly different political and philosophical values, in all of them there are few opportunities for the learners or community to participate in policy making. Fifth, teachers generally have no training in adult education. In Canada, highly professional teachers trained to work with children and youth have a patronizing and paternalistic attitude regarding adult learners. In Mexico and Tanzania, paraprofessional and poorly trained teachers present high rates of job turnover and absenteeism, which in turn lead to high student dropout rates. Last, there is evidence that in Canada, Mexico, and Tanzania, adult education programs are organized in a two-track system: a more prestigious one that focuses on programs for upgrading skills, and a marginal one that emphasizes adult basic education and literacy training (see Torres, 1989b, 1991c, 1996 1998c; Torres & Schugurensky, 1993).

THEORIES OF THE STATE AND EDUCATION

A second focus of my empirical work has been to study the complexities of the relationships of education to the state in the context of development (and underdevelopment) and social change in Latin America in comparative perspective. This research, eventually, grew to apply theories of the state to understand the complexities of the interactions of class, race, gender, and religion in education, and the complexity of the interplay between power, money, influence, and interest in policy formation and educational reform in comparative perspective.

A focus on the state is important because I have argued in my research that the nature of educational change is related to the nature of the state. The *state* can be defined as the totality of the political authority in a given society. In Latin America, political authority implies the capacity to impose a course of action by means of a decision-making process in societies that are highly heterogeneous and characterized by very contradictory interests. As an expression of a given political coalition and/or alliance of groups and classes, the democratic state is in itself an actor but, at the same time, an arena where political struggles "have the potential to constantly reshape lines of political conflict or coalition" (Block, 1987, p. 17). While the state represents the basic pact of domination that exists between social classes or factions of the dominant classes and the norms that guarantee its domination over the subordinate groups, at the same time the state is a self-regulating administrative system, an organization that produces a system of selective and self-regulating rules. As Vincent (1987) describes it, "The state is a public power above both ruler and ruled which provides order and continuity to the polity" (p. 218).

The basic tenet of my analysis is that the nature of educational change is related to the nature of the state, more so in Latin America. I have used the notion of compensatory legitimation to refer to the need of the state to cope with a deficit of legitimacy in the overall system. This crisis of legitimation has several sources. One of the most important is the disparity between growing social demands on welfare policies and diminishing fiscal revenues to meet those demands. To confront the crisis of legitimation, the state calls upon scientific and technical knowledge and expertise, increasing policies of participation, and legalization of educational policies with a growing role for the judicial system in education. Therefore, education as compensatory legitimation implies that the state may use educational policies as a substitute for political rights and for increased material consumption while, simultaneously, creating a system of legitimacy beliefs, which will assure the loyalty of its citizens.

Using a political sociology of nonformal education, I have discussed the following questions: What are the relationships among economy, politics, and education? How did the economic crises of the 1980s affect educational policy? How has educational research become entangled with international agendas—particularly the World Bank agenda—promoting a neoliberal model of policy making and setting of priorities. What lessons can be learned from the interaction between research and policy that may help in understanding the developmental role of education in the 1990s? I present here just a brief summary of my theoretical and empirical findings (see also Arnove, Torres, Franz, & Morse, 1996; Morrow & Torres, 2007; Torres, 1990a, 1999).

I argue that past efforts and available resources have made possible basic education for all children, helped to extend the years of schooling, provided early and preschool education, facilitated the access of disabled children to education, and improved the chances of the poor, migrants, girls, and indigenous children to attend public schools in Latin America. In addition to improving the equality of educational opportunities, schools have improved their overall capacity to retain students and even to promote them to higher education (see Torres, 2000b; Torres & Antikainen, 2003).

However, equality, quality (including effectiveness, equity, and efficiency) and relevance of educational provision in the region continue to be critical issues, especially now that Latin American states are financially pressed. Elementary and secondary schooling in the region continue to be segregated by class, with the poor attending public schools, and middle and upper classes attending private institutions. With few exceptions preschooling, decisive in shaping the cognitive structure of children, is not widely available for the children of the poor in the region. Illiteracy continues to plague educational planners, with the gender gap ever widening to the disadvantage of women. Illiteracy and the educational condition of the rural populations, particularly those of indigenous origin, continue to be pressing issues, with adult education remaining at the top of the agenda for policy making. *Popular education,* an indigenous paradigm of nonformal education developed in the region, is facing serious challenges in the context of postmodernism and post-Marxism in Latin America. Teachers' training, their political views and technical skills, continue to be central for educational reform in the region. Current social, political, and economic changes in Latin America underscore the pace, texture, and scope of educational development, educational quality, and the relevance of education. In this context, educational planners, children, youth, parents and communities deal with the implications of the lack of economic growth in the 1980s, the growing external debt, increasing fiscal constraints, and intended and unintended impacts of structural adjustment of economies and neoliberal states. Alas, the relationships between education and social change continue to be revisited by those seeking educational reform, but the challenges of poverty remain seemingly intractable for public policies—especially education—and democracy.

The research agenda presented in the special issue of *Comparative Education Review* (Torres & Puiggrós, 1995) and in my book with Puiggrós (Torres & Puiggrós, 1996) offers a relevant sample of the current research on Latin American education in comparative perspective. Throughout the different articles and chapters, the most relevant topics, research agendas, and some of the key theoretical and political problems of Latin American education are presented, discussed, and analyzed. In my work with Puiggrós I have emphasized that understanding the theoretical and political problems of Latin American education needs greater conceptual sophistication than traditional theories and methodologies in comparative education. Recent scholarship in the region incorporates concepts that may be employed in understanding the complexities of education, including the notions of unequal and combined development of Latin American educational systems, the notion of an organic crisis, the presence of new subjects of education, the role of the democratic state, and the presence of "fractures" and "borders" in modern education.

The notion of unequal and combined development suggests the intersection of pockets of modern, highly educated populations, including postmodernist expressions in art, humanities, and science, side by side with premodern, peripheral, marginal, and even pre-Columbian cultures and populations. These cultures are marked by deep cultural and linguistic discontinuities with the dominant cultural capital prevailing in schools and societies. Public schools were conceived by the state as central tools and tenets of a modernist discourse. Their goals were to produce a homogeneous citizenry and highly trained workers in the framework of an unequal and combined development of Latin America. Thus the Marxist concept of unequal and combined development popularized in the 1960s and 1970s, the emblematic notion of dependency utilized to assess the interconnections between external and domestic factors as a leitmotif of underdevelopment, and the notion of hybrid cultures—a cultural melange of mestizos, indigenous, and Spanish and/or Portuguese people that García Canclini (1982, 1990) so aptly has discussed in his anthropological studies—all point to the intersection of modern and traditional cultures. These modern and traditional cultures through constant cultural border crossings (Giroux, 1992) produce and reproduce new identities and the "asynchronic development of Latin American educational models" (Weinberg, 1984). Theoretically, the notion of multiple identities also relates to Dérrida's (1989) notion of *diférénce* and the feminist notion of "otherness," essential concepts to capture the magnitude of this unequal and combined cultural development in the region.

Puiggrós and Torres claim that it was Paulo Freire who very early in his "pedagogy of the oppressed" addressed the meanings of border crossings, otherness, hybrid cultures, and asynchronic development in Latin America. In so doing, he showed the political implications of pedagogical work. Freire argues that notions of oppression and domination are part and parcel of the pedagogical relationships between teachers and pupils in traditional classrooms. Thus the notion of *extensionism*, the provision of the dominant educational discourse to peasants in the context of agrarian reforms, was expressed not only as part and parcel of a pedagogical discourse but also as part and parcel of a political discourse. A fundamental insight of Freire is that the social and pedagogical subjects of education are not fixed, essential, or inflexible—that is, the teacher is a student and the student a teacher. The cultural and pedagogical implications are that the place and role of a teacher is not always and necessarily the extension of the role of adult White men, or conversely a role performed by a female teacher subsumed under the discourse of hegemonic masculinity.[4] Similarly, as a product of European logocentric thought, school knowledge is not always reproduced in schools, but is subject to contestation and resistance. While Freire criticized the Western school in Latin America as banking education and as an *authoritarian device*, that is, as a device transmitting official knowledge and at the same time eliminating pupils as subjects of their own education, his pedagogy of liberation invites a dialogue in the context of multiple political and social struggles for liberation. Dialogue appears not only as a pedagogical tool, but also as a method of deconstruction of the way pedagogical and political discourses are constructed.[5] More than 30 years after Freire's main books were published (see Freire, 1978a, 1978b; Torres, 1995a), the concept of dialogical education still appear as a democratic tool for dealing with complex cultural conflicts in the context of unequal and combined development of Latin American education.

The notion of crisis of hegemony implies also finding new concepts to take stock of the new subjects—teachers and pupils—in the new political and cultural formations emerging in Latin America (see Martín-Barbero, 1987a; Vilches, 1987). Similarly, it is important to understand how the crisis of hegemony relates to the problem of national identity; what role the state attributes to the school system and teachers' professional work; how the public/private cleavage in education is changing in the context of neoliberalism; and how the new social problems drastically depart from the social problems school systems faced in the past. These new social problems in Latin American education include, but are not limited to, the educational needs and the educational alternatives for street children, how the culture of drug trafficking is affecting educational establishments, and how private networks of communication and informatics are changing the status, reliability, and accessibility of school knowledge in the region (see Apple, 1993).

The concept of subjects refers to the notion of social and pedagogical subjects and their relationships with knowledge and structures. In Latin America the notion of a pedagogical and social subject (see Pereyra, 1988; Aguilar, 1990) involves an analysis of a complex cultural and social milieu that is the result of multiple parallel determinations, including class, gender, race, ethnicity, religion, and regionalisms (Morrow & Torres, 1995). At the same time, by placing the notion of the pedagogical subject at the center of competing educational discourses, it is possible to find a heuristic device to understand the complex determinations—actions and reactions—resulting from the decadence of the old political order (and their social agents). It also helps to understand the progressive breakdown of national identities while at the same time local and regional identities emerge as relevant in decision making and political and social struggles. Finally, the concept of subject is useful for exploring the disappearance of cultural and educational traditions in schools and societies.

The role of the conditioned state—the subject of my research in the last decade discussing the interactions between politics, political power, and educational policy in the region—continues to be problematic for democracy and public education in Latin America. While we have argued that the institutional identity of the state is crucial in understanding the role education has played in development and social change, the notion of the dependent or conditioned state helps in understanding not only the contradictions in public policy formation, but also the disparate roles and functions that the Latin American states play in the context of peripheral capitalism. Conditioned by the dynamic of metropolitan capitalism, the significant noncapitalist (although perhaps postfeudal) elements in its own political system, and the political alliance in power, the nature of the democratic state in the region continues to pose serious constraints to the political and economic democratization of civil societies. This is especially true when, despite the political shortcomings of the Latin American democracies and their limitations in endowments and resources, the liberal state in the region attempted to develop a system of public education that provided access and permanence to the system for vast sectors of the population, including the poor. The policy rational was clearly synthesized by Sarmiento's premise that the state should "educate the sovereign" (1956). A critical extension but also deconstruction of this premise emerged in the 1960s with the notion of a pedagogy of the oppressed, conscientization, and popular education. The current debate in the region is, on the one hand, whether the systematic withdraw of resources from public education under the political economy of neoliberalism has deeply affected the traditional educational role of the states, the performance of the systems vis-à-vis equality of educational opportunity and quality of education, and by implication the nature of the democratic pact. On the other hand, the prevailing theories and methodologies and the political-technical rationale for educational planning are seen as subsidiary to the main goals of neoliberalism (Torres, 2006).

These goals are currently expressed by international institutions like the IMF and World Bank with their political economy of conditionalities and policy preferences, but also are accepted and graciously implemented by neoliberal states in the region. In this context, many scholars, teachers, policy activists, and communities wonder whether the dynamics and dominant institutions of metropolitan capitalism are shaping the discourse and praxis of education in the region. The question is whether, given the process of globalization, these internationally induced policies are compatible with fundamental notions of democratic accountability, national sovereignty, and community empowerment. The question about the nature of the state and public policy is also a question about the future of public education in Latin America.

"Fractures" and "borders" in education refers to the way education is produced, and the way official knowledge is selected, organized, and hierarchically ranked in the curricula as well as to the nature of the prevailing pedagogical practices. Fractures and borders in education refer to conflicts between means of production, distribution, and use of knowledge originated (and validated) in different cultures and across hybrid cultures as well. Old and new political and cultural struggles resulting from the confrontation of new subjects will continue to besiege the public school in Latin America. Different ways of imaging, understanding, and theoretically analyzing (and seeing) reality will clash in the schools. Thus a discussion is just beginning in educational settings, addressing the rights of the various social subjects to participate in decision making, and in the production, development, and evaluation of the process of teaching and learning. Most likely, this discussion will remain central in the pedagogical and political thought of the region and internationally.

The risk of further fragmentation of the school system and the exacerbation of cultural *diférénce* and otherness, given the withdrawal of the state from the pedagogical utopia of public education in Latin America, will become critical in the unequal and combined development of schooling and societies. Therefore, the possibility of establishing a basic democratic consensus, and the articulation of *diférénce* in the constitution of identities will become even more remote and certainly more costly.

PAULO FREIRE'S POLITICAL PHILOSOPHY OF EDUCATION

The third major focus of my work in the last 3 decades has been the social foundations of Paulo Freire's political philosophy of education. I have argued in my work on nonformal education and the dependent state that compensatory legitimation is an attempt to incorporate disenfranchised populations within corporatist political representation, using low-cost educational alternatives (such as adult education and literacy training) as a symbolic substitution instead of real improvement in their quality of life, social mobility or income. I have extensively documented that equality, quality, and relevance in adult education programs remained outside the main goals of adult education reform in Mexico, other countries in Latin America, Canada, and Tanzania. Is there, then, any possible alternative to nonformal education as compensatory legitimation and extension of state authority? The answer to this question entails a discussion of Paulo Freire's proposals.

I have used the work of Paulo Freire and produced over the years a systematic criticism of his theoretical, metatheoretical, epistemological, and pedagogical positions, as an attempt to bridge the gaps separating critical theory à la Frankfurt school, sociologies of education, and critical education theories (see, e.g., Gadotti, Freire, Ciseski, Torres et al., 1996; O'Cadiz, Wong, & Torres, 1998; Torres, 1978a, 1978b, 1980a, 1980b, 1995a, 1998a, 2005c).

The philosophical origins of Freire can be traced to the *Escola Nova* movement in Brazil in the 1930s and 1940s, promoted by several Brazilian disciples of John Dewey. Thus, as an extension and reelaboration of Dewey's educational proposals, Freire's analyses are relevant to U.S. education and address questions and issues I have raised elsewhere in my own work.

Freire, a Brazilian philosopher and educator who became famous in the early 1960s due to his powerful method of literacy training (the method of the generative word), has become a landmark for critical pedagogy all over the world. The method of the generative word is based on discovering a "community generative theme," that is, an existential and crucial everyday-life situation for members of a given "oppressed" community, such as affordable housing, health care, homelessness, unemployment, and so on. This method allows for the selection of 18–24 generative words. Starting by discussing "existential situations" of the community, Freire's method uses generative words that are codified and presented graphically; and through dialogue between facilitators and students, they allow for quick literacy training. In the original experiences of Freire in Angiços, Rio Grande do Norte, in northeast Brazil, 40 hours of instruction were sufficient for allowing people to begin reading and writing, achieving literacy proficiency (Brown, 1975).

The importance of Freire's work is conveyed by the fact that his most important books—*Pedagogy of the Oppressed* (1970b), *Education for Critical Consciousness* (1973), *Pedagogy in Process: The Letters to Guinea-Bissau* (1977)—have been translated into many languages including German, Italian,

Spanish, Korean, Japanese, and French; and some of them—especially *Pedagogy of the Oppressed*, which has been translated into 18 languages—have more than 35 reprints in Spanish, 19 in Portuguese, and 20 in English, which amounts to more than half a million volumes in sales.

What has made Freire's political philosophy of education so current and universal, placing him and some of the "generative themes" suggested by his method at the center of educational debates in critical pedagogy for the last few decades? Influenced by the work of psychotherapists such as Franz Fanon and Erich Fromm, Freire argues in his *Pedagogy of the Oppressed* that few human interpersonal relations are exempt from oppression of one kind or another; by reason of race, class, or gender, people tend to be perpetrators and/or victims of oppression. He points out that class exploitation, racism, and sexism are the most conspicuous forms of dominance and oppression, but he recognizes that there exists oppression on other grounds such as religious beliefs or political affiliation.

Freire's *Pedagogy of the Oppressed* was influenced by a myriad of philosophical currents including phenomenology, existentialism, Christian personalism, humanist Marxism, and Hegelianism. Freire's new philosophical synthesis calls for dialogue and ultimately social awareness as a way to overcome domination and oppression among and between human beings. A key influence in Freire's philosophy is German philosopher G. W. F. Hegel. Since John Dewey himself has argued strongly against Hegel, Freire's paradoxical combination of Hegel and Dewey in a new synthesis makes Freire's contribution even more intriguing.

What are the implications of *Pedagogy of the Oppressed* for contemporary education and critical pedagogy? Freire introduces an epistemological perspective in pedagogy. Knowing for Freire, like Dewey, starts from lived experience. Problem-posing education, which is at odds with problem-solving education models, starts by discovering the theory hidden in the practice of human agency and social movements. Freire's epistemological perspective seeks, in turn, to produce new knowledge that will guide, inspire, redefine, and assist in the comprehension of praxis. However, this unknown theory is not yet knowledge. It has to be discovered, invented, or re-created in an intelligent dialogue between the logic of critical social theory and the demands of tension-ridden, contradictory practices. This epistemological stance has at least two major implications. On the one hand, critical pedagogy emerging from Freire's contribution—and critical theory à la Frankfurt—is concerned with how emancipatory education can validate the learners' own culture and discourse while at the same time empowering them. On the other hand, Freire's recognition of the tensions between objectivity and subjectivity and between theory and practice—as autonomous and legitimate spheres of human endeavor—lead him (departing once again from Dewey) to recognize that these dichotomies and tensions cannot be overcome. Nor can they be captured in their entire complexity through empiricist methodologies.

In Latin America, models of popular education spring from the original Freirean "pedagogy of the oppressed" developed in the early 1960s (see Gadotti & Torres, 1992, 1993, 1994; O'Cadiz, Wong, & Torres, 1998; Torres, 1990b; Torres & Morrow, 2002a). The following four points define "popular education." First, popular education arose from a political and social analysis of the living conditions of the poor and their outstanding problems (such as unemployment, malnourishment, poor health), and attempted to engage the poor in individual and collective awareness of those conditions. Second, this strategy bases its educational practices on collective and individual previous experiences (understood as previous knowledge) and stresses work in groups rather than individualistic approaches. Third, the notion of education provided by these projects is related to the concrete skills or abilities that they try to instill in the poor (i.e., literacy or numeracy), and these projects strive to arouse pride, a sense of dignity, personal confidence, and self-reliance among the participants. Finally, these projects can be originated by governments, as in Colombia and Dominican Republic, with projects related to integrated rural development, or, as in Nicaragua, with the collective of popular education; and they may be directed toward adults as well as children. U.S. examples can be found in the newsletter *Seeds of Fire* from the Network of North American Popular Educators, or in the popular education graduate program at the Lindeman Center, Northern Illinois University, Chicago, Illinois.

In short, my work on Freire has concentrated on understanding the philosophical, historical, and critical roots of the Brazilian philosopher and educator Paulo Freire (e.g., see Freire & Torres, 1993, 1994; Gadotti & Torres, 1991; Morrow & Torres, 1999; O'Cadiz & Torres, 1994; Torres, 1994a, 1994b, 1994c, 1995a, 1998b, 2007; Torres & Freire, 1994; Torres & Morrow, 2002b; Torres et al., 2001). The book that I edited with M. Gadotti, Director of the Paulo Freire Institute–São Paulo, and other colleagues in Brazil provides the first international biography and bibliography on Paulo Freire. It contains also *depoimentos* (testimonies) from more than 100 scholars all over the world about the influence of Paulo Freire and Freire's pedagogy and philosophy in their own scholarship and practice (Gadotti, Freire, Ciseski, Torres et al., 1996).

There is no question that the contributions of Freire and a host of other critics of models of banking education, were among the first to provide a systematic description and analysis of neoliberalism as a comprehensive model of domination and capitalist hegemony of worldwide reach, and also signaled with their critique the need to produce alternatives to neo-liberal policies. Yet Freire was also one of the first theoreticians to identify and critically analyze the problematique of diversity in education and the possibilities of what metaphorically has been designated as "border cross-ing in education"—in fact a theoretical meditation to the question of the pedagogical subject.

EDUCATION, DEMOCRACY, AND MULTICULTURALISM: DILEMMAS OF CITIZENSHIP IN A GLOBAL WORLD

As a natural outgrowth of my work on Freire and his notion of the "peda-gogy of the oppressed," and also because of my engagement with and study of debates in the United States, I have been discussing the question of multiculturalism in education for more than a decade (see Chapter 3 of this volume and Torres, 1998a). Starting with an exploration of some of the key themes of multiculturalism, I have provided a critical reading of the multiculturalist movement as it is reflected in multicultural educa-tion through a relevant sample of criticisms from liberal quarters, from the neoconservative movement, and from the Left.

Focusing on the question of cultural difference and class distinctions, I have shown some of the contradictions associated with theories of mul-ticulturalism in education. I consider both multiculturalism as a social movement and multicultural education. Citizenship education entails what traditionally was called "civics education," that is, the teaching of constitutional democracy. Three categories are usually associated with civics education: *civic knowledge,* which in the context of constitutional de-mocracy usually entails the knowledge of basic concepts informing the practice of democracy such as public elections, majority rule, citizenship rights and obligations, constitutional separation of power, and the place-ment of democracy in a market economy that is used as the basic premises of civil society; *civic skills,* which usually mean the intellectual and partici-patory skills that facilitate citizenship's judgment and actions; and *civic virtues,* usually defined around liberal principles such as self-discipline, compassion, civility, tolerance, and respect.

An important point, therefore, is to emphasize that citizenship edu-cation is wedded to politics and by implication is a contested concept, one that relates to what sociologists call "political socialization," a notion that, in turn, links the formation of individuals to state policies. There are questions of whether citizenship education should emphasize civic knowledge, civic skills, and civic virtues as defined by the political estab-lishment, and

if they conceptualize the citizen role mainly as one of compliance and cooperation, they may reward these behaviors and teach about law and government; if they define the role in more participatory terms, however, educators might teach students how to influence public affairs and deliberate
public policy. Both viewpoints are plentiful in U.S. citizenship education
literature. (Parker, 1997, pp. 39–40)

Perhaps, rather than synthesizing here the complexity of the theories,
hypothesis, and analysis presented in my book, *Democracy, Education,
and Multiculturalism* (1998a), it will be sufficient to describe the intellectual project behind the book. In the book I look at developments that are
changing our understanding of the role of education in citizenship and
the possibilities of democratic participation. The first chapter introduces
the key themes of the book and the theses. The second chapter challenges
educators to think more politically about education. It is based on a seminal analysis that shows the role education plays in the liberal, neoliberal,
and neoconservative state, incorporating critical perspectives from neo-
Marxism, postmodernism, and feminism. Chapter 3 reviews theories
of globalization and how they affect the nation-state. Two contrasting
perspectives are analyzed, including the conservative perspective that
understand citizens as consumers, and the progressive understanding
of human rights in the world system, and how these two contradictory
trends redefine the context, meaning and dynamics of citizenship in the
global world. With the analysis provided in Chapters 2 and 3 as background, Chapter 4 discusses the connections between democracy and
education, based mostly on the classical contributions to political theory
of C. B. MacPherson and the notion of participatory democracy. Chapter
5, based on a critical analysis of T. H. Marshall's contributions, discusses
the connections between theories of citizenship and democracy, drawing
from several critiques to the notion of liberal citizenship, including the
feminist critique, postcolonialism and subaltern spaces theory, critical
race theory, and social movements theory. In Chapter 6, I analyze the
critical reception of theories of multiculturalism from the perspectives
of liberalism, neoconservativism, and the New Left. In my conclusion
of this richly textured chapter, I offer a challenging analysis of the politics of identity in education. Finally, in the concluding chapter, I offer a
comprehensive summary of the thesis of the book and advance a set of
arguments of how to develop, from a progressive political economy perspective, a democratic multicultural citizenship as civic virtues. In short,
this is a book that draws from Hobbes, Locke, Jefferson, Kant, Hegel,
Marx, MacPherson, Mouffe, Pateman, Marshall, and many other political theorists, but is also influenced by the work of political philosopher

of education Paulo Freire. It brings back the question of theories of the state, globalization, and democracy; outlines contemporary approaches to multiculturalism in education and citizenship; and discusses the transition from the welfare state to the neoliberal state in education.

TEACHERS UNIONS AND THE STATE:
ALTERNATIVES TO NEOLIBERALISM

Also in the last 10 years, I have been preoccupied with questions of how different teachers unions and social movements respond to the neoliberal agenda. Hence I had focused my work in the political sociology of education, dealing with the interactions between teachers unions, women leaders, and the state in Latin America in the context of structural adjustment in the developing world, and in the context of the changed political orientations in the United States.

Focusing on the dynamics and rationality of educational policy, innovative educational policies and practices, and the effective contribution of education to development, I have been concerned particularly with the poorer sectors of Latin American societies and with the question of how multiculturalism can help to promote the goals of crossing the lines of diversity in searching for a politics of liberation (see Torres, 2000b, 2000c; Torres & Boron, 1996). My research analyzes the quality and development of education in Latin America in the context of dramatic regional economic and political changes of the past 2 decades. My focus has been on Argentina, Brazil, and Mexico in comparative perspective. Together, these three countries represent approximately two thirds of the Latin American population and are among the top 20 industrial countries in the world system. In addition, they have large, complex and conflictive schooling and adult education systems, have experimented for more than 50 years with radical educational alternatives to the establishment, particularly the presence of popular education paradigms, and are the home to a multitude of social movements challenging capitalism and particularly neoliberal policies. In terms of their governments, these three countries are part of a region that has in the last 10 years elected social democratic governments not completely allied to the policies of the United States in the international system.[6]

It is imperative to situate the national and regional reality of Latin American education in the context of a global economy, which operates in very different ways from the former industrial economy. This new global economy is more fluid and flexible, with multiple lines of power and decision making. The old economy was based on high-volume and highly standardized production with a few managers controlling the production process from above and a great number of workers following orders. This economy of mass production was stable as long as it could reduce its costs of production, including the price of labor, and retool quickly enough to stay competitive. Because of advancements in transportation and communications technology and the growth of the service industry, production has become fragmented around the world. Production moves to locations where there is either cheaper or more highly trained productive labor, favorable political conditions, access to better infrastructure and national resources, and larger markets and/or tax incentives. While the public education system in the old capitalist order was oriented toward the production of a disciplined and reliable work force, the new global economy seems to have redefined labor relations, challenging our perception of the role of education in development.

How do these transformations in the world economy specifically affect education in Latin America? The oil and debt crisis of the 1970s and early 1980s spurred the introduction of structural adjustment policies under IMF and World Bank supervision, intended to "fix" ailing economies. Structural adjustment policies require financial and public sector restructuring in order to stabilize economies and sustain economic growth. They are based on principles of free trade, reduction of public expenditures, and privatization.

The state in Latin America is redefining its role given the economic constraints under structural adjustment. Historically, the state in Latin America has actively intervened in the development of national economies by means of redistributionist policies, extending social benefits to vast sectors of the population. Education played a key role in these social programs, because mass schooling was viewed as a means of building a national citizenry, a productive labor base, and increasing social mobility. Ultimately mass schooling was seen as a prerequisite for liberal democracy. In contrast to the previous achievements in the expansion of public schooling, the past 2 decades have witnessed a decline in quantity and quality of schooling in the region.

Yet a number of research questions remain unanswered: Has the state made a significant change in its political commitment to educate all citizens, or are we simply witnessing a "pause" in educational development as a result of an economic crisis? Given the requirements to decrease educational spending under structural adjustment programs, are the new national educational policies a temporary response to the crisis or do they represent the foundation for a new conception of the role of the state in providing public education? What educational programs, curricular reforms, and pedagogic practices have educators at the local school site level created in reaction to the economic circumstances under structural adjustment?

To answer these questions, I have coordinated in the last decade two major international studies on educational reform, teachers and teachers unions, and globalization. The first study analyzes the relationships between the state, education reform, and teachers unions, particularly women teachers, in Latin America. This study also offers insights into the role of teachers unions, in Latin American, the United States and Canada, and Korea and Japan. The second study concentrates in understanding the impact of globalization on teachers' lives, curriculum, educational reform, and policy in 18 countries, and affecting K–12, higher education, and adult education systems and practices.

School reform agendas have been launched in the United States, Pacific Rim countries, and many Latin American countries, focusing on "restructuring" rather than merely transforming the efficiency of existing systems. Restructuring attempts the transformation of purposes, assumptions, and methods of schools systems (Darling-Hammond, 1993). Not surprisingly, this reform agenda is being implemented in times of serious financial retrenchment in public education everywhere. Because much of the "schools-are-failing" literature blames the teachers for the ills of education, the relationships between teachers and educational authorities are also being reconsidered. Even where there is less focus on blame, there is considerable attention to competency testing, certification, and national standards; in short, diverse attempts to improve excellence in instruction and learning. Trying to reduce expenses of financially overburdened school districts and attempting to make the systems more cost-effective often involves layoffs and substitution of lower-paid instructional personal for fully trained, more expensive teachers. This situation, along with recent initiatives for alternative school finance, such as vouchers, has placed teachers' organization at the center of disputes on educational policy and practice.[7]

Teachers, as state employees, are important actors who fulfill a leading role in the welfare state.[8] As such, many of them think of themselves as the main public employees responsible for the transmission of a nation's collective values to its children. This self-perceived mission, coupled with similar roles attributed by the state in Latin America, created a mystique of spiritual satisfaction, self-esteem, and professional status, and gave their professional organizations an opportunity to participate in the formulation of educational policy and curricula (Lomnitz & Melnick, 1991). It is this unstable consensus between teachers and the state and the perception of the mission of teachers that is being eroded by changes in the role of the state and by drastic changes in the living and working conditions of teachers in

Latin America. As a result, new areas of conflict in the interaction between teachers, teachers' organizations, and the state are developing. Of particular relevance is the role of women teachers and women leaders, their lives, views, and political actions in the context of educational restructuring. For instance, for the first time in Mexico's labor union history, a woman, Elba Esther Gordillo, was elected General Secretary of the powerful national teachers union (SNTE). In Argentina many female teachers constitute the top leadership of the confederation of teachers (CTERA), including Mary Sánchez, former CTERA General Secretary, and a prominent political leader in the country.

This research explored the patterns of behavior of teacher's organizations and the state's educational policies in Latin America. Examples and illustrations of these patterns were drawn from the changing political and economic environments of Argentina, Brazil, and Mexico during the last 2 decades. Early in their history as independent nations, Argentina and Mexico were relatively successful in providing universal public elementary education for their populations. In contrast, Brazil, despite its significant economic development in the last 4 decades, has failed to provide a basic education for vast sectors of its population.[9]

A premise of the analysis is that the state is an arena displaying the interaction of domestic and international institutions and actors.[10] Therefore, the state reflects the microcosmic condensation of power relations in civil society, and to some extent the implications of trends of globalization of the economy and culture. A focus on tensions, contradictions, and conflict will offer a privileged vantage point from which to observe changes in educational policies in the context of renewed international and domestic efforts to modernize schools and societies. These changes have many implications for economic growth, social welfare, and political democracy.

It is with a view to the changing role of the state and to the current economic and sociopolitical repercussions of structural adjustment policies that I will study the educational systems and teachers' organizations in Latin America. How have teachers' organizations and trade unions—particularly women teachers and union women leaders—defined the role of public education in the overall process of democratization of their societies which are facing neoliberal structural adjustment policies?

This research agenda has suggested a number of research dimensions and research questions that need to be addressed in further research. I list here the very important questions I have pursued:

1. There is a debate in Latin America about whether the change from a type of welfare state to a neoliberal state more responsive to market demands has also altered the role and

functions of public education. Given the requirements to decrease educational spending under structural adjustment programs, are the new national educational policies a temporary response to the crisis or has the state diminished its political commitment to educate all citizens? What are the views and policies of teachers' organizations?

2. What is the role that women teachers play in shaping new educational policies? Did teachers unions with an increasing female leadership better articulate women's interests in teaching and educational policies? Did women union leaders define the problems of teaching as related to larger social movements and gender relations?

3. What actually happened in the last 2 decades in terms of educational expansion and financing? How have the debates surrounding educational expansion and financing been perceived by teachers' organizations and state officials? Are teachers' organizations concerned with deskilling, standardization, and rationalization of the teaching profession? What positions have teachers' organizations taken, particularly women leaders, on educational restructuring?

4. Are there shared "visions" among teachers' organizations and state agencies about the role public education should play in terms of equity, equality of educational opportunity, and quality of education? What are the views of the functionaries responsible for public education and leadership of teachers unions, particularly those representing primary and secondary education teachers, a great majority of them women?

5. Finally, an important preoccupation of research on teachers unions in Latin America is the need to understand the new role of women teachers as union leaders. Feminist scholars have argued that women are more nurturing than men, and that having been excluded from the networks of power, women leaders will be less compromising with the status quo and more prominent in the defense of the poor and the underclass, particularly children (Butler & Scott, 1992). In considering these arguments, a number of issues and questions emerge. Do female union leaders manage to specifically articulate women's interests in the practice of teaching and educational policies, defining the problems of teaching as related to larger social movements and gender relations? Is there a change of guard from an "old-boys" teachers trade-unionism, to a new facilitating female teachers' leadership? Do women leaders

perceive their role as resisting work intensification? Do they perceive a loss in the autonomy and skills of teachers?

Considering these questions and the great degree of uncertainty regarding the implications of policies of structural adjustment and stabilization in public education, more research is needed. Particularly, it is necessary to understand what is really happening to women teachers and specifically to female teachers' leaders in the context of a growing conflict in the relationship between teachers unions and the state, a relationship that may be drastically changing from historical patterns of an unstable consensual relationship into an abrasive political conflict, especially in the formulation of public educational policies (see Torres, 2003, 2004a).

THE COMPARATIVE STUDIES
OF GLOBALIZATION AND EDUCATION

A central question of this new research agenda is how structural changes in schooling and the growing impact of neoliberalism resulting from the processes of globalization differentially affects social change, national development, and the betterment of individuals and families in several regions of the world.[11]

Presently, I am studying the connections between globalization and education in three continents. This research project seeks to understand how globalization has affected educational reform in K–12 and higher education systems in several countries in Latin America, North America, Europe, Africa, and Asia. The countries selected for the study are the United States, Canada, Mexico, Argentina, Brazil, Portugal, Spain, Italy, France, Finland, Korea, Japan, Taiwan, Egypt, South Africa, and China.[12]

The dominant neoliberal agenda for globalization in K–12 education includes a drive toward privatization and decentralization of public forms of education, a movement toward educational standards, a strong emphasis on testing, and a focus on accountability. Specific to higher education reform, neoliberal versions of globalization suggest reforms for universities in four primary areas: efficiency and accountability, accreditation and universalization, international competitiveness, and privatization.

The reforms associated with international competitiveness could be described as "competition-based reforms," characterized by efforts to create measurable performance standards through extensive standardized testing (the new standards and accountability movement), introduction of new teaching and learning methods purported to create better performance at lower cost (e.g., universalization of textbooks), and improvements in the selection and training of teachers. Competition-based reforms in higher education tend to adopt a vocational orientation and reflect the point of view that colleges and university exist largely to serve the economic well-being of a society. With regard to accreditation and universalization, major efforts are under way throughout the world to reform academic programs through accreditation processes and various strategies that produce increased homogeneity across national boundaries.

The privatization of higher education in debt-ridden countries such as Mexico, Brazil, and Argentina typically is advanced by the IMF and the World Bank as a precondition to further lending to these countries. A precondition of such lending involves the transfer of educational financing from higher education to lower levels of education based on the premise that to subsidize higher education is to subsidize the rich, since the majority of students enrolled in higher education are from the middle classes and affluent families. Needless to say, these reforms are actively resisted in some of these countries by faculty, unions, parents, social movements, and students. Indeed, globalization has had a major impact in education since international institutions have promoted finance-driven reforms, which eventually clash with the possibility of equity-driven reforms in many countries.

There are, to be sure, differential processes of implementation and adaptations of these financially driven, competition-based educational reforms in different countries. Differences depend on the history of each educational system, the type of government in power, and the role of teachers unions and professional organizations, and so on. Yet, while these reforms are implemented and adopted, there is also growing resistance to globalization. Resistance, controversies, contradictions, and even activist confrontation to what is perceived as top-down imposed reforms through globalization policies and priorities take place in diverse domains, including curriculum and instruction, teacher training, and school governance, and are also reflected in the public debates about schooling reform. Yet a central focus of these debates are the specific cultural values that need to be preserved in each nation-state in terms of citizenship building facing the prevailing cultural globalization through mass media and the trends of competition-based educational reforms. Hence the question of educating the global citizen remains a central question hitherto not carefully explored and with little, if any, available historical and empirical evidence.

Let me now highlight some of the key research questions. This comparative research project focuses on K–12 and higher education. We would like to know what, if anything, is happening in the classrooms of the selected countries, particularly in K–12, when one considers the processes associated with globalization. There are then three levels of inquiry: The first is exemplified in the following simple question: What happens when the door of the classroom is closed and the teacher is in charge of the lesson plan? Are the processes associated with globalization playing any role within the classroom? How is globalization affecting the lives and work of teachers in each of the countries?

The second question pertains to policy and planning along with financing, administration, and governance. Is globalization affecting the curriculum, teacher training, and overall educational policy in the society? How are these changes being perceived by the different stakeholders in educational reform? What alternatives, if any, are being advanced to resist, transform, and challenge the rationale and implementation of financially driven, competition-based reforms? How are people taking advantage of the processes unleashed by debates about globalization and reform to advance an agenda of social inclusion, equity, and equality in education and communities?

A third issue is the key question regarding globalization, education, and citizenship. The complexity of this issue is revealed when one identifies the presence of a form of globalization centered on advancing the universal movement toward human rights rather than international competitiveness. The movement toward universal human rights is a powerful force, and the idea of global human rights has also become a central issue in considering citizenship and democracy. I have analyzed in my previous work the limits of citizenship in the era of globalization and highlighted some of the issues.

If the agenda for human rights is reconfiguring the boundaries of nations and the individual rights of citizens, and these are seen as preconditions for attaining basic equality worldwide, then educational systems will need to confront the tension between human rights as a globalized project of cosmopolitan democracies and the long-standing influence of nationalism. This tension also is projected in questions of identity and whether the particular rights of cultural and religious groups will be upheld in the face of an ideology of global human rights.

Key concerns of global human rights advocates center largely on the universal rights to food, water, and health care. Others suggest that the right to participate in a society's governance structure and the right to a quality education also ought to be universal. In terms of the latter two rights, as concerns about what constitutes "quality" and the role that educational institutions play in shaping expectations and dispositions relative to civic participation come to the forefront, schools and universities become key sites of struggle. Teachers unions have played major roles in this struggle. A key question specifically tied to higher education is the question of whether education is a privilege or a right. This has become a major point of contention in countries such as Mexico and Argentina, where structural adjustments clearly situate participation in higher education as a privilege, while long-standing social contracts within these two countries suggest otherwise. Here we see a clear clash of two oppositional agendas, one focused on privatization and advancing a competition-based social structure, and the other focused on social intervention and advancing a spirit of collectivism. This is the premise of my analysis with R. Rhoads in a new book (Rhoads & Torres, 2006). Hence the question of cosmopolitan or global citizenship, nationalism, and tolerance as mainstays of liberalism in the context of democracy has achieved center stage in the debates about citizenship and education.

EPILOGUE

This *racconto* of the last 3 decades of my research will be incomplete without mentioning that social sciences and humanities share much in common. Hence it is not unusual that scholars working in the social sciences delve into the social collective imagination by exploring fiction (for my work in fiction, see Torres, 2004b, 2005a, 2005b). Perhaps it is in fiction and poetry where we may find our true self. Or at least it may be true that by reading and writing fiction we can conceive and re-create a different sociological imagination, one of worlds that exist while they may not be mentioned or even known, or of struggles that are deeply imprinted in our soul while we may not be able to fully and consciously recognize them, let alone resolve them.

Whatever the reason we explore fiction as writers, there is always a sense of utopia when words, characters, and arguments are made and re-made at our will, while they, in turn, transform our own emotions and feelings in the process. Some people may argue that this is exactly what happens in the academic discourse and intellectual debates, but that is another matter.

For some people, fiction could be an escape from a suffocating reality of unjust worlds, lack of tenderness in social exchanges, painful feelings, anger or rebellion against intolerance, violence, oppression, and exploitation or domination of human beings by human beings. In a way, fiction could be a way to face the fundamental tensions, contradictions, and challenges of our lives: love, madness, and death, though all of them mediated by power.

Yet for others, fiction doesn't have to have a therapeutical role. On the contrary, fiction could be another way to emancipation, another way to express our dreams and our fears, without having to explain to anybody why we feel that way, or what is the actual truth of our feelings. Perhaps, we may need to answer the question that Sir Charles, the principal character of my novel, *O Manuscrito de Sir Charles*, posed to the readers in his manuscript, apparently written in the thirteen century:

> We seek the truth because we require an inextinguishable principle of reason on which to base our vision of the world and our individual conduct. But is this, in the final instance, anything more than the self-complacent posing of a principle of rationality? (Torres, 2005b, p. 50)

NOTES

1. Broad schools of development include modernization, dependency, bureaucratic authoritarianism, postimperialism, and interactive local political economy perspectives. Modernization focuses on the nature and characteristics of the social structure of less developed countries as causes of underdevelopment. Dependency theories instead focus on the structure of international capitalism and the lack of availability of capital for autonomous expansion of a less developed economy. Bureaucratic authoritarianism explains "dependent development" as a result of problems in the model of import-substitution industrialization implemented by several Latin American countries. A key factor of instability is the growing demands of the working class undermining both the legitimacy of the overall model of development and its ability for capital accumulation. The answer to this development crisis is the emergence of an authoritarian state. Dependent-development theories spring from dependency theories and are compatible with world system analysis. Dependent development points to the centrality of the state for the accumulation in the periphery of the capitalist world system. Postimperialism theories attempt to explain underdevelopment as part of a process of transnational class formation in the developing world. Finally, the perspective that focuses on the interaction of social domestic forces using a modern political economy emphasizes that the complex interaction of domestic socioeconomic and political trends determine policy outcomes, insisting on the centrality of economic pressures by domestic socioeconomic actors in the determination of policy options and outcomes. In this brief statement I cannot provide a comprehensive discussion of these schools of development which I have described in rather technical terms. For a good summary of these approaches, see Frieden (1991).

2. The concept of relative autonomy implies that schooling in capitalist societies is not totally independent but operates with some autonomy from the actions and programs of the ruling classes.

3. For Habermas, the pursuit of knowledge in the human sciences can be better understood as guided by three fundamental knowledge-guiding interests rather than a single explanatory one. There is an empirical-analytical knowledge, but there are also historical-hermeneutic interests and critical-emancipatory

knowledge. Similarly, cognitive-instrumental rationality can be differentiated from moral-practical rationality, and from aesthetic-practical rationality.

4. This concept, developed by Robert W. Connell (1983, 1987), refers to the historical association of masculinity with universalistic modes of thought.

5. The notion of pedagogical subject is related to the notion of social subject developed by Ernesto Laclau in several of his works (Laclau, 1991; Laclau & Mouffe, 1987).

6. The 2006 highly disputed election in Mexico, with the Mexican Supreme Court determining that the candidate of the ruling party (PAN), Felipe Calderon, should be sworn as president of Mexico shows a departure from the trend of electing social democratic governments. Yet, with less than 400,000 votes over his left-leaning contender, and the pervasive complaint that there had been election fraud, he will rule amid serious social conflict, highlighting the difficulties for neoconservative and neoliberal governments to establish their legitimacy in Latin America.

7. It is no secret that teachers unions in the United States were enthusiastic and energetic supporters and major contributors to President Clinton's campaign and its message for change. In 1993, Californian teachers invested heavily in defeating a statewide voucher initiative, and teachers unions have been a most important and strong opposition to the many attempts to install vouchers systems in the United States.

8. The *welfare state* is considered a particular form of the democratic liberal state in industrialized societies. Its origins have been associated with the industrial and financial reconstitution of the post-Depression era in the United States, which was based on a "social pact" (New Deal) and concertation policies between employers and labor. A striking feature of the welfare state is the interventionist role of the state in the economy and enlarged public spending in both productive and nonproductive sectors of the economy. *Welfare polices* are defined as government protection of minimum standards of income, nutrition, health, housing, and education. As Wilensky (1975, 1976) argued, these welfare benefits were assured to every citizen as a political right rather than as charity (see also Popkewitz, 1991).

9. Although the adult illiteracy rate in Costa Rica and Argentina is as low as 5% and 6%, respectively, and 10% for Mexico, in Brazil it remains as high as 22% (World Development Report, 1991). For a detailed analysis of the Brazilian case, see D. Plank (1987).

10. For a discussion on the relationship between the state and education, see Torres (1995c).

11. There are many definitions of globalization, or perhaps more accurately, there are many globalizations. For example, *globalization* has been defined by British political scientist David Held (1991), following Giddenss, as the intensification of worldwide social relations that link distant localities in such a way that local happenings are shaped by events occurring many miles away and vice versa. Another view presented in the work of Australian social scientists Luke and Luke (2000) sees globalization as a feature of late capitalism, or the condition of postmodernity, and, more important, as the emergence of a world system driven in large part by a global capitalist economy. Urry (2000) sees globalization as the transformation of time and space in which complex interactions and

exchanges once impossible become everyday activities. Still influential sociologists like Manuel Castells (1996) or Alain Touraine (1981) see globalization as an assault on traditional notions of society and the nation-state whereby the very nature of citizenship and social change is dramatically altered. For the purposes of my research,

> globalization may be defined quite simply as increasing global interconnectedness; a number of complex and interlinked processes are theorized under the heading of "globalization," principally economic, technological, cultural, environmental, and political processes. Globalization involves flows of goods, capital, people, information, ideas, images, and risks across national borders, combined with the emergence of social networks and political institutions which constrain the nation-state. (Nash, 2000, p. 47)

12. Many of the principal investigators are associated with the growing network of Paulo Freire Institutes in the world. Presently, in addition to the Paulo Freire Institute originally founded in São Paulo, Brazil, in 1991, there is the Paulo Freire Institute in Porto and Lisbon, Portugal (created in 1999); Xativa, Valença, Spain (created in 2000); the PFI–UCLA (created in 2002); the PFI–Italy (created in 2006); the PFI–Argentina (created in 2003); the PFI–Taiwan (inaugurated December, 2003); the Paulo Freire Institute–South Africa (inaugurated in Pietermaritzburg in 2006); and the Paulo Freire Institute–India (inaugurated in New Delhi in 2005). The Paulo Freire Institute–Korea will be inaugurated at the National University of Seoul soon. The rest of the principal investigators are associated with the work of the PFI–UCLA and in some cases have previously collaborated among themselves.

CHAPTER 1

Critical Theory and Political Sociology of Education: Arguments

The objective of this chapter is twofold. The first objective is to analyze the relevance of critical theory for education and its connections with neo-Marxism and other forms of theorizing embedded in the critical modernist tradition. I argue that despite poststructuralist critiques of representation, it is still possible to theorize about social reality, albeit in more self-reflexive and less totalizing ways than in the past. Critical modernism relates intimately to critical theory in the specific German tradition of the Frankfurt School, but it also takes into account contributions from a handful of neo-Marxists, such as Antonio Gramsci, Karel Kosic, Georg Lukacs, or Claus Offe, the work of Max Weber in political theory, and the continuation of the Frankfurt School in the work of Jürgen Habermas. Other strong influences relate to critical theories of democracy by C. B. McPherson or the early John Dewey, and critical contributions from postcolonial traditions such as Paulo Freire's work. In this context, and as an attempt to differentiate critical theory from "traditional or positivist theory," the early Frankfurt School, following a critical modernist perspective, proposed that "an alternative conception of social science was required, one that could grasp the nature of society as a historical totality, rather than an aggregate of mechanical determinants or abstract foundations. Further, it was argued that such analysis could not take the form of an indifferent, value-free contemplation of social reality, but should be engaged consciously with the process of its transformation" (Morrow & Brown, 1994, p. 14).

The second objective of this chapter is to develop a series of theoretical arguments about the relevance of a political sociology of education to comprehend, understand, and critique, in a macro, historical, and structural perspective, educational policy and planning. A particular focus of the critique is the notion of educational policy based on instrumental rationalization.

CRITICAL THEORY: DEFINITIONS

Critical Theory as Negative Philosophy

The term *critical theory* is employed here following the tradition of the
Frankfurt School, and particularly the work of Herbert Marcuse and his
interpretation of the political and social philosophy of Hegel and Marx.
Discussing the contribution of G. W. F. Hegel to social theory, Marcuse
(1941/1968) argued that

> Hegel's system brings to a close the entire epoch in modern philosophy
> that had begun with Descartes and had embodied the basic ideas of mo-
> dern society. Hegel was the last to interpret the world as reason, subjecting
> nature and history alike to the standards of thought and freedom. At the
> same time, he recognized the social and political order men had achieved
> as the basis on which reason had to be realized. His system brought phi-
> losophy to the threshold of its negation and thus constituted the sole link
> between the old and the new form of critical theory, between philosophy
> and social theory. (pp. 252–253)

Marcuse is right when he argues that Hegel's determinate negation
is the foundation of Marx when he advocates the "merciless criticism of
everything existing" (Lenin, n.d., p. 10). What is the role of determinate
negation? As Smith (1989) explains,

> The logic of "determinate negation" is the principle of development which
> exhibits the movement from one category or form of consciousness to an-
> other. It constitutes a method for moving from one stage to another that is
> not externally imposed. . . . The logic of determinate negation has both a
> critical and a constructive aspect. It is critical because it does not merely
> accept what a body of thought, a philosophical system, or even an entire
> culture says about itself, but is concerned to confront that thought, system,
> or culture with its own internal tensions, incoherences, and anomalies. It
> is constructive because out of this negation or confrontation we are able
> to arrive at ever more complete, comprehensive, and coherent bodies of
> propositions and forms of life. (pp. 188–189)

This notion of negative philosophy is intimately associated to the notion of negation of negation in dialectics, and to the concept of determinate negation developed by Hegel and later transformed by Marx in *Das
Kapital*. As I have argued elsewhere following Marcuse's analysis (Torres,
1994a), Hegelian dialectic is the rational construction of reality by which
the subject assimilates his vital experience in an ongoing fashion until
it finds itself again through the positivity of the determinate negation.

Hegel foresaw that the subject would not only appropriate things (basic property) but that it was trying to appropriate the subjects as well (the struggle of the opposed consciousnesses); when the conflict of the two self-consciousnesses was brought to bear (that of each consciousness that had gone out of itself and was for itself), both fighting to appropriate the same good, a road toward a solution was being established. This road was the Pact, a pact in which one of the two consciousnesses submitted to the other so as not to die. In this way, there came to light an independent consciousness and a dependent consciousness (dependent on the first one); in classical terms, the Master (Lord) and the Slave (Servant).

This notion of *determinate negation* has become a centerpiece of early critical theory. Herbert Marcuse draws from this notion of determinate negation when he speaks of the power of negative reason and how it is being obliterated in the context of authoritarian industrial societies (Marcuse, 1966/1991; Kellner, 1984). Therefore, the rational nucleus of Hegelian dialectic is the notion of positivity of the determinate negation. For Hegel, self-consciousness tended to negate the actual forms that it would find along its way (as a notion and not the truth of thinghood), in search of the emergence of the immanent unfolding of the mind (which is its very self), present in daily life. This negation is called the positivity of the determinate negation. History would thus be the road of the mind, wholly self-conscious, which identifies with the totality of the historical process, whereas this historical process, in its logic, is nothing more than the manifestation—in itself already a historical—of immanent life at the historical unfolding of the mind. The philosophizing consciousness (or the mind) upon negating in a determinate fashion the objects that confront it, with the aim of clearing a path on the road of rationality, in reality will be constructing an infinite totality, which is nothing more than its own life.

It is in Hegel that Marx found the substantial premises for the elaboration of his dialectical-historical philosophy, and the basic concepts that he cleverly employed to study the relationships between and among human beings and historically constituted structures. In so doing, Marx challenges the traditional epistemology in the subject-object relation, drawing from the Hegelian premise that material reality is a concrete totality constituted through social antagonisms. Within this Hegelian-Marxist framework that underpins the work of critical theory, the concept of labor is posited as determining the development of consciousness because human beings transform (and appropriate the fruits of) nature through their labor. This notion, in turn, is a central Hegelian contribution to Marx, particularly Hegel's suggestion that the opposition of consciousnesses is the result of the confrontation resulting from the desire of ego to appropriate things and even consciousness itself.

Marcuse (1941/1968) argues that:

> The traditional epistemological antagonism between subject (conscious-
> ness) and object, Hegel makes into a reflection of a definite historical
> antagonism. The object first appears as an object of desire, something to
> be worked up and appropriated in order to satisfy a human want. In the
> course of the appropriation, the object becomes manifest as the "otherness"
> of man. (p. 259)

This Hegelian premise is taken up by Marx who would argue that

> the realization of labor appears as negation to such an extent that the work-
> er is negated to the point of starvation. The objectification appears as a
> loss of the objects to such an extent that the worker is deprived of the most
> necessary objects of life and labor. Moreover, labor itself becomes an object
> of which he can make himself master only by the greatest effort and with
> incalculable interruption. Appropriation of the object appears as alienation
> to such an extent that the more objects the worker produces the less he
> possesses and the more he comes under the sway of his product, of capital.
> (Marx, cited by Marcuse, 1941/1968, p. 277)

Hence Marcuse's argument is that Marx found in Hegel's premises
the foundations for his philosophy of history, which challenged relativism and positivism alike (Marcuse, 1941/1968, p. 322). Marcuse sees the
rise of modern social theory in the linkage established by Hegel between
philosophy and social theory. The post-Hegelian philosophical thought
was dominated by positivism (or the positive philosophy in Marcuse's
terminology), until Marx managed to deconstruct Hegel's philosophy of
history, philosophy of rights, and dialectics, establishing the foundations
of a negative philosophy:

> Hegel's critical and rational standards, and especially his dialectics, had
> to come into conflict with the prevailing social reality. For this reason, his
> system could well be called a *negative philosophy*, the name given to it by its
> contemporary opponents. To counteract its destructive tendencies, there
> arose, in the decade following Hegel's death, a positive philosophy which
> undertook to subordinate reason to the authority of established fact. The
> struggle that developed between the negative and the positive philosophy
> offers . . . many clues for understanding the rise of modern social theory in
> Europe. (Marcuse, 1941/1968, p. vii)

In short, critical theory appears as a negative philosophy because it
challenges the tenets of the philosophy of positivism (a positive philosophy). However, it is a negative philosophy as well because, as it has been

argued independently from critical theory by the Italian Marxist Antonio Gramsci (1971), critical theory helps to deconstruct and critique the premises of the principle of common sense—which guides the daily construction of social interactions—as contradictory and building hegemony. Or as Horkheimer puts it, "Among the vast majority of the ruled there is the unconscious fear that theoretical thinking might show their painfully won adaptation to reality to be perverse and unnecessary" (Horkheimer, 1937/1972, p. 323).

Yet for critical theory, culture—as defined in the work of Gramsci and a host of neo-Marxist writers—plays a central role in the production of hegemony and common sense interpretations of everyday life. The notion of negation and criticism implies the presumption that, in Ricoeur's (1981) hermeneutical analysis, all cultural relationships involve subtle codes of domination and discrimination. In so doing, the state appears as a site for contradictions and a contested terrain, and therefore changes in the political alliances controlling the states are central for neo-Marxist analysis (Bowles & Gintis, 1986). The role of theories of the state must therefore be brought to the forefront of the debate (Carnoy, 1984, 1992; Torres, 1985, 1995c), which explains the need for a political sociology of education to understand educational policy formation.

Critical Theory and Neo-Marxism

The connections between the original brand of critical theory that inspired the origins of the Frankfurt School and its many associates (Walter Benjamin, Theodor Adorno, Max Horkheimer, Erich Fromm, Herbert Marcuse, and, most important for education, Karl Mannheim) and the original production of Marxism, built on three theoretical traditions (British political economy, German philosophy, and French socialism) are well documented and need no further analysis (Morrow & Torres, 1995). What is important, however, is to link the developments of the original critical theory with recent social theory as elaborated in the work of Jürgen Habermas or Claus Offe, and thus to relate critical theory to neo-Marxism.

A central tenet of critical theory is Marx's analysis of the social production of material and symbolic life. Marx (1935) argued:

> In the social production which men carry on they enter into definitive relations that are indispensable and independent of their will; these relations of production correspond to a definite stage of development of their material forces of production. The sum total of these relations of production constitute the economic structure of society—the real foundation, on which rises the legal and political superstructure and to which correspond definite forms of social consciousness. The mode of production in material

life determines the social, political and intellectual life in general. It is not the consciousness of men that determines their being, but, on the contrary, their social being that determines their consciousness. (p. 356)

The concepts of contradiction, dialectics, exploitation, domination, and legitimation are pivotal in the arsenal of critical theory and neo-Marxism. Most recent theoretical developments have pushed the limits of original analyses based mostly on rigid notions of class as the ultimate determinant of collective social behavior, making the concept of class analytically compatible with (but not subordinated to) processes of discrimination and exploitation based on other key dimensions of human life, most prominently race, ethnicity, and gender relationships.

Critical theory, however, has been more a tool for analysis and criticism than an attempt to undertake a journey of prophetism and utopia. Critical theory has not tried to delineate the future developments of human interactions that it may deem most relevant for empowerment and liberation— which are indeed seen as the ultimate goals of any human experience, including scientific work. The role of socialism and the importance of the proletariat as the class that will eliminate all classes have been drastically tempered, if not simply abandoned, as a political program. Many people who work closely with the critical theory tradition have decreed that Marxism, for practical and theoretical purposes, is dead (Laclau, 1990; Laclau & Mouffe, 1985). Alas, it is important to emphasize that neo-Marxism is not a monolithic approach. Moreover, looking at the specific political dimensions of analysis, neo-Marxism and critical theory perspectives include a call for democratic renewal, highlighting the importance of emancipatory social movements to democracy in contemporary capitalist societies.

The Notion of *Critical* in Critical Theory

But what is the meaning and nature of the concept of *critical* in critical theory? Morrow and Brown (1994) offer an insightful set of distinctions when they argue that

the term *critical* itself, in the context of "critical theory" has a range of meanings not apparent in common sense where critique implies negative evaluations. This is, to be sure, one sense of critique in critical theory, given its concern with unveiling ideological mystifications in social relations; but another even more fundamental connotation is methodological, given a concern with critique as involving establishing the presuppositions of approaches to the nature of reality, knowledge, and explanation; yet another dimension of critique is associated with the self-reflexivity of the investigator and the linguistic basis of representation. (p. 7)

Following Morrow and Brown's contribution, I would like to argue that as a research program, critical theory implies three dimensions: First, it is a human science, hence providing a humanistic, antipositivist approach to social theory. Next, it is a historical science of society; hence it is a form of historical sociology. Finally, it is a sociocultural critique that is concerned with normative theory, that is, a "theory about values and what ought to be. Critical imagination is required to avoid identifying where we live here and now as somehow cast in stone by natural laws" (Morrow & Brown, 1994, p. 11).

These three dimensions notwithstanding, there is no unitary critical theory as Douglas Kellner (1989) has forcefully argued in his comprehensive study of the critical tradition initiated by the Frankfurt. A definitive feature of this theoretical cluster and research program, and what makes critical theory so relevant for the study of education is its interdisciplinary nature, defying the logic of separate disciplines analyzing discrete objects of study: "Critical theory has refused to situate itself within an arbitrary or conventional division of labor. It thus traverses and undermines boundaries between competing disciplines, and stresses interconnections between philosophy, economics and policies, and culture and society" (Kellner, 1989, p. 7). Hence critical theory emerges as a seminal framework to understand education, curriculum and instruction, classroom practices and educational policies.

Another important insight from Kellner's (1989) analysis is the notion that critical theory attempts a synthesis that, as a research program, can only be accomplished through collective groups of intellectuals aiming at social transformation:

> [A critical theory] project requires a collective, supradisciplinary synthesis of philosophy, the science and politics, in which critical social theory is produced by groups of theorists and scientists from various disciplines working together to produce a critical theory of the present age aimed at radical social-political transformation. (p. 7)

This notion of critical theory has serious implications for the role of intellectuals in contemporary capitalist societies, for the role of social theory in the context of debates about modernism and postmodernism, and for the role that education can play in social transformation. For the critical theory tradition, theory cannot be easily separated from practice, a premise of emerging perspectives in sociology of education (Torres & Mitchell, 1998). A political sociology of education is a pristine example of the application of critical theory for the study of educational policy.

The aim of a political sociology of education is not only to understand educational policies and practices (as in the logic of enlightenment) or to improve the epistemological, logical, and analytical perspectives of metatheory, theory, and empirical research, (as in the logic of theorizing). A political sociology of education is not only an extension of a critique, drawing from the notion of negative philosophy, but also an invitation to change at a macrolevel, contributing to improve the practice of policy makers, policy brokers, and policy constituencies; and at a microlevel, contributing to improve both the cognitive and noncognitive outcomes of teaching and learning.

Unfortunately, there are serious problems for apolitical sociology of education to be as effective as it could be in educational establishments. One problem is the incommensurability of discourses between critical theory and the dominant positivist and behaviorist paradigms in education. Mainstream scholars and policy makers find the language of critical theory obscure, convoluted, and opaque. Likewise, many of the theoretical concepts in critical theory cannot be operationalized with conventional categories for empirical analysis. Indeed, the notion of dialectics, and the logic-in-use associated with it, sharply differs from the logic of policy analysis based on linear developments rejecting notions of profound discontinuities (Torres & Mitchell, 1998). A second problem is the assumption, by mainstream analysts and policy makers, that politics has no place in education. In this vein, teaching and learning are based on premises of objectivity and the separation of facts from opinions, hence a sharp separation between science and ideology. As we shall see below, these are antinomical premises to the way that critical theory and a political sociology of education construct explanations and advance alternative policies.

A POLITICAL SOCIOLOGY OF EDUCATION:
A CRITICAL MODERNIST PERSPECTIVE

A political sociology of education is an interdisciplinary hybrid. As I have argued elsewhere, this notion aims to study power and relations of authority in education, and the political underpinnings and implications of educational policies:

> It suggests an analytical approach concerned with the connections among religion, kinship relations, social classes, interest groups (of the most diverse type), and the political culture (ideology, value system, *weltanschauung*) of actors and social groups in the determination of political decisions and in the constitution of social consensus—or, failing that, a confrontation or distancing—of actors and social classes with respect to the legitimation of public policy. Obviously, any study in political sociology has to consider questions of bureaucracy and rationalization, power, influence, authority,

and the constitutive aspects of such social interactions (clients and political and social actors, their perceptions of the fundamental questions of political conflict, and the alternative programs that derive from these). Similarly, at the heart of a political sociology are the connections between civil and political society, as well as the complex interactions among individual subjects, collective subjects, and social practices. A political sociology of education implies considering all of these topics, theoretical questions, and problematics in a specific program of investigation to understand why a given educational policy is created; how it is planned, constructed, and implemented; who are the most relevant actors in its formulation and operationalization; what are the repercussions of such policy for both its clienteles and its social questions; and what are the fundamental, systemic, and organizational processes involved from its origins to the implementation and evaluation of the policy. (Torres, 1990b, p. xvii)

A political sociology of education has marked features including its structural historical analysis focus; its emphasis on the political raison d être of educational practices and policies; its reliance on theories of the state as a theoretical backbone; its critique of instrumental rationalization as the only feasible, practical, and cost-effective way to adequate means to ends; its focus on the politicity of education and educational policy formation as its theoretical and practical leitmotif; its concern for multicentered (but not decentered) notions of power (and hence interest and privilege); and finally the attempt to frame the research questions, theoretical rationale, and policy implications in terms of the importance of ideology and the scholarship of class, race, gender, and the state in comparative perspective.

A HISTORICAL-STRUCTURAL PERSPECTIVE: THE DIALECTICS OF POLICY FORMATION

Common criticisms to conventional approaches in policy making are that they lack an understanding of theory of the state, a critical conceptualization of issues such as domination, power, rules, and political representation in analyzing policy making, and a historical perspective of class, race, and gender relationships in education. But perhaps they are especially faulty in the methodological individualism of these approaches. Hence prevailing methodological individualism in social theory and pragmatic empiricist epistemological assumptions in educational administration have defined the study of educational policy as a political process where constraints and opportunities are a function of the power exercised by individual decision makers who operate with basic ideological values. This assumption, which I would like to term *methodological individualism*, will be challenged by a critical, historical, sociological, and comparative perspective informed by critical theory.

Moreover, the obsession of mainstream analysts and government officials with efficiency has led to an underestimation of the constraints (or restraints) on policy makers' actions, and particularly the importance of their worldviews in policy decisions and implementation, hence the importance of issues of class, race, and gender. In short, conventional studies on policy making (inspired by the rational paradigm of educational administration), on incrementalist perspectives, and/or on structural functionalist approaches, lack the theoretical sophistication needed to understand a very complex and rather sophisticated political process of public policy making in capitalist advanced and dependent societies.

The importance of critical theory informing a political sociology of education lies in its theoretical impetus, which suggests a dual, mutually inclusive and interactive focus on the structural constraints of human action and on the historicity of human relations. Therefore, if structural constraints shape behavior, rationalities, values, expectations, and aspirations, this modeling or patterning of human behavior, a notion closely associated with structuration theory as advanced by Giddenss,[1] is neither complete nor irresistible. Human subjects are a complex embodiment of passions, rationality, and desire (expressed as ideology and theory but also as body aesthetics and sensations). As human subjects, we are able and occasionally willing to muddle through structural constraints and historical limitations to strive toward the transformation of social reality—sometimes in revolutionary terms. In other words, the role of human agency appears as a fundamental element in the dialectics between structural and historical conditionalities and the perhaps seemingly unlimited capacity of women and men to intervene and eventually change the historical, cultural, symbolic, and structural circumstances that contributed to shape them.

A historical-structural approach to policy formation and social change has moved beyond simplistic versions of reproduction theories without ignoring the central critique and practical implications of social and cultural reproduction as a theoretical problematique. The implication of moving beyond classical reproduction theory, as by Althusser (1971) or the early Bowles and Gintis (1977, 1981) approach has been the emergence of theories of resistance that could account for the possibilities of change.

Morrow and Torres (1995) have argued, showing the importance of a historical-structural analysis in education, that theories of resistance

> required a theory of social action that endowed subjects with at least the potential for transformative action, a theme closely related to "new social movements" theory. Though enjoying particular prominence in critical

pedagogy, this theme was part of a more general rethinking of popular culture, structure, and agency in critical social theory. Within critical social theory the key step has been reconceptualizing society in terms of the distinctions between analysis at the level of "system integration" as opposed to "social integration," a strategy shared by both Habermas and Giddenss. . . . The methodological consequence of linking systemic and social-action analysis in critical theories have been twofold: attention to the agency-structure dialectic in analyzing processes of social and cultural reproduction; and a turn to historically specific (though often explicitly comparative) and ethnographic investigations capable of integrating, generalizing, and case-study analysis—something quite distinct from the neo-Foucauldian opposition of the universal and local, as if regional analysis could dispense with generalizing (though not in the sense of ahistorical, invariant laws) social theory. (p. 373)

THEORIES OF THE
STATE AND EDUCATIONAL POLICY FORMATION

A political sociology of education draws from theories of the state, criticizing the conventional or mainstream policy analysis approaches for they lack a holistic or comprehensive approach to determinants of policy making. At the highest level of abstraction, for instance, conventional approaches to policy formation lack the ability to link what happens in schools and nonformal education settings with what happens in society in terms of the dynamics of the processes of capital accumulation and political legitimation.

Above all, these approaches have a practical and rather pragmatic bias in which the guiding *knowledge interest* of research—borrowing the term from Jürgen Habermas—is almost exclusively empirical-analytical, thus oriented toward potential technical control, rather than, or in addition to, a historical-hermeneutic interest, or a critical-emancipatory one.

The need to focus on the role of the state is not foreign to mainstream institutions. For instance, in a letter to Deans of Education that discussed the woes of budget wrangling in Washington in 1996 and its implications for higher education, C. Peter Magrath, president of the National Association of State Universities and Land-Grant Colleges stated unequivocally that:

As we face a changed environment because of the changing demographics of our students, the exploding communications and technological revolution, and growing competing from for-profit educational entrepreneurs, the state agenda becomes ever more critical to our universities. This is why I am more convinced than ever that this association must expand its focus on addressing state and local government relations. (p. 3)

A critical theory of power and the state is a necessary starting point to study educational policy making (or public policy in general). The analysis is hence moved from the strict realm of individual choice and preference, somehow modeled by organizational behavior, to a more historical-structural approach where individuals indeed have choices, but they are prescribed or constrained by historical circumstances, conjunctural processes, and the diverse expressions of power and authority (at the micro- and macrolevels) through concrete rules of policy formation. Any study of education as public policy should deal with issues of the organizational context in which power (as an expression of domination) is exercised.

The concept of the state has become a fashionable term in political science. However, some authors would refer to political authority and policy making as the role of the government or the public sector, and some may even be inclined to use a more comprehensive notion such as the political system rather than the state. For a political sociology of education informed by critical theory a central focus is to consider the state to be an actor in policy making with purposeful and relatively independent action while, at the same time, becoming a terrain or an arena where public policy is negotiated or fought over (Arnove, 1994; Carnoy, 1984; Morrow & Torres, 1995; Offe, 1975; Torres, 1985, 1995c). This notion of the state as an arena of negotiation questions the notion of educational policy as the product of instrumental reason; yet it is the logic of instrumental reason that underlies the rationale for policy decisions.

THE CRITIQUE OF INSTRUMENTAL REASON

The notion of *instrumental rationality* is central to critical theory. It is defined here combining the Weberian notions of rationality as purposive-instrumental action and Habermas's notion of instrumental action. For Max Weber, purposive-instrumental action is "determined by expectations as to the behavior of external objects and of other men, and making use of these expectations as 'conditions' or 'means' for the rational success-oriented pursuit of the agent's own rationally considered ends" (quoted by McCarthy, 1979, p. 28).

The notion of instrumental action in Habermas "is governed by technical rules based on empirical knowledge. In every case they imply empirical predictions about observable events, physical or social" (quoted by McCarthy, 1979, p. 391). I should add, following Marcuse's criticism of technical reason, that every form of instrumental rationality—insofar as it represents an adequate means to a given end and is governed by technical rules based on empirical knowledge that seek to forecast and control so-cial and physical events—involves a substantive purpose of domination. This domination, however, is exercised through methodical, scientific, cal-culating, and calculated control. To understand and critique this techno-cratic position in the analysis and design/implementation of policy, criti-cal theory is led to emphasize the political dimension of human relations, which is of particular importance in education.

I have argued elsewhere studying instrumental rationality in adult education (Torres & Schugurensky, 1995) that individual (and collec-tive) experiences—considered in broader moral, cognitive, and daily-life dimensions—constitute individuals' rationales, including their narra-tives and metanarratives (Mezirow, 1978, 1981; Welton, 1990). Human experience is brought into being through language. As Freire has said innumerable times, it is the word that allows human beings to name the world. Analytical and descriptive perspectives involve institutionalized ideologies that predicate descriptive categories and rules or conventions governing their use. Previous research in Canada, Mexico, and Tanzania indicated that the dominant rationality of policy makers is technocratic thinking informed with a mixture of populist traditions and conserva-tive politics (Torres, 1990a).

Technocratic thinking constructs a model of the world with a system of categories that come to expect certain relationships and behavior to occur and then experience those categories. Technocratic thinking is also a meta-learning that has taken place by being exposed to a set of institutionalized experiences (Mezirow, 1985, 1997). Metalearning as a cognitive process is in-timately related to power and domination, emphasizing thus the relational nature of power. Ira Shor, in a conversation with Freire, has argued that

> domination is more than being ordered around impersonally in school, and more than the social relations of discourse in the transfer-of-knowledge pedagogy. Domination is also the very structure of knowing; concepts are presented irrelevant to reality; descriptions of reality achieve no critical in-tegration; critical thought is separated from living. This dichotomy is the interior dynamic of a pedagogy that disempowers students politically and psychologically. (Shor & Freire, 1987, p. 37)

Technocratic thinking can be discussed in the framework of guiding knowledge interests postulated by German social scientist Jürgen Haber-mas. According to Habermas, there are three guiding-knowledge interests that "determine the mode of discovering knowledge and for establishing whether knowledge claims are warranted" (Mezirow, 1979, p. 19; see also Morrow, 1989). These three distinct but interrelated learning domains are: the technical, the practical, and the emancipatory. The *technical* relates to the world of work and essentially refers to the way one controls and manipulates his or her own environment. Instrumental action is the empirical way that effective control can be achieved through planning in capitalistic societies. The empirical analytical sciences (including hypothetical deductive theories, deduction of empirical generalizations through controlled observation and experimentation) are central for forecasting, predicting, and manipulating the exercise of planning and administration-technical control and manipulation of nature and culture. Thus the technical guiding-knowledge interest will construct a basic instrumental learning domain, and individuals will be taught to learn within prevailing meaning schemes.

The *practical* guiding-knowledge interest refers essentially to the interaction between human beings. This interaction is eminently practical as long as it involves communicative action, the basis for any social action. Its aim is not technical control and manipulation but rather the clarification of conditions of communication and intersubjectivity. The typical examples of this knowledge interest are expressed in the historical-hermeneutic sciences. Thus the practical guiding-knowledge interest will construct a dialogical learning domain, and individuals will be encouraged to learn new meaning schemes.

Finally, the *emancipatory* guiding-knowledge interest refers to the notion of power. Typically, sociologists identify five sources of power: Physical force, the basis for coercion; control of necessary material resources, the basis for domination; the strength of the better argument, the basis for influence; the capacity to deliberately misrepresent, the basis for manipulation; and advantageous location within a system of meanings, the basis for authority (Lengermann & Niebrugge-Brantley, 1990, p. 334).

While recognizing the importance of coercion, influence, manipulation, and authority, power as domination has been a more central concern of critical theory, feminist theory, critical pedagogy, postmodernism, and other contemporary theoretical brands. Emancipatory guiding-knowledge interest challenges power as domination. This guiding-knowledge interest is emancipatory because it attempts to emancipate social beings from reified forces. A key tool to produce such an emancipation is self-reflection (Habermas, 1975). Planning is not the central goal. What is sought is liberation from human alienation by means of increasing enlightenment through analysis, explanation, and knowledge construction (Adorno & Horkheimer, 1972). There are a number of examples of critical social sciences that can help this process of emancipation, including the Frankfurt School and critical theory, feminist theory, postcolonial theories, hermeneutics, and psychoanalysis. Thus the emancipatory guiding-knowledge interest will construct a self-reflective learning domain, and individuals will be encouraged to learn through meaning transformation schemes.

In short, I argue that in adult education policy formation—but I presume in the majority of domains of policy formation, instrumental rationality underpins technocratic thinking, and that technocratic thinking is the dominant weltanschauung in policy planning. What are the dominant characteristics of technocratic thinking? The guiding-knowledge interest is eminently technical, centered in the notion of work and control (planning) of the environment, forecast, effective control, and reliance on the empirical analytical sciences. Likewise, the model of the world constructed is dependent upon a process of metalearning to which policy makers have been exposed due to their institutionalized experience. This model refuses to take seriously the notion of interaction-at the practical level or intersubjective communication including in the process of representation multiple voices—unless this process of participation implies a reinforcement of the cultural hegemony based either on liberal pluralism or neoconservatism. Finally, this technocratic model rests on the ideology of possessive individualism. Popkewitz (1988) has argued:

> The view of society as composed by "possessive" individuals provides a basis for organizing schooling. Attitudes, knowledge, and skills were conceived of as the personal property of the individual. The psychology of a possessive individual is incorporated into contemporary curriculum through the use of behavioral objectives, notions of affective and cognitive learning, taxonomies of knowledge and processes, and psychological testing and measurement. Methods of teaching are to enable individuals to develop particular attributes and abilities and to internalize some logical state which they "own" as one would objects or commodities. (p. 86)

The preceding analysis offers some clues as to how instrumental rationalization leads to depolitization of policy makers' views regarding the social world. Following Weber, we should remember that instrumental rationality "does not lead to the concrete realization of universal freedom but to the creation of an iron cage of bureaucratic rationality from which there is no escape" (Bernstein, 1985, p. 5). A large number of policy makers and teachers, consultants and international experts working for bilateral and multilateral agencies, and a growing number of intellectuals have adopted the technocratic language and rationality in their day-to-day operation, having a genuine vision that social and educational problems can be defined as technical problems and, given the right amount of resources, can be solved through adequate planning (Levin, 1980, p. 33). Perhaps it is this depoliticization of state apparatuses that facilitated the emergence of a less consensual and more confrontational neoconservative politics (Torres, 1995c). Public sectors, in their attempts to avoid traditional or clientelist ways or promoting the routinization of charisma through scientific administration and the failures of public policies, coupled with the contradictions of liberalism and the welfare state, may have paved the way for new political views, yet of neoconservative character, texture, and orientation, to gain a foothold in public sectors and civil societies alike.

I am aware that this suggestion is at odds with Marcuse's perception that technological rationality is always ideological and, as such, political, and therefore it "protects rather than cancels the legitimacy of domination" (Habermas, quoted in McCarthy, 1979, p. 21). However, I would argue that the slippage between administration and politics in public sectors under the guise of welfare states arises as a product of two main trends widely criticized by Habermas. First, there is the abandonment of a project of a comprehensive notion of reason, and its reduction to the exclusive validity of scientific and technological thought—thus, my criticism of technocratic thinking as reductionist of human praxis. Second, the neglect of emancipatory and heuristic knowledge in favor of instrumental rationality overlooks the intersubjective character of human interactions, and, in Habermas perspective, undermines the possibility of undistorted communicative action. Finally, I shall emphasize that Habermas, reviewing Daniel Bell's claims of the split between culture and society, recognizes the tension between a modern society governed in terms of economic and administrative rationality, and a modernist culture "which contributes to the destruction of the moral bases of rationalized society" (Habermas, 1985, p. 82). Critical theory however, relentlessly argues that education is not only a technical enterprise but it is also apolitical arena.

THE POLITICITY OF EDUCATION

A theory of the state that can systematically criticize the prevailing models of policy analysis and policy design based on instrumental rationality is needed to study what Paulo Freire so aptly has termed the "politicity of education" (1998). However, what are the relationships between politics and education from a critical theory perspective?

Commonsense language despises politics, and the political is thus seen as spurious social action. Political action is treated as either irrational, manipulative, or intrinsically perverse. It is often the case that in academic and government environments the notion of political action is opposed to the notion of technical action. This contradistinction has an epistemological bedrock in positivism along similar lines of the epistemological distinction between empirical judgments and value judgments. Technical assessments are considered always based on a theoretical framework devoid of social interests, created in the dispassionate environment of technical reasoning through the manipulation of empirical data that, despite potential problems of reliability, generalization, and sample size, cannot be suspected to be social constructions. By and large, technical assessments are always seen at the service of the truth and technocratic planning becomes an exercise of social engineering and ingenuity. Political assessments, on the contrary, are seen as always embedded in social interests and partisanship. Political views are seen as representative of either the passion of political competition between individuals, cliques, groups, factions, parties, or ideologies, or a cold-blooded calculating behavior by individuals attempting to attain a privilege for some group in society rather than the independent pursuit of truth and virtue.

Critical theory challenges this commonsense distinction, offering a sophisticated analysis. Politics is intimately linked to power and is concerned with the control of the means of producing, distributing, consuming, reproducing, and accumulating material and symbolic resources. Politics and "the political" should not be restricted to political parties, the activities of the governments and its critics, voting, and so on. Political activities take place in private and public spheres and are related to all aspects of human experience that involve power. Hence, as long as educational interaction involves power, politics and education are enmeshed in a complex intertwinement not easily separated as the clear-cut, but much wanting, distinction implied in the empirical and value judgment dichotomy. Critical theory, however, does not consider all educational activities regulated by top-down power interactions and hence inescapably political. There is ample room in critical theory for a constructivist perspective of technical assessment that, neither free from ideology nor devoid of human values, constitutes a relatively autonomous sphere seeking to understand reality beyond the weak objectivity of positivism (Harding, 1986, 1987). There are numerous instances where, while still reflecting power relations, the content, process, and product of teaching and learning acquire an autonomous nature that is educational and not merely political.

For instance, while there are multiple experiences of power involved in traditional Western philosophy, and while the canon of Western philosophy —from Aristotle and Plato to Erasmus, Vico, Rousseau, Kant, Hegel, Marx, Dilthey, and Foucault—is the product of White, male, and mostly heterosexual thinkers, there is a wealth of knowledge to be discovered and pursued in that corpus of thought. Yet it cannot be considered a single canon, nor can it be dissociated from the cultural reception of any theoretical analysis. This corpus of knowledge reflected in the word *canon* is indeed too strongly biased to be useful here yet with the appropriate contextualization and deconstruction it could be extremely useful to inspire and underscore what is known as Western thought. We know, however, from the contributions of feminism and postcolonial discourses, that we can make a substantive critique and reading of that corpus of work. We also know that no theoretical corpus is ever dissociated from power and power relations, and no theoretical construct can ever be considered the sum of the book of virtues. A critical understanding of this corpus—made a canon by traditionalists—is emblematic for critical theory that draws from an old heritage in philosophy. In other terms, a critical reading, rereading, and public debate of the Western theoretical corpus can be extremely educational for the twin aims of achieving undistorted communication and social political empowerment.

Moreover, the pursuit of philosophical understanding brings to some of us enjoyment and freedom in the delight of struggling to comprehend a theoretical construction or to make sense of an analogical puzzle or a categorical syllogism. This joy is also part of the educational and philosophical enterprise, adding a dimension of satisfaction and plenitude to the intellectual task. This satisfaction is similar to the feelings that contemplation of a work of art or listening to preferred music can elicit in connoisseurs and neophytes alike. Finally, while there are limits to traditional logic as a method of thinking, there should be no discussion that a rigorous training in logical thought could enhance our ability to think clearly, to develop insightful interpretations and analysis, and eventually to understand complex processes with greater intellectual refinement. This is exactly Gramsci's argument when he suggested that classical education and the learning of Latin constitute major assets in revolutionary politics (Gramsci, 1971; Entwistle, 1979).

In this context, considering politics as a set of relations of force in a given society including the politicity of education, the relationships between education and politics are examined by a political sociology of education, including the interactions between class, race, gender, and the state in education. A central consideration, however, is the notion of power for education and the implications of postmodernism.

POSTMODERNISM AND MULTICENTERED NOTIONS OF POWER

I have argued elsewhere (Torres, 1995c) that several postmodernist currents claim that power has become decentered and fragmented in contemporary societies. In so doing, the argument goes, social subjects have also become decentered. A political sociology of education, while taking into account the importance of considering different notions of power and the multiplicity of power situations in society, will question this notion of powering decentration and fragmentation. Does this imply that we cannot speak of a power elite, or a ruling elite conducting its business, having decisive influence in the formulation of public policy or education? How does one define power that is fragmented and lacking a unifying principle? Does this undermine the nonsynchronous, parallelist conception advanced by McCarthy and Apple (1988) of the relations of class, gender, and race in cultural reproduction? In short, does the fragmentation of power undermine conceptual frameworks and "grand narratives" such as of hegemony and domination?

The notion of the decentering of social subjects implies an uncoupling of the close link between objective social interests and subjective expressions (or class consciousness) assumed by much modernist social theory. The resulting contradictory loyalties of individuals increasingly undermines a central organizing principle of struggle. One often-noted consequence of this relative uncoupling of social position and political action is that the "new" social movements are more concerned with cultural (and ethical-political) demands than distributional ones. Decentered individuals are not supposed to have "class consciousness" in classical terms, yet they strive to achieve "self-actualization" in Giddenss's social psychological analysis (Morrow & Torres, 1995).

Of course, if individuals are decentered, classical educational notions of socialization in democratic behavior can also be considered obsolete. Critical theory, however, contends that notions of ideology and socialization cannot be abandoned or trashed so quickly that they remain no longer useful. On the contrary, they still play a major role in explaining educational policies and practices.

WELTANSCHAUUNG AND THE SEDUCTION
OF IDEOLOGY IN EDUCATIONAL POLICY FORMATION

Destutt de Tracy introduced in 1796 the notion of ideology within the realm of political philosophy. For de Tracy, ideology was a general doctrine about the ideas, using the concept of idea in a manner similar to that in use by Anglo-Saxon and French empiricist philosophy (e.g., John Locke or Condillac). According to de Tracy (1801), the term has neither a laudable nor a pejorative meaning:

> If we only give attention to the subject, this science can be named ideology; it can be named general grammatics if we put our attention only to the medium; finally, it can be named logic if we do not consider other dimensions than the object. This term does include, no matter which label we choose, these three parts, since we cannot reasonably treat each

one without including the other two. I believe that ideology is the generic term, since it is the science of ideas, including the expression of the ideas and their deduction. At the same time, it is the specific name of the first part. (quoted in Naes, Christophersen, & Kvale, 1956, p. 4).

Therefore, following this early formulation, *ideology* has been understood as a term that indicates a system of conceptual connections of any kind but with logic and internal articulation. However, with the development of the formal German sociology, the term *ideology* was very often translated as *weltanschauung*, giving it a different use and relevance and also interpreting ideology in a more restricted and specific way than before.

Weltanschauung means a synthesis of the forms of social consciousness in a defined historical moment. Werner Sombart (1939) states:

> I understand by *Weltanschauung* the totality of our interpretation of the world and our life in the world (then, it is a problem of knowledge); similarly, It means the totality of values according to which we are living (a problems of willingness). The religion, politics, epistemology or morality of any individual is just a part of this *Weltanschauung*. (n.p.)

It is clear that the concept of weltanschauung relates to the discussion about objectivity in social science, and the positivist claim of sociological knowledge to be value-free. Considering that weltanschauung represents the spirit of the epoch, each social scientist, as the traditional formal German sociology postulates, has a particular weltanschauung. This means that every social scientist has a pool of ideas, prejudgments, or prenotions that are conditioning the purpose of research, the choice of the research problem, the basic analytical framework, and even the method of analysis.

Thus it is evident that the possibility of isolating any "ideological" notion within a weltanschauung, and of separating these notions from true scientific knowledge has been—for the formal sociology paradigm—a precondition for the legitimacy of the scientific task in itself. A typical methodological outcome of this rationality is the distinction between value judgment—which is reserved for the ideological domain—and empirical judgment—which is reserved for the scientific domain. The legacy of this historicist formal German sociology, whose best expression had been Max Weber's writings, is to look for a clear demarcation between science and ideology. Hence ideology as weltanschauung can be considered an expression of human thought, which doesn't accord to the scientific and rational appraisal of reality, and science is thought as a true systematic approach to reality.

Growing out of nineteenth-century political philosophy, but anchored in the Hegelian-Marxist heritage, another contrasting approach to ideology can be detected: ideology as false consciousness. In this sense, ideology will not only be something distinct but the antitheses of the "Science of the Experience of the Consciousness," the provocative subtitle of G. W. F. Hegel's seminal book *The Phenomenology of Mind* (1967). The identification of ideology with false consciousness is attributed to the young Marx, particularly in his early writings prior to 1845, and specifically in his work with Engels entitled *The German Ideology* (1970). That is to say, ideological forms of consciousness are just the material dominant relationships captured at the level of thought by any social agent. These mental constructions, however, inasmuch as they reflect the fetishism of commodity production, are unable to understand, let alone to explain, the linkages between social and material forces. Despite this widespread belief, even in his earlier writings Marx in fact sustained a dual categorization of ideology. On the one hand, Marx indeed understood ideology as pure speculation, as facts separated from real praxis that was at the core of his criticism to Stirner's anarchism. On the other hand, however, Marx stressed the fact that ideology does simultaneously represent the conscious being, the imperatives of social daily practice, and could eventually represent the ideal expression of the social conditions of existence of social classes. Thereby, ideology may be seen just as the replica, at the spiritual level, of the process of alienation or the fetishism of commodities that result from the economic sphere. Yet Marx argues that ideology, even if it reflects the condition of existence of the people in a distortioned fashion, it is somehow expressing real relationships by codes yet to be deciphered. In short, for Marx, ideology is not just pure speculation or false consciousness but a rational appraisal of reality that, given certain conditions, could be used for rational and analytical purposes.

This dual character of ideology in Marx can be thought of as a theoretical tension by which Marx simultaneously considered ideology as false consciousness and as a real expression of the material conditions of human experience. Karl Kautsky and Edward Bernstein, main representatives of the Marxism of the Second International, also known as "vulgar Marxism"—while retaining the notion of ideology as false consciousness, that is, as simply a pure reflection of material relations, diluted Marx's understanding of the notion of ideology as expression of real material forces. Hence, and not surprisingly, the Marxism of the Second International defined *ideology* as a mere instrument of class domination, which is exercised by the bourgeoisie through the ruling action of the *state*, which in turn is defined as the ruling committee of the bourgeoisie. Ideology is then opposed to the true science of the proletariat—that is

Marxism—and the richness of cultural and social-symbolic struggles are cast aside as irrelevant.

It did not take long for a strong reaction against this vulgar Marxist notion of ideology to come about from two somewhat different but nonetheless intertwined theoretical responses: the critical theory of society represented in the work of the Frankfurt School, and the work of other prominent neo-Marxists such as Karl Korch, George Lukacs, and Antonio Gramsci. Undoubtedly, the most influential approach to the discussion of ideology from a neo-Marxist standpoint is Gramsci's theoretical formula. Gramsci introduces the notion of hegemony as a more "extensive" notion to assess the "ideological" phenomena in capitalist societies. Insofar as hegemony is founded on coercion and consensus, it is an educative relationship. Similarly, despite the fact that hegemony is exerted by the ruling class, it is organized in capitalist society by a particular social category, the intellectuals (Gramsci, 1971; Torres, 1985, 1995c).

The notion of *hegemony*, then, refers to the relationships between groups, especially social classes. A social class can be thought of as exercising hegemony over other "subaltern" classes. However, hegemonic domination does not rest exclusively on ideology but on the material relationships in society that inspire the basic values portrayed as legitimate and successful. Hugues Portelli (1972) argues that Gramsci's notion of ideology as a worldview, and hence a concept close to the notion of weltanschauung, is manifested in art, the law, the economic activity, and any manifestation of intellectual and collective life. Portelli emphasizes that Gramsci suggests a threefold approach: (a) ideology as such, as content; (b) the ideological structure of society, such as the cultural organizations that create and transmit ideology; (c) the ideological material, that is the language that is structuring a conversation in terms of a determinate syntax or grammar but exercising only partial control over the content of the communicate exchange (Bowles & Gintis, 1981, p. 28; Portelli, 1972).

Drawing heavily on the Gramscian production while simultaneously making a philological interpretation of Marx's writings, Louis Althusser provided an alternative interpretation of ideology. For Althusser's structuralist Marxism, ideology does operate as a regional meaningful instance of the social edifice. For Althusser, ideology, in contrast to scientific knowledge, has the function of hiding the real contradictions of social life, reconstructing, in an imaginary plane, a relative coherent discourse that can operate as the skyline of the lived experience of each social agent. Ideology then gives shape to the social processes of representation that, in turn, contributes to insert the social agent in the social formation.

Despite the complex and obscure formulation of Althusser's analysis, it is clear in structuralist Marxism that ideology will have several features.

First, ideology has an opaque character: It contributes to shatter the rational perceptions of individuals regarding the content of social practices in society. Second, ideology validates, legitimates, and hides the relationships of exploitation in the capitalist mode of production. Third, ideology has a technical character: It helps individuals to articulate a normative framework and behavior that orient their own practices in society.

Advancing the agenda of structuralist Marxism, but going beyond the Althusserian's formulations, Poulantzas (1978) provides a set of powerful insights in his argument:

> Ideology does not consist merely in a system of ideas or representations: it also involves a series of material practices, embracing the customs and life style of the agents and setting like cement in the totality of social (including political and social) practices. Ideological relations are themselves essential to the constitution of the relations of possessions and economic property, and to the social division of labor at the heart of the relations of production. The state cannot enshrine and reproduce political domination exclusively through repression, force or "naked" violence, but directly calls upon ideology to legitimize violence and contribute to a consensus of those classes and fractions which are dominated from the point of view of political power. Ideology is always class ideology, never socially neutral. In particular, the ruling ideology constitutes an essential power of the ruling class. (p. 28)

What should be retained from this theoretical discussion and incorporated into a political sociology of education studying the ideological dimension of policy making are the following six points: First, ideology is linked to processes of social alienation that, in turn, are deeply rooted into the material and symbolic practices and social relations of production. Second, ideology is part of the process of social reproduction, and as such plays key roles in the further materialization and reproduction of social relations of production but also, given the dual nature of ideology, in its challenge toward social transformation. Third, in a more restricted and historical sense, ideology can also be considered a system of thought or conceptual connections of any kind, having an inner logic and internal articulations of concepts. Hence it is possible to speak of an ideological framework or to decode the notion of ideology in the traditional sense of weltanschauung.[2] Fourth, the dominant ideology in a social formation, while related to the ideology of the dominant class, is also the outcome of social struggles. Obviously, the notion of ideology may refer to the set of values, beliefs, ideas that is at the level of rational understanding but also incorporating the affective component of human behavior.[3] Fifth, ideology can also be considered false consciousness since it contributes to hide or obscure key laws of motion of reality at the level of meaning, which is always a social construction but has strong material bases. Finally, it is possible to understand "ideological structures" as a system of representations by which social agents express a particular mode of appraising reality, codifying information and processing it in practical outcomes. The ideology (and any ideological framework) henceforth contributes to organizing information and underlying the effective action of individuals, groups, and classes. In this sense, ideologies are in correspondence with social structures and with forms of social consciousness but never are a mere reflection of those structures.

Considering this discussion on ideology, a political sociology of education will move beyond individual preferences, experiences, views, or technical qualifications of policy makers, policy brokers, and clienteles. Another area of concern for a political sociology of education, taking particularly into account the concept of ideological framework, are the key elements of policy planning, namely: (a) goals, objectives, and philosophies underscoring a specific program; (b) general strategy followed to implement educational reform; (c) models of financing of the programs; (d) models used and implemented in planning and administration; (e) structures of coordination implemented (centralized versus decentralized structures); (f) production of didactic material (orientation, quantity, dissemination, content, and so on); (g) type of evaluation implemented; (h) measures of productivity considered for the overall system and programs; (i) degrees of coordination achieved with other governmental or nongovernmental institutions; (j) types of training programs organized for the personnel; (k) perception of outcomes in terms of the same bureaucratic structure, the mission of the institution, the social content of the programs, and the teaching and learning dimension.

CRITICAL THEORY, CRITICAL INTELLECTUALS, AND A POLITICAL SOCIOLOGY OF EDUCATION: IN THE GUISE OF A CONCLUSION

Critical theory and political sociology of education strive to develop a scholarship of class, race, gender, and the state in comparative perspective. The goal is to work toward an integrative theory, producing comparative studies incorporating the categories above defined, the epistemological principles embodied in the connections between metatheory, theory, and empirical research, and the role of intellectuals seeking an education for empowerment.

Antinomical to neoliberal and neoconservative intellectuals employing mainstream theories, critical intellectuals assume to be critics of the system following the logic of determinate negation—not to be a critic who is necessarily intransigent or intolerant by definition, but one who is able to offer to society, like a mirror, the critical aspects that need to be considered and improved in dealing with mechanisms of sociability, production, and political exchanges. Universities as institutions historically constituted and inhabited by intellectuals and not only by technocrats, have a role to play in developing critical modes of thinking for society. This implies, additionally, a critique of the commodification of human relations and hence a critique of educational models that are merely based on instrumental rationality. In so doing, critical intellectuals highlight the role of education as enlightenment, empowerment, and helping to achieve higher levels of human freedom in societies that have become subject to commodity exchanges to the benefit of the privileged few.

The role of intellectuals in the critical modernist tradition has been aptly captured by Gramsci's suggestion that a central role of intellectuals is to create a social imaginary. The creation of a social imaginary implies, for critical intellectuals, a moral responsibility and a political commitment. The moral responsibility is to imagine social scenarios where people can deliberate and construct mechanisms of participation that may expand the workings of democracy. The political commitment is to create a sphere of public debate, as suggested by Habermas: an autonomous sphere of public deliberation that is neither controlled by the market nor controlled by the state.

Gramsci proposed a forceful hypothesis when he argued that everybody has the capacity to do intellectual work, but only a few recognize that they have that capacity or actually work in intellectual professions. Hence two key elements emerge from Gramsci's suggestion: First, intellectual work is not only a trade, a set of techniques, or a profession but also the capacity to realize refined analysis that may lead to praxis and social transformation. Second, a good critical intellectual in the tradition of critical modernism is one who is able not only to teach but also to learn from the people, from the popular sectors. Paraphrasing Mao Zidong, a critical intellectual is one who is able to capture the collective imagination of the people, in all its disorganized richness and insightfulness, and is able to return this knowledge back to the people in a more systematic and organized fashion so the very same producers of the knowledge would be able to appraise, reinterpret, and rethink their own knowledge and insights, both conceptually and practically.

Any process of teaching and learning, as well as the production of knowledge in the human sciences, involves a great deal of persuasion. People in general, and intellectuals in particular, are always trying to persuade each other, trying to show that they have a better explanation and a more powerful, far-reaching, and/or completed analysis than previous explanations or competing ones. Many critical intellectuals working in the tradition of critical theory have embraced a constructivist perspective as the polar opposite to positivism. A constructivist model of social science reflects a strong alternative vision in which reality appears as a product of discontinuities and unpredictable effects. Learners in the view of constructivists actively participate in learning, a notion that applies to the most elementary forms of learning and the most advance forms of research. Viewing all knowledge and learning as a social activity does not necessarily mean, as some post-modernists argue, that we cannot potentially represent reality, but it does imply that we must acknowledge the diversity of perspectives involved in the formation of a community, and a community of inquirers and teachers in particular. Abandoning the "quest for certainty" does not require abandoning the search for knowledge.

From a constructivist perspective, critical intellectuals, despite their attempt to persuade, are convinced that there is never a perfect, definitive, or comprehensive interpretation or understanding nor a conclusive analysis that cannot be challenged or be subject to serious debate and criticism. Perhaps the best way to put it is the Hegelian notion of *Aufhebung:* Knowledge creation is always the negation of the previous negation, the criticism of previous knowledge that in and by itself is a criticism of previous knowledge.

Assuming this notion of *Aufhebung* invites one to a sense of humility and humbleness in intellectual and creative work. Intellectuals always work with knowledge produced by someone else, not only individuals but collectivities. Hence critical intellectuals see their work as part of a social process, and always provisory and limited. Critical intellectuals cannot be detached clinicians offering objective advice. While intellectual work is seen by conventional wisdom as eminently individual work or the work of a team of individuals who share similar analytical, theoretical, and methodological premises, for critical intellectuals what they do is also part of collective work because they always draw from previous knowledge and the criticism of previous knowledge. Therefore, the notion of learning is as important as the notion of teaching in knowledge construction. Critical intellectuals do not assume that their expertise based on esoteric knowledge is theirs and theirs alone, and that their commitment is simply the pursuit of a profession or trade. Facing the notion of the Mannheimean intellectual, such as an independent or detached intellectual working above the fray of power and social interests, critical intellectuals assume that they are enabled and constrained by the conditions of their time, but that they should pursue a dream, or a utopia, one which cannot be simply defined by their own wishes or desires, but rather by a set of collective conditions and aspirations that they may assume as theirs. Obviously, this cannot be achieved unless critical intellectuals assume their role as part of a community effort for social transformation. Critical intellectuals assume an agonic perspective in knowledge production. Assuming that no intellectual work can provide a definitive answer to virtually any domain or problematique of the human sciences, critical intellectuals cannot, for moral and political reasons, give up continuing the process of mutual persuasion, even if their intellectual product may be short lived. Marcuse offers a compelling argument to justify the moral dimensions of the work of critical intellectuals. Speaking, perhaps for the last time, to his disciple Jürgen Habermas, Marcuse said "Look, I know wherein our most basic value judgment are rooted—in compassion, in our sense for the suffering of others" (quoted in Habermas, 1981, p. 77).

Politically, critical intellectuals pay as much attention to the process as they do to the product of intellectual work—both as individual and collective endeavors. In so doing, critical modernist intellectuals remain key facilitators of intellectual exchanges in the production of collective symbolism and rituals. They remain key to facilitate the creation of spaces for public conversation, as Paulo Freire has exemplified throughout his own life. A few years ago I was interviewing Freire and asked him what he would like his legacy to be. He answered that when he died, he would like people to say of him: "Paulo Freire lived, loved, and wanted to know." Freire, in his poetic style, provided a simple and yet powerful message about the role of critical intellectuals. For Freire, critical intellectuals should live passionately their own ideas, building spaces of deliberation and tolerance in their quest for knowledge and empowerment. They love what they do and those with whom they interact. Love, then, become another central element of the political project of intellectuals agonizing in producing knowledge for empowerment and liberation.

Finally, it is their love for knowledge itself that makes them sensitive to the popular knowledge and common sense. Following Gramsci, critical intellectuals know that always common sense has a nucleus of "good sense." From this "good sense" of the common sense, critical intellectuals can develop a criticism of conventional wisdom, knowledge, and practices. In educational policy and planning, this "good sense" could be a starting point for a critique of instrumental rationalization.

For critical theory, the critique of education should lead to change, and the construction of better lives for children. That is what matters. It is then appropriate to conclude this chapter with a letter I received recently from Mike Rose, a friend and colleague of mine at UCLA, and author of the classic book *Lives on the Boundary*. Mike just released his second book, *Possible Lives,* a book that has been received with a note of optimism and hope by critical intellectuals in the United States. Mike's letter is, at the same time, the beginning of a critique of the ideas presented in this chapter, and a reaffirmation of some of its intimate—and I must say, most fundamental—premises:

Carlos,

I've been thinking about the kind things you said about *Possible Lives* after last week's faculty meeting. At the time, I said to you that one problem the Left has is its inability to critique and celebrate simultaneously. (Somewhere in *Lives on the Boundary,* I call for a binocular vision, the capacity to see both degradation and hope at the same moment.) What we also have trouble doing—and I hope I do a bit of this in *Possible Lives*—is crafting a critique out of exemplars rather than out of images of oppression. Given our critical traditions, I think this is hard for us to do. But it seems we're at a historical moment when it's necessary. For all the intellectual work being done in Marxist, poststructuralist, and other critical fields, little of it seems to move widely beyond the academy.

Of course, intellectual work doesn't have to gain its final measure of worth by how widely it sweeps. Of course not. But I'm also concerned by what I see happening *within* the academy with these critical enterprises. I don't claim to know a lot about critical theory and cultural studies, but the little I do know seems, at times, to be pretty unsupple, rigid, and grounded in a kind of anger that constricts possibility. I watch some of the more politically oriented members of our profession, and as much as I like and admire them, they sometimes don't seem to be able to use their critical tools to ponder, reflect, strategically select . . . rather, they judge quickly, assuredly, dismissively. There's a place for that in any social movement, of course, but there has to be more—especially to build. To nurture possibility. To appreciate the astounding variability in each community. To keep from reproducing yet another set of limitations and hatreds in a different guise. Somehow, trying to develop different ways of engaging in social critique seems necessary. What I see around me—and I may be talking out of ignorance here—seems too brittle, too self-referenced, too ungenerous, both conceptually and socially.

Anyway, these are the thoughts that your kind words sparked. Somehow we need to craft critiques that begin with an affirmation of what people can do—real, concrete images of intellectual, social, economic possibility. This critique needs to move back and forth from historical, social analysis to detailed, everyday moments of achievement: kids adding numbers, people planting a garden, and so on. So much of the critical literature I read holds up only one standard for social change: major social transformation. There's something arrogant about that, it seems to me, for it discounts the daily good work that thousands of people do to effect microlevel change, to incrementally build community. Such change gets dismissed (or patronized) in way too much radical literature. There was something very powerful about those teachers I visited— doing the hard, consistent day-to-day work they were doing— and I don't see it represented very often in the critical literature. Your confirmation of those portraits touched me deeply, emotionally and intellectually, . . . and, dare I say it, politically. (Mike Rose, personal letter to the author, March 14, 1996)

Very powerful words written in the spirit of critical theory. Words that should resonate with critical intellectuals thinking about possibilities of critique and change. Words that invite to dialogue about common ground, about the celebration of exemplars and not only the critique of oppression, and about finding ways to link the power of abstract theory thinking macroscopic changes with the daily life of the schools and the dreams of children, teachers, and parents for a quality public education.

NOTES

1. Morrow and Torres (1995) have argued that Giddens's structuration theory is a sophisticated formulation of Marx's transformational dialectical model that attempts "to go beyond a formal analysis to historically analyze the intersection of systemic crisis and group-based mobilization and counter-mobilization, thus effectively coupling the analysis of social and system integration" (p. 33).

2. Two observations are in order. There is an important distinction between the notion of ideology as weltanschauung and the appraisal that within a given weltanschauung there could be competing ideologies interacting and/or confronting the same definition of that weltanschauung. The example of Christianity as ideology serves well.

Without doubt, as a summary of moral, philosophical theological, and spiritual religious perceptions Christianity is a weltanschauung. However, several ideologies compete for the definition of this weltanschauung, some of them drastically different, such as the ideology of Christendom (the traditional perspective associated with the Catholic Church) or a populist and even socialist orientation as represented in theology of liberation (Torres, 1992a). At a more abstract level however, some authors have suggested the existence of a "class weltanschauung" which may comprise also several alternative ideologies or ideological momentums. For instance, this is the point in the distinction of an economic-corporatist phase and a political phase in Gramsci's analysis of correlations of forces between social classes, or Lukac's distinction between class instinct and class consciousness. It seems that some commentators of Gramsci, such as H. Portelli (1972), interpret ideology in Gramsci as class weltanschauung.

3. This dominant ideology helps the ruling classes in two ways: first, by legitimating the dominant values as the central values within the overall society; and second, by justifying a particular class situation (e.g., class role, class positions. and class dynamics) of a ruling class in society. In short, it contributes to justify the reasonableness of the ruling politics on the basis of class habitus. That is the reason that the patterning of a given set of ideologies, within class societies, is determined by a given set of class constellations and class relations, and hence subject to class struggle (Therborn, 1980).

CHAPTER 2

The State and Public Education in Latin America

with Adriana Puiggrós

Past efforts and available resources have made basic education possible in Latin America for the majority of children, helped to extend the years of schooling, provided early and preschool education, facilitated educational access for disabled children, and improved the chances for the poor, migrants, girls, and indigenous children to attend public schools. In addition to increasing the equality of educational opportunities, schools have also improved their overall capacity to retain students and even promote them to higher education. Nevertheless, the equality, quality (including effectiveness, equity, and efficiency), and relevance of educational provision continue to be critical issues, especially now that Latin American states are financially pressed. Elementary and secondary schooling continue to be segregated by class, with the poor attending public schools, while middle- and upper-class students are largely educated at private institutions. With few exceptions, preschooling—decisive in shaping the cognitive structure of children—is not widely available for the region's poor, while illiteracy (especially among women) also continues to plague the efforts of educational planners. This illiteracy and the rural educational conditions, particularly among indigenous groups, continue to be pressing issues, with adult education remaining at the top of the policy agenda. *Popular education,* an indigenous paradigm of nonformal education developed in the region, is facing serious challenges in the context of postmodernism and post-Marxism in Latin America. Teachers' training, their political views, and their technical skills continue to be central for educational reform. Current social, political, and economic changes in Latin America underscore the pace, texture, and scope of educational development, quality, and relevance. In this context, educational planners, children, youth, parents, and communities must deal with the implications of

63

stagnant economic growth during the 1980s, the growing external debt, increasing fiscal constraints, and both the intended and unintended impacts of structural economic adjustments and neoliberal states. Although the relationships between education and social change continue to be revisited by those seeking educational reform, unfortunately the challenges of poverty remain seemingly intractable for public policies—especially education—and democracy.

THE STATE IN LATIN AMERICA: FROM THE OLIGARCHICAL STATE TO NEOLIBERALISM

During the second half of the nineteenth century and the first three decades of this century, the predominant state model in Latin America was a liberal state, which has been defined as "oligarchical"(Boron, 1976). The oligarchical state consolidated the nation and generated relative political stability. In this model, the oligarchy maintained tight control over the political process, at times by directly controlling the state and at other times through control of the parliament and important political parties. In order to implement this control, on occasion electoral fraud or simply open repression was employed (Collier & Collier, 1991).

Systems of public education were developed as part of the project of liberal states that sought under the control of a landowning oligarchy to establish the foundations of the nation and citizenship. When the oligarchical state collapsed in the early 1930s, it was replaced by several variants that shared a fundamentally corporatist orientation. In some cases, the state models followed a Keynesian or welfare-state orientation. Despite these changes, however, the role and function of public education remained largely unchanged. Nevertheless, since public education attempts to create a citizen as a "disciplined pedagogical subject," the role, mission, ideology, and training of teachers—including the prevailing notions of curriculum and school knowledge—are all marked by the prevailing philosophy of the state (Puiggrós, 1986, 1990b; Puiggrós et al., 1992a).

A reorganization of the state took place in Latin America following the collapse of the oligarchical pattern. These new models included experiences as diverse as the Mexican postrevolutionary state, the democratic state that emerged in Costa Rica after the 1948 revolution, the liberal-democratic states that were implemented by pacts between liberal and conservative parties in Venezuela and Colombia, and modernizing developmentalist regimes in Chile, Uruguay, Brazil, and Argentina that arose after the 1950s. A key element in the debate about state-society relationships was the experience of populism and the growing presence of trade unions. In addition to populism, a central element of the Latin American state has been the implementation of public policies with a welfare orientation. State interventionism in the modernization of societies followed similar although not identical paths to the construction of the welfare state.

The *welfare state* is a particular form of the democratic-liberal state in industrialized societies, whose origins have been associated with the industrial and financial changes in post-Depression United States, based on a "social pact" (New Deal) between employers and labor. A striking feature of the welfare state is its interventionist role, including enlarged public spending in both productive and nonproductive sectors of the economy. *Welfare policies* are defined as government protection of minimum standards of income, nutrition, health, housing, and education. As Harold Wilensky (1975, 1976) has argued, these welfare benefits were assured to every citizen as a political right rather than as charity (see also Popkewitz, 1991).

However, several elements—some intrinsic to Latin America's structure and political culture and some the result of external pressures—conspired against the full implementation of the welfare state model in Latin America. First is the extremely unequal distribution of income, in part due to the resiliency and power of elite landowners and the new bourgeoisie that emerged as the region industrialized. Second is the economic vulnerability of states and economies facing pressure from multinational corporations and even foreign governments—an issue at the core of "dependency" theory developed largely by Latin American scholars. Third is the lack of unemployment insurance and welfare benefits. The final element is the impact of populist experiences that disorganized the state's bureaucratic control, creating diverse constraints but also inducements for specific public policies. In short, the Latin American state that propels economic and political modernization is still a dependent development capitalist state (Carnoy, 1984, ch. 8; Carnoy & Samoff, 1990; Sonntag & Valecillos, 1977.

The 1970s were a decade of state authoritarianism—what Argentine scholar Guillermo O'Donnell (1987) defines as the "bureaucratic-authoritarian state." This new authoritarianism had clear expressions in the military dictatorships in Brazil and Argentina. The 1980s were marked by the demise of authoritarian military dictatorships and the implementation of new liberal-democratic forms of government. In the political-economic arena, however, a grave crisis of capital accumulation and income distribution, coupled with a fiscal crisis of the state and growing external debt, threatened the region's return to democracy. Hence the 1980s were the "lost decade" for development, a period marked by high (even hyper-) inflation and recession of a severity never before experienced. The oil crises of 1973 and 1982 left the region in a state of economic disarray, a situation exacerbated by rising international interest rates that made it increasingly difficult for Latin American countries to meet their debt repayment schedules. International agencies—specifically the International Monetary Fund (IMF) and the World Bank—exhorted governments in the region to adopt structural adjustment policies to address these balance-of-payment difficulties and fiscal deficits. The attempt to restore economic stability by restructuring the economy and the relationships between state and society prompted numerous scholars, politicians, and informed observers to notice the formation of a new social pact of domination controlling capitalist states in Latin America: the neoliberal state (Lomnitz & Melnick, 1991, pp. 9–47).

Neoliberalism is a term employed to characterize a new type of state that emerged in the region during the last 2 decades, the first example of which is usually associated with the policies implemented in Chile after 1973. Neoliberal policies typically advocate free trade and small public sectors and oppose excessive state interventionism and tight market regulation. Neoliberalism has historically and philosophically been associated with structural adjustment programs. Structural adjustment, in turn, usually entails a broad range of policies recommended by the World Bank, the IMF, and other financial organizations. Although the World Bank differentiates among stabilization, structural adjustment, and adjustment policies, it acknowledges that the general use of these terms is often imprecise and inconsistent (Samoff, 1990, p. 21).

The neoliberal model of stabilization and adjustment has resulted in a number of policy recommendations, including the reduction of government expenditures, currency devaluations to promote exports, a reduction in import tariffs, and an increase in public and private savings. Key aims of this model include a drastic reduction in the state sector, the liberalization of salaries and prices, and the reorientation of industrial and agricultural production toward exports. In the short run, the goals are to reduce fiscal deficits and public expenditures, to drastically cut inflation, and to lower exchange rates and tariffs. In the medium term, structural adjustment relies on exports as the engine of growth. To that extent, structural adjustment and subsequent stabilization policies seek to liberalize trade, to reduce any distortion in price structures, to end any "protectionist" policies, and therefore to facilitate the rule of the market in the Latin American economies (Bitar, 1988, p. 45). Variations exist in the implementation of these models of economic liberalization and structural adjustments, of course. Some countries benefit from their economic endowments, aggressive policies, or successful performance of their exports commodities (e.g., Chile); others gain from specific free trade deals within larger regional markets (e.g., Mexico, with the North American Free Trade Agreement [NAFTA]; and Brazil, Argentina, Paraguay, and Uruguay, with Mercosur); while still others, such as Argentinean capital markets, benefit from the political instability of Eastern Europe.

The Sociopolitical Background

Latin American societies have a long tradition of political authoritarianism that has to some extent permeated many different policy arenas, including education. The historical irony is that the return to democracy in the 1980s and 1990s is being marked by unusual economic constraints. The political debacle of the region's Left, the failure of socialist revolution in Central America during the 1980s (i.e., Nicaragua, El Salvador, and Guatemala), and the broader collapse of socialism worldwide created the "right conditions" for structural adjustment policies to be fully implemented throughout Latin America. Thus the deadlock that had existed between the programs of lower-class sectors (particularly trade unions) and the economic and political preferences of elites was finally broken with the onset of this adjustment period (Raban & Sturzenegger, n.d.).

While the full extent of the social consequences from the economic crisis and subsequent stabilization policies is still a matter of debate, a number of international agencies have concluded that the overall welfare of many Latin Americans is worse than 20 years earlier. According to the Economic Commission of Latin America (ECLA), for instance, approximately 44% (183 million) of the region's population in 1990 were living below the poverty line—an increase of 112 million over 1970. The ECLA attributed this growing impoverishment to "the dramatic fall in average income, which marked a tremendous step backwards in the material standard of living of the Latin American and Caribbean population" (Rosenthal, 1989, p. 1). Similar analyses and forecasts are presented in a recent report by the Inter-American Dialogue (Aspen Institute, 1992; see also United Nations Development Program [UNDP], n.d.a, n.d.b).

In response to the second items, stabilization and structural adjustment programs have been carried out under different names—by regimes with diverse ideological orientations—within the context of a general and deep crisis. Economic stabilization occurred in Latin America as a response to debt crisis, fiscal crisis, industrial recession, and inflation (in some cases hyperinflation). This stabilization happened, however, only after key social actors in the distributional conflict (the working class, campesinos, and even sectors of the middle classes) lost, by default or purposely, their will to challenge cuts in public expenditures. Reform reduced the state's interventionist role in welfare policies and facilitated, through privatization and diminishing welfare expenditures, the rule of market forces in Latin American societies. This, of course, has implications for state legitimacy and the role of public education in the region.

The State and Public Education

In the nineteenth-century liberal state and under the diverse state models that emerged in the wake of struggles during the 1920s and the Depression of the 1930s, Latin American public education played a major role in political integration and legitimation as well as modernization (Puiggrós, 1986).[1] To facilitate development, the state extended social benefits to vast sectors of the population, particularly in Argentina, Costa Rica, and Mexico. Education played a key role in these social programs because mass schooling was viewed as a means of creating responsible citizens, training skilled labor, and increasing the opportunity for social mobility. In the early 1960s, human capital theories and educational planning justified educational expansion not only as a good investment in skill training but also as a prerequisite for liberal democracy.

This educational expansion during the early phase of industrialization in the 1960s produced the highest rates of educational growth in the world (United Nations Educational, Scientific and Cultural Organization, 1974, pp. 167, 227). Between 1960 and 1970, higher education and secondary education expanded by 248% and 258%, respectively; however, the enrollment in primary basic education grew only 168%, while the region's illiteracy rate remained basically unchanged (United Nations Educational, Scientific and Cultural Organization, 1971). In the last 4 decades, Latin America made significant progress toward democracy by "(i) expanding access to education for most of the children reaching school age; (ii) extending the years of schooling; (iii) improving timely entrance to school; (iv) providing early care to an increasing number of deprived children; and (v) increasing the provision of minimum inputs and eliminating tracks for social levels" (Schiefelbein, 1991, p. 4; see also United Nations Educational, Scientific and Cultural Organization/CEPAL, 1981).

Enrollment in elementary education has grown steadily in Latin America, but while this trend continues, the growth rate of educational expenditures adjusted for inflation diminished in the 1980s. Fernando Reimers (1990) shows that between 1975 and 1980, total educational expenditures increased in all countries in the region. From 1980 to 1985, however, the total in real terms diminished in 12 of the 18 countries he studied. In contrast to previous educational expansion then, the past 2 decades have witnessed a decline in both the quantity and quality of schooling (Avalos, 1986; Lockheed & Verspoor, 1991). Reimers (1991) argues that the constraints of structural adjustment policies have forced ministries of education to sacrifice equity and efficiency in order to reduce their educational expenditures—cuts that have disproportionately affected primary education and are reflected in the limited resources available for teaching materials, school facilities, and falling rates of enrollment. These reductions have alienated teachers' organizations, forcing them to develop defensive actions and occasionally putting them into conflict with the state over the formulation of educational policies (see Carnoy & Torres, 1992; Samoff, 1994).

Reimers and Luis Tiburcio (1993) offer these conclusions about educational spending in Latin America:

> An analysis of the changes in public government financing of education in Latin America between 1970 and 1985 concludes that the adjustment led to disproportionate cuts in expenditures on education as a percentage of government expenditure or of GNP [gross national product]. Within education, capital expenditure suffered disproportionately as did expenditure on non-salary items, while increasingly more countries reduced expenditure at the level of primary education disproportionately. A study of the financing crisis in Central America between 1979–1989 concludes that most of the countries (except Honduras) show a tendency to spend a smaller percentage of GDP [gross domestic product] on education, that teachers' salaries have depreciated in real terms with losses of about two-thirds, and that at the end of the decade most of the budget in primary education goes to salaries. (p. 22)

Their analysis of Brazil and Mexico shows similar declines in educational expenditures "against the background of a growing government sector, relative to GDP" (p. 37).

These changes are occurring in the context, and are perhaps the result of an emerging global economy that operates very differently from the former industrial economy. The old economy was based on high volume and highly standardized production, with a few managers controlling the production process from above and a great number of workers following orders. This economy of mass production was stable as long as it could reduce its costs (including the price of labor) and retool quickly enough to stay competitive. But because of advancements in transportation and communications technology as well as the growth of the service industry, industrial production has become fragmented around the world. Production now moves to locations where there is either cheaper or more highly trained productive labor, favorable political conditions, access to better infrastructure and national resources, larger markets, and/or tax incentives (O'Reilly, 1992).

The new global economy is more fluid and flexible, with multiple lines of power and decision making analogous to a spider web as opposed to the static pyramidal organization of the traditionalist capitalist system (Reich, 1991). In this context, a public education oriented toward the production of a disciplined and reliable workforce is no longer as firm a goal in the new global economy as it was under the old capitalist order.

The performance of the economy is a major issue underpinning educational policies, and the question is to what extent the recipes for structural adjustment will either help or hinder educational expansion, quality, and equality of opportunity in the region. This is the bedrock concern underscoring the political behavior of the main actors involved with Latin American education today, particularly teachers' organizations, the neoliberal state and its agencies, and international organizations, especially the World Bank.

It is imperative to situate the national and regional educational policies of Latin America within the context of recent global changes including the rise of the newly industrialized countries in Asia and the Pacific Rim and the impact of this shift on the models of economic development in Latin America; the promise of consolidation of regional economic markets (European Economic Commission, NAFTA, and Mercosur); the intensification of competition among the major industrial powers of Germany, Japan, and the United States; the opening of Eastern Europe; and the resurgence of regional ethnic and religious conflicts (Ohmae, 1990; Przeworski, 1991; Thurow, 1992). These changes and contradictions are increasingly related to the globalization of economies, cultures, and societies, showing how very powerful the structural forces involved in education can be at times of severe crisis and restructuring of policy priorities and systems.

State Corporatism and Dependency

Public education also plays a major role in the legitimation of the political systems and the integration and modernization of Latin American countries in the context of corporatism and dependency (Collier & Collier, 1991). The dependency perspective should be considered alongside other broad schools of development, which include modernization, bureaucratic authoritarianism, postimperialism, and interactive local political economy. While modernization focuses on the nature and characteristics of the social structure in less developed countries as causes of underdevelopment, dependency theories instead emphasize the structure of international capitalism and the lack of capital available for autonomous expansion. Bureaucratic authoritarianism explains dependent development as a result of problems stemming from the model of import-substitution industrialization implemented by several Latin American countries. A key factor contributing to instability is growing working-class demands that undermine both the legitimacy of the overall model of development and its ability for capital accumulation. The answer to this development crisis at times has been the emergence of an authoritarian state. Dependent-development theories, which point to the centrality of the state for the capital accumulation in the periphery of the capitalist world system, spring from dependency theories, and are compatible with world-system analysis (Wallerstein, 1987). Postimperialism theories attempt to explain underdevelopment as part of a process of transnational class formation in the developing world. Finally, the interactive local political economy perspective, which focuses on the interaction of social domestic forces within a modern political economy, claims that the complex interaction of domestic socioeconomic and political trends determines policy outcomes. In this perspective, economic pressures from domestic socioeconomic actors are considered central in the determination of policy options and outcomes (see Cardoso & Faletto, 1979; Evans, 1979; Frieden, 1991; Prebisch, 1985).

The theory of "conditioned states" in the Third World—expanding on and clarifying the notion of the dependent state—argues that the state is shaped

> by the nature of the peripheral role that its economy plays in the world system and the corresponding enormous influence that the dynamic of metropolitan capitalism has on its development process. The Third World state is also conditioned by the significant noncapitalist (postfeudal) elements in its own political system. (Carnoy & Samoff, 1990, p. 20)

Latin America's conditioned states have been unable properly to carry out their public functions for a number of reasons. On the one hand, the fragility of local economies has made local dominant groups unwilling to allow pluralist participation by the masses in selecting the state bureaucracy. On the other hand, since the popular sectors have historically identified the state primarily as a pact of domination by the elite or a surrogate state, the state has not been seen as an independent entity working on behalf of the citizenry (see Carnoy & Torres, 1990; Torres, 1991c; see also Morales-Gómez & Torres, 1992).

Similarly, the vast social gap between the rich and poor, both in material and cultural terms, has prevented the state from administering laws on behalf of the entire citizenry. When a state's performance is not regularly overseen by conventional means such as elections, the state runs the risk of increasing its degree of repression of civil society instead of improving its own legitimation through consensus.[2]

Another question is the state's ability to consolidate the nation and the market. Since the market's boundaries are externally defined by the presence of outside powers and multinational corporations, the definition of the nation is continually and historically respecified by a complex matrix of exogenous-endogenous processes. More often than not, the conditioned state has little control over the dynamics of its own political economy.

Finally, the state's position on the periphery of technological creation and the use of science and technology for improving capital accumulation make it impotent to link the capitalist division of labor with science and technology. The brain drain of a nation's intellectuals is a typical example of this difficulty.

While theories of dependency, dependent-development, and the conditioned state have set the tone for a discussion on the nature of the state in Latin America, the perspectives of state corporatism and the political sociology of education have been employed to study the peculiar characteristics of the region's political regimes, particularly the formation of educational policy in Mexico. Corporatism has been defined by political scientist Philippe C. Schmitter (1974) as

> a system of interest representation in which the constituent units are organized into a limited number of singular, compulsory, noncompetitive, hierarchically ordered and functionally differentiated categories, recognized or licensed (if not created) by the state and granted a deliberated representational monopoly within their respective categories in exchange for observing certain controls on their selection of leaders and articulation of demands and supports. (pp. 93–94)

Corporatism, particularly as seen in the intimate relationship between teachers' unions and the state, as well as in the ideology of "normalism" in some countries, helps to explain the nature of educational policy formation in Latin America. For instance, the development of Mexico's educational system has depended on the consolidation of the corporatist state as a mode of governance and political legitimation. Corporatism in Mexico refers to a form of state that has a mass base of popular support because of its revolutionary origins. The Mexican concept of corporatism also refers to the incorporation of peasants, workers, and middle-class sectors into the official political party—the Revolutionary Institutional Party—and into a system of distributing power and influence in the state. Thus corporatism in Mexico refers specifically to the organizational characteristics of the state structure, party, and political control that depend to a certain degree on popular participation and mobilization, although both have traditionally been carefully controlled and manipulated for nondemocratic ends.

The basic premises of the postrevolutionary state are the redistribution of land, strengthening of labor unions, massive education, and the principle of non-reelection (Morales-Gómez & Torres, 1990). Education has played a fundamental role in legitimating the postrevolutionary state and strengthening its hegemony. Furthermore, the corporatist nature of this state has deeply conditioned the way educational policy has been organized, implemented, and evaluated, and Mexican education (particularly adult education) is part of a comprehensive project of compensatory legitimation. While the Mexican case is perhaps too specific—and this may in part explain the country's political stability within the turmoil of recent Latin American history—it could be argued that historical changes in the patterns of relationships between state and society during this century created the conditions for the widespread implementation of corporatist arrangements and for the development of corporatist states. Similarly, educational expansion and the accompanying premise of social mobility for the lower classes through education—even if this rarely occurred—were important components of the democratic pact in Latin America.

Educational systems, and particularly adult education, have been usually co-opted by the state and employed as an instrument of social legitimation and the extension of state authority, rather than as a tool to increase the self-reliance of individuals and poor communities. This has serious implications for policy, planning, and the quality of education. Education has become an arena of struggle among competing political agendas.

THE PEDAGOGICAL SUBJECT

The region's school systems were founded during the second half of the nineteenth century under the guidance of the educational philosophy of cultural liberalism, which considers the state to be the main agent of education. Because cultural liberalism holds that educational systems should prepare modern citizens, integrate the nation, and culturally homogenize the population, achieving some degree of uniformity in pupils' behavior, customs, ways of thinking, and political and cultural language was a desirable goal. This pedagogy was imposed on earlier generations, who faced an inflexible school atmosphere, full of fear, where voices could not be raised and students could not move out of line or have a creased or ink-stained paper from the primary through secondary level. Students wrote with pen and ink and did not dare to speak to teachers without permission (Puiggrós, 1990b).

School enrollment reached significant levels in Latin America, but the success of the liberal project in each country was linked to the degree and type of development of society as a whole. Therefore, there were different pedagogical subjects in each country, who also differed from the image that nineteenth-century liberals held of students as citizens. In fact, cultural homogenization did not take place. Rather, the partial, unequal participation of each subject in public culture stimulated the growth of subjects characterized by different structures.

In the 1960s the Alliance for the Progress program, which borrowed from the experience of the War on Poverty in the United States, promised a social engineering solution in Latin America to poverty, inequality, and inequality of educational opportunity. However, despite such programs, social inequalities continued to increase between developed and developing countries. In 1968, for example, the world's developed nations (with almost one third of the globe's inhabitants and one fourth of the youth population) invested $120 billion in education, while the developing countries invested less than $12 billion. Differences increased, and educational expenditures declined in the underdeveloped world. In 1980 total public spending on education in relation to GNP was 3.6% in Argentina, 4.4% in Bolivia, 4.4% in Mexico, and 7.8% in Costa Rica; in 1985 Argentina had dropped to 2.2%, Bolivia to 0.5%, Mexico to 2.6%, and Costa Rica to 4.7% (United Nations Educational, Scientific and Cultural Organization, 1988).

Concern over the crisis in education acquired an international dimension in the late 1960s with the publication of the classic works of Philip Coombs (1971) and Edgar Faure (1974). They reflected the concern over the increasing quantitative and qualitative deficits in education, caused by the urgent educational needs in the Third World, particularly among the population which remained outside the school system. The crisis those authors reported did not question the existence of the school system, nor did the solutions they proposed reduce education to the needs of the market. Yet they supported state responsibility for public education and proposed that both the state and international organizations increase their investment in this area.

In the late 1960s, educational systems faced an explosion of demand at all levels, a serious lag in curricular content in relation to the cultural, scientific, and technological advances that were occurring worldwide, and a lack of training for work and of preparation for political participation of citizens. With the exception of Mexico, and to a lesser extent Venezuela and Brazil, countries did not carry out the reforms necessary to respond to the demand. Instead, most of the systems accentuated these problems, and it was public knowledge by the late 1980s that educational quality was inadequate (CEPAL, 1990).

Indeed, there was an unprecedented crisis in the region, a real dislocation between the discourse of teachers and pupils, between adults and the younger generation, and between leaders and followers (Puiggrós, 1990a, 1993). This crisis differed from the one in the late 1960s, however, as it was more than the mere repetition of problems that had affected schooling systems for a century (such as dropping out or repetition) but involved others that reflected a profound "ineffectiveness" among the agents of education (teachers, parents, and public and private educational institutions) and a break of cultural links between generations. The gravity of this crisis suggests that it is organic and that Latin American education as a whole is affected.

The globalization process, that is, "the intensification of worldwide social relations which link distant localities in such a way that local happenings are shaped by events occurring many miles away and vice versa" (Held, 1991, p. 9), has expanded modern culture among the high, middle, and working urban sectors in Latin America.[3] However, through the mass media and political, cultural, and educational programs, this process of globalization has also begun to reach the most economically backward and culturally remote groups in Latin America, such as villagers in the Andean cordillera, inhabitants of Argentina's Patagonia, and the alienated urban populations in the shanty towns in Rio de Janeiro, Caracas, and Bogota. Consequently, the global culture is reaching places where the school has not arrived in full force (Coraggio, 1993; Ezcurra, 1991). Globalization also explains the heterogeneity of production, which in turn, increases inequalities of income distribution (ECLA, 1993). Consequently, there are new combinations mixing traditional popular cultures, the cultural makeup of the states in the region, and a trans-nationalized mass culture. The result is the establishment of new subjects who are the product of multiple ethnic, linguistic, social, and ideological amalgamations. This situation can be illustrated by a tour around the numerous cafes and bars in the city of Buenos Aires, which in recent years have been filled by a population of begging children, the so-called street children. Although they cannot read since they have either dropped out or never attended school, they understand the rules of city life and can look after themselves, perhaps better than can middle-class children. Their discourse reflects peasant and working-class language, but language tinged by the experience of city violence. Although they reason like adults, their images are childish. They love and hate schools, that privileged place from which they have been excluded. Their imagination is full of television images and characters from their neighborhood. They have not learned geography and have no idea that their country is located in Latin America, but they refer confidently to situations that they have seen on television in faraway countries (Gadotti & Manfio, 1993).

These changes are also reflected in the appearance of new school rituals. In 1991, for example, the Argentine rock singer Charly Garcia made a respectful musical arrangement of the national anthem. This arrangement scandalized Argentinean society, however, and few schools played it in this rock music version. Nevertheless, youngsters who previously had refused to learn the traditional hymn began to enthusiastically sing the new arrangement, illustrating how an important ritual for reproducing the collective conscience had been rescued for a new generation by articulating it with musical statements that resonate and give an identity to the Argentine youth of today.

School boundaries have been broken, the walls of educational establishments are unable to protect children from external influences, and perhaps much teaching and learning have ceased to be done in schools. There is a fracture between teachers and pupils, and among adults, children, and youth. The concept of organic crisis developed by Antonio Gramsci (1985) suggests that the discourses of traditional teachers no longer articulate the discourses of the new pupils. Thus teachers complain that "nobody listens," that "children are on another wavelength," and that "they don't read, they don't learn anything" (Puiggrós et al., 1992b).

In fact, the distance between adults and young people has widened so much during the last 15 years that this gap now seems, in the eyes of the older generation, to be nothing but a vacuum: "Children today have got empty minds"; "they don't read and they are not interested in culture"; "they are not interested in politics"; "they don't feel like responsible citizens"; "there are no bridges between their language and ours." These are common complaints by parents and teachers (Puiggrós et al., 1992b, pp. 2–3).

These are not sudden cultural changes, however, but the product of long-simmering processes that are the product of numerous ruptures of words, of myths, and of painful changes in values. Trained in the typical logic of modernity, adults seek coherence, continuity, and similarity between cultures. Influenced by functionalist thought and having inherited the ideas of evolutionism and positivism, many intellectuals and pedagogues in particular have difficulties in understanding "border" situations, that is, those where the limits of modern culture appear in their broadest meanings. The inadequacy of customs, rituals, and organizational forms that affect traditional knowledge is disruptive, altering the transmission chain of culture from adult to younger generations. In short, the Latin American school system is going through an organic crisis.

This organic crisis afflicting education requires a thorough analysis of the categories involved, including a multidisciplinary examination from the perspectives of the political sociology of education and historiography.[4] Among other features, this crisis involves increasing difficulties in the teaching and learning of reading and writing, in the secondary importance that students give to reading books and to writing as a means of expression and communication at schools and elsewhere, and in the obstacles in the use of reading and writing among university students in learning scientific and technical disciplines, despite the fact that they have become proficient in the new technologies through self-teaching. In addition, there is a gap between the basic languages taught at schools (e.g., alphabetic, graphic) and the new languages of modern culture (e.g., mass media images, music, and so on) that students learn and appropriate with unusual speed. At the same time, students are increasingly ignorant of both their own national past and world history, reflecting profound gaps in the transmission of culture (and official knowledge) between generations. While younger generations accept fundamentalist explanations of the beginning of life and fundamental values, they are indifferent to collective values or notions of solidarity. Most of them are apolitical in their attitudes—a sharp contrast to Latin American youth in the 1960s and 1970s—but they reject the ideological and cultural essentialism, logocentrism, and authoritarianism of the older generation.

Despite this organic crisis, schools continue to be the designated institution for socializing children into the official knowledge of the nation and the culture of older generations. Social differences now have symbolic values in the contrasting experiences of nighttime musical entertainment, attendance at soccer matches, or the middle- and upper-class pastime of gathering in the paddle and tennis courts. Traditional clubs, neighborhood streets, and even political party activities do not attract young people, nor do they have appealing cultural offerings for them.

This organic crisis is quite different from the endemic crisis of educational quality that was perceived worldwide by reformers in the 1960s and 1970s. Do children's and youth's perceptions of reading and writing as obsolete indicate an organic crisis rather than representing mere symptoms of systemic dysfunction? How does this crisis affect the definition of the term *education*? In other words, can we expand the educational system when the elements that make up the educational landscape in the traditional and modern pedagogical imagination are disappearing or have little if any meaning to new generations? In answering these questions, it should be borne in mind that the organic crisis affects not only modernist educational discourses but also pedagogy per se. The concepts that constitute the training of pedagogues and scientists responded to the laws of standardized grammar and modernist expressions of schooling, either reflected in the New School movement or in the different strains of pedagogical liberalism, socialism, and popular education approaches. If pedagogues cannot question their own premises and concepts, they will only be able to receive the mirror image of their (our) own decadence as teachers, while lamenting the decadence of the school system or the poor quality of education. In so doing, educators and policy makers will be unable to understand the complexity of phenomena that have caused this crisis or develop new theoretical and programmatic strategies. Retaining old discourses without deconstructing them prevents social transformation, even though the concept that pedagogues and policy makers employ may have been the most progressive of their time.

In this context, teachers are questioned on two fronts by the cultural changes. They are questioned first as social subjects in general (i.e., as citizens, heads of family, workers, or consumers) and second as citizens responsible for the professional transmission of basic cultural norms and values to younger generations.[5] They are overwhelmed by their responsibility in today's world. For over a century, they were responsible for transmitting the legal and legitimate modern cultural capital, that is, the transmission of culture. At present, however, the definition of the "subject" of the educational process, and the articulation among teachers, students, and knowledge, seems to be disintegrating. The "pupils" imagined by modern education are deeply fractured, and new combinations of identities arise with different perspectives. Instead of being unified by the same pedagogical discourse in the classroom, school rituals connect teachers, students, and knowledge combining bits of different cultural origins and statements from dissimilar discourses. This is perhaps best exemplified by the Latino school population near the U.S.-Mexican border, the *pachuco* culture that is the product of complex political, cultural, and pedagogical subjects and, by implication, diverse identities (Prieto, 1992).

In Southern Cone countries—Chile, Uruguay, and Argentina—that had developed some of the region's earliest modern educational systems, the experience of authoritarian governments in the 1970s, coupled with economic collapse during the 1980s and early 1990s, brought about the collapse of pedagogical circuits that connected with school knowledge. The public school discourse that educated so many generations of immigrants and native-born in these nations was the product of a pedagogical consensus constructed by the state—hence the ideology of normalism and its implications for pedagogical practices (Bernetti & Puiggrós, 1993). This discourse has become less comprehensible for the new impoverished social classes—the sons and daughters of immigrants from neighboring countries who speak indigenous languages—and for vast sectors of urban youth.

While the organic crisis is a profound fracture in the operation of educational systems, it is not so different from the cultural gap that prevailed in the foundations of the school system in countries with large indigenous populations, including Guatemala, Bolivia, Peru, Ecuador, and, to a lesser extent, Mexico. In many of these countries, because the educational system has been unable to cross linguistic and cultural barriers, the culture of society has been fractured for more than a century.

Dissimilar pedagogical discourses deeply wounded Domingo Faustino Sarmiento's (1850/1989) notion of public, compulsory, and massive schooling as the answer to the conflict between civilization and barbarism. The notion of public education as a state political mandate is now under siege by the neoliberal drive, which proposes that the logic of the market and market exchanges should regulate educational investment. Previous inequalities and the growing distinctions between schooling for the poor and for the rich mark the educational landscape of Latin America. This dualization of schooling is the result of many political decisions, including the relinquishment of the state's responsibility to educate all its citizens. Today, some Latin American states seek only to provide a basic education for the majority of the population, but even this is not the case in countries such as Peru. Drastic reductions in funding for public schools and growing out-of-pocket costs for parents increase inequalities. New fees for previously free services—including access to libraries, exams, and salaries for teachers in special subjects— leave the main school expenditures to the ability of parents' cooperatives and associations (in some countries they are termed *cooperativas escolares;* in others, school "foundations") to raise revenues to supplement dwindling state subsidies. Decentralization, including the transfer of schools from the federal to the municipal system, often leaves many poor provinces and local municipal authorities in charge of educational systems for which they lack the appropriate material, financial, and even human resources. Some even claim that this transference of schools from federal to municipal authority condemns many educational systems to poverty (Nuñez, 1984b). In some cases, funds are released only after the efficiency of establishments is assessed or when mechanisms for nationally centralized systems of control over the teaching profession are established, paradoxically, in the context of increasingly decentralized systems of public education (First Sectorial Education Investment Project, 1993; Kubler, 1991).

Private education may not be the ultimate solution for the educational crisis. Many parents and students are unable to meet the cost of their own education, and the investment of private education (either in its religious, business, or professional corporation orientation) may be insufficient to meet the social demand. Increasing unemployment, growing numbers of

children living in the streets and/or alienated from the cultural foundations of their societies, and poverty place educational development at risk.
In Venezuela, for example, a recent study shows that 43.7% of the population live in poverty and that malnutrition affects 16% of children under
age 15 (Instituto Interregional de las Naciones Unidas, 1991). Despite the
lack of reliable statistics for countries such as Argentina and Uruguay,
educators not surprisingly suspect that illiteracy—an educational problem once considered virtually solved—is growing. In this context, some
researchers, evaluating the neoliberal experiment applied in Chile, argue
that the strategy implied in the reduction of the state's economic, political, and technical investment in public education attempts to eliminate
the public school as a privileged space for the preparation of political
and cultural subjects. The outcome is the segmentation of the population
into different and unequal cultural configurations and educational levels
(Nuñez, 1984a, 1984b).

CONCLUSION: RETHINKING/UNTHINKING
LATIN AMERICAN EDUCATION IN COMPARATIVE PERSPECTIVE

Understanding the theoretical and political problems of Latin American
education demands greater conceptual sophistication than that found in
traditional theories and methodologies of comparative education. Deconstructed notions of unequal and combined development of Latin American educational systems, organic crisis, the presence of new subjects of
education, the role of the democratic state, and the presence of "fractures"
and "borders" in modern education will provide unusual breadth and
depth for knowledge in comparative education.

   The notion of unequal and combined development suggests an intersection between pockets of modern, highly educated populations (including postmodernist expressions in art, humanities, and science) and
premodern, peripheral, marginal, and even pre-Columbian cultures and
populations. These societies are marked by deep cultural and linguistic
discontinuities, with the dominant cultural capital prevailing in schools
and societies. Public schools were conceived of by the state as central tools
in an effort to produce a homogeneous citizenry and highly trained workers in the framework of an unequal and combined development of Latin
America. Thus the Marxist concept of such development popularized in
the 1960s and 1970s, the emblematic notion of dependency utilized to highlight the interconnections between external and domestic factors in underdevelopment, and the notion of hybrid cultures—a cultural melange of
mestizos, indigenous, and Spanish and/or Portuguese people that Néstor

García Canclini (1982, 1990) so aptly has discussed in his anthropological studies—all point to the intersection of modern and traditional cultures. These modern and traditional cultures, through constant cultural border crossings (Giroux, 1992; McLaren, 1993), produce and reproduce new identities and the asynchronic development of Latin American educational models (Weinberg, 1984). Theoretically, the notion of multiple identities also relates to Dérrida's (1989) notion of "difference" and the feminist notion of "otherness," concepts essential to capturing the magnitude of this unequal and combined cultural development in the region.

Paulo Freire very early in his *Pedagogy of the Oppressed* addressed the meanings of border crossings, otherness, hybrid cultures, and asynchronic development in Latin America. In so doing, he showed the political implications of pedagogical work. Freire argues that notions of oppression and domination are part and parcel of the pedagogical relationships between teachers and pupils in traditional classrooms. Thus the notion of *extensionism*, that is, the provision of the dominant educational discourse to peasants in the context of agrarian reforms, was expressed not only as part of a pedagogical discourse but also as a political discourse.

A fundamental insight of Freire is that the social and pedagogical subjects of education are not fixed, essential, or inflexible—that is, the teacher is a student and the student is a teacher. The cultural and pedagogical implications of this observation are that the place and role of teachers are not always and necessarily an extension of the role of adult White men, or conversely, a role performed by female teachers subsumed under the discourse of hegemonic masculinity.[6] Similarly, as a product of European logocentric thought, school knowledge is not always reproduced in schools, but is subject to contestation and resistance. While Freire criticized the Western school in Latin America as banking education and an authoritarian device (i.e., as a device transmitting official knowledge while simultaneously eliminating pupils as subjects of their own education), his pedagogy of liberation is an invitation to dialogue in the context of multiple political and social struggles for liberation. Dialogue appears not only as a pedagogical tool, but also as a method of deconstruction of the way pedagogical and political discourses are constructed.[7] More than 30 years after Freire's main books were published, the concept of dialogical education still appears as a democratic tool for dealing with complex cultural conflicts in Latin American education (Freire, 1978a, 1978b; Torres, 1995a).

The notion of a hegemonic crisis implies also finding new concepts to take stock of the "new subjects"—teachers and pupils—in the changing political and cultural formations emerging in Latin America (Martín-Barbero, 1987a; Vilches, 1987). Similarly, it is important to understand how the crisis of hegemony relates to the problem of national identity; what role the state attributes to the school system and teachers' professional work; how the public/private cleavage in education is changing in the context of neoliberalism; and whether (and if so, how) the new social problems differ from those that school systems in Latin America faced in the past. These new social problems include, but are not limited to, the educational needs and the educational alternatives for street children, how the culture of drug trafficking is affecting educational establishments, and how private networks of communication and informatics are changing the status, reliability, and accessibility of school knowledge in the region.[8]

The concept of subjects refers to the notion of social and pedagogical subjects and their relationships with knowledge and structures. In Latin America, the notion of a pedagogical and social subject involves the analysis of a complex cultural and social milieu that results from multiple parallel determinations, including class, gender, race, ethnicity, religion, and regionalisms (Aguilar, 1990; Morrow & Torres, 1995; Pereyra, 1988). At the same time, by placing the notion of the pedagogical subject at the center of competing educational discourses, it is possible to find a heuristic device to understand the complex determinations—actions and reactions—resulting from the decadence of the old political order (and its social agents). It also helps to understand the progressive breakdown of national identities while local and regional identities simultaneously emerge as relevant in decision making and political and social struggles. Finally, the concept of subject is useful for exploring the disappearance of cultural and educational traditions in schools and societies.

The role of the conditioned state continues to be problematic for democracy and public education in the region. The state's institutional identity is crucial in understanding the role education has played in development and social change. The notion of the dependent or "conditioned" state helps to explain not only the contradictions in public policy formation but also the disparate roles and functions that Latin American states play in the context of peripheral capitalism. Conditioned by the dynamic of metropolitan capitalism, the significant noncapitalist (although perhaps postfeudal) elements in its own political system, and the political alliance in power, the nature of the democratic state in Latin America continues to pose serious constraints to the political and economic democratization of civil societies, even more so than when, despite the political shortcomings of Latin American democracies and their limitations in endowments and resources, the liberal states in the region attempted to develop public educational systems that provided access to vast sectors of the population, including the poor. The policy rationale was clearly synthesized by Sarmiento's premise that the state should "educate the sovereign," that is, the people. A critical extension, but also deconstruction, of this premise emerged in the 1960s with the notions of a pedagogy of the oppressed, conscientization, and popular education. Popular education approaches have employed structuralist methodological strategies in ways highly sensitive to history, agency, and social practices, thus challenging the enlightenment projects reflected in modernist schooling and arguing instead for emancipatory pedagogical practices grounded in normative and practical discourses oriented toward social transformation.

> In the Freirean perspective, the objective is to link education with a historical project of social emancipation: Educational practices should be related to a theory of knowledge. Consequently, education appears as the act of knowing rather than a simple transmission of knowledge or the cultural baggage of society. Since knowledge and power are considered to be intimately related, cultural traditions and practices in schooling, for example, are suspected of concealing relations of domination. Thus, critical appropriation of knowledge by the working class also implies a criticism of the culturally arbitrary. (Torres, 1994, pp. 198–199)

The current debate in the region is, on the one hand, over whether the systematic withdrawal of resources from public education under neoliberalism has deeply affected the state's traditional educational role, the performance of the systems vis-à-vis equality of educational opportunity and quality, and, by implication, the nature of the democratic pact. On the other hand, the prevailing theories and methodologies and the political-technical rationale for educational planning are seen as subsidiary to the main goals of neoliberalism. These goals are currently expressed by international institutions like the IMF and World Bank with their political economy of conditionalities and policy preferences, but also are accepted and graciously implemented by neoliberal states in the region. In this context, many scholars, teachers, policy activists, and communities wonder if the dynamics and dominant institutions of metropolitan capitalism are shaping the discourse and praxis of Latin American education. The question is whether, given the process of globalization, these internationally induced policies are compatible with fundamental notions of democratic accountability, national sovereignty, and community empowerment. In short, the question about the nature of the state and public policy is also a question about the future of public education in Latin America.

"Fractures" and "borders" in education refer to the way education is produced and the way official knowledge is selected, organized, and hierarchically ranked in the curricula, as well as to the nature of prevailing pedagogical practices. Such fractures and borders also refer to conflicts among means of production, distribution, and the use of knowledge originated (and validated) both in different cultures and across hybrid cultures. Old and new political and cultural struggles resulting from the confrontation of new subjects will continue to besiege the public school in Latin America. Different ways of imaging, understanding, and theoretically analyzing (and seeing) reality will clash in the schools. Thus a discussion is just beginning in educational settings, addressing the rights of the various social subjects to participate in decision making and in the production, development, and evaluation of the process of teaching and learning—a discussion that will likely remain central in the region's pedagogical and political thought.

The risk of further fragmentation of the school system and—given the state's withdrawal from the pedagogical utopia of public education in Latin America—the exacerbation of cultural difference and otherness will become critical in the unequal and combined development of schooling and societies. Therefore, the possibility of establishing a basic democratic consensus, and the articulation of difference in the constitution of identities, will become even more remote and certainly more costly.

NOTES

1. For an alternative explanation using a world-system framework, see the work of representatives of the institutionalist school (e.g., Boli & Ramirez, 1992).

2. Particularly in authoritarian governments usually resulting from military dictatorships, the sociology of fear, not the law, rules, and property rights always predominate over personal rights.

3. Among other things, Held (1991) suggests that globalization is the product of the emergence of a global economy, expansion of transnational linkages between economic units creating new forms of collective decision making, development of intergovernmental and quasi-supranational institutions, intensifications of transnational communications, and the creation of new regional and military orders.

4. The study conducted at the Universidad Nacional de Entre Rios, in Parana, Entre Rios, Argentina, under the sponsorship of the project APPEAL (Alternativas Pedagógicas en América Latina) by pedagogues from the National Autonomous University of Mexico (UNAM), the Universidad de Buenos Aires (UBA), and the Universidad Nacional de Entre Rios (UNER) has used historical analysis to understand the relationships between education, modernism, and postmodernism, and particularly the emerging university curricula for the twenty-first century. These researchers have reconstructed educational processes in recent history, discussing some of the crucial features of contemporary problems and their future development. Among other sources, this study draws from the theoretical proposals of Jacques Dérrida and Jacques Lacan and attempts to

approach the problems from a postmodernist standpoint. Dérrida and Lacan are particularly interested in the "deconstruction" of pedagogical discourses and in the analysis of the transformation of the subjects within those discourses. For a theoretical formulation and exegesis of Dérrida's work which can be applied to education, see R. Gasche (1986).

5. The concept of social and pedagogical subject refers also to the theoretical problematique of life, options, dreams, and actions of the social agency in the context of structural determination.

6. This concept, developed by Robert W. Connell (1983, 1987), refers to the historical association of masculinity with universalistic modes of thought.

7. The notion of pedagogical subject is related to the notion of social subject developed by Ernesto Laclau in several of his works (see Laclau, 1990; Laclau & Mouffe, 1987).

8. For a discussion of the implications of official knowledge for policy, see M. Apple (1993).

CHAPTER 3

Democracy, Education, and Multiculturalism

Dilemmas of Citizenship in a Global World

THE THEORETICAL PROBLEM

The questions of citizenship, democracy, and multiculturalism are at the heart of the discussion worldwide on educational reform, deeply affecting the academic discourse and the practice of comparative and international education. Cloaked in different robes, questions about citizenship, the connections between education and democracy, or the problem of multiculturalism affect most of the decisions that we face in dealing with the challenges of contemporary education. In this chapter I outline some of the problems that occur in trying to reconcile the tensions among theories of citizenship, democracy, and multiculturalism in the context of capitalist societies, and I try to pinpoint some of the gaps and omissions in the discussion. In the closing section, I focus on one key aspect of this exploration: the question of the canon, culture, and constitution of a democratic multicultural citizenship.

Theories of citizenship and theories of democracy mark the advent of modern political science and reflect, in their complexities, the theoretical and practical challenges to democracy in contemporary societies. Both also underline the dilemmas of negotiating power in democratic societies.

Theories of citizenship relate to every problem of the relations between citizens and the state and among citizens themselves, while theories of democracy relate clearly to the connection between established—hidden and explicit forms of social and political power, the intersection between systems of democratic representation and participation with systems of political administrative organization of public governance, and with political party systems. Ultimately, theories of democracy need to address the overall interaction between democracy and capitalism.

Finally, theories of multiculturalism, so prevalent in the educational field in the last 20 years, have emerged not only as a particular response to the constitution of the pedagogical subject in schools or to the interaction between the pedagogical subject and the political subject in democratic societies, but also as a way to identify the importance of multiple identities in education and culture. In short, theories of multiculturalism are intimately connected to the politics of culture and education.

Thus theories of multiculturalism relate to the main analytical purpose of theories of citizenship. Both attempt to identify the sense and sources of identity and the competing forms of national, regional, ethnic, or religious identity. Yet theories of multiculturalism have addressed the implications of class, race, and gender for the constitution of identities and the role of the state in a way that, by and large, mainstream theories of citizenship have not. While the interconnections between identity and citizenship are not at all evident in the specialized bibliography, they have a practical grounding that also brings them closer to theories of democracy. This is so because, not only are theories of democracy preoccupied with participation, representation, and checks and balances of power, but some brands also are concerned with ways to promote solidarity beyond particular interests of specific forms of identity.

Theories of citizenship, democracy, and multiculturalism, in their specific spheres of influence and empirical locus, not only strive to identify a sense of identity (for the notion of a democratic citizen and a multicultural political subject) including all its contradictory sources but also seek to define vigorously the limits and possibilities of forms of sociability that will promote the ability of individuals to tolerate and work together with people who are different from themselves. Likewise, these theories may enhance people's (or in a more restricted formulation, citizens') ability and desire to participate in the political process of promoting the public good and accountability. Finally, these theories will help individuals' willingness to exercise self-restraint and personal responsibility in their economic demands and in personal choices that affect the health and wealth of society and the environment as well as the process of community(ies) formation. This is so because, as Jürgen Habermas (1992) so aptly has argued, "The institutions of constitutional freedom are only worth as much as a population makes of them" (p. 7).

The dilemmas of citizenship in a democratic diverse multicultural society can be outlined, at the beginning of our analysis, as follows: Theories of citizenship had been advanced—in the tradition of Western political theory—by White, heterosexual males who identified a homogeneous citizenship through a process of systematic exclusion rather than inclusion in the polity.[1] That is, women, identifiable social groups (e.g., Jews, Gypsies), working-class people, members of specific ethnic and racial groups (i.e., people of color) and individuals lacking certain attributes or skills (i.e., literacy or numeracy abilities) were in principle excluded from the definition of citizens in numerous societies.

Theories of democracy, while effective in identifying the sources of democratic power, participation, and representation in legitimate political democratic systems, had been unable to prevent the systemic exclusion of large segments of the citizenship. Thus formal democracy drastically differs from substantive democracy. More worrisome still is the fact that theories of democracy had been unable to differentiate the roots of representative democracy (based on the notions of equal representation, equity, and equality) from their immersion in the foundational principles that articulate capitalist societies. By definition, capitalism requires differential representation in power and politics, fostering inequity formation through hierarchies and competing interests and inequality through the workings of a profit-seeking system.

Theories of multiculturalism, while effective in discussing the politics of culture and identity and the differential sources of solidarity across and within specific forms of identity, and even insightful in showing the remarkable complexity of multiple identities, had been unable or unwilling to embrace a theory of citizenship and a theory of democracy that could be workable, in practical, procedural terms; ethically viable, in moral terms; and politically feasible in the context of capitalist civil societies.

We need a theory of multicultural democratic citizenship that will take seriously the need to develop a theory of democracy that will help to ameliorate, if not eliminate altogether, the social differences, inequality, and inequity pervasive in capitalist societies and a theory of democracy able to address the draconian tensions between democracy and capitalism, on the one hand, and among social, political, and economic democratic forms, on the other. Finally, we really need a theory of democratic multicultural citizenship that can provide a reasonable theoretical answer to the neoconservative cry about the ungovernability of modern democracies in capitalist societies.

CITIZENSHIP AND EDUCATION

In discussing theories of citizenship and their importance to education, it is important to move beyond historical or legal considerations. Likewise, it is important to move beyond the notion of citizenship as a kind of personal status, a combination of rights and duties that all legal members of a nation-state hold. The discussion of theories of citizenship requires stating a premise from the outset: A theory of a "good citizen" should be relatively independent from the formal premises of the legal question of what it is to be a citizen. This is so because of the dual theoretical concerns of citizenship: as identity and as civic virtues. However, without considering the political economy dimension and the need for a historical-structural analysis of citizenship, any suggestion that citizenship is primarily a function of civic virtues could be seen as an idealistic undertaking. Civic virtues need a civil minimum that can only be found in a historical-structural context where these civil minimums overlap with basic material conditions.

The Enlightenment as the Foundation of and the Proposal of T. H. Marshall

The movement of the Enlightenment suggests a historical and social construction of human identities, and therefore socialization in rational principles is considered important, with educational institutions—as key institutions of the Enlightenment—playing a central role.

There are three elemental aspects of a theory of citizenship for the Enlightenment. First, the Kantian proposal that sustains the hypothesis that socialization processes, especially as related to cognitive thinking, have a place within structures that preceded individuals becoming knowledgeable. Second, the Hegelian proposition that suggests the capacity to be socialized should be recognized as a civilizing technique, that is, as part of a process that largely depends on the circumstances that inhibit or facilitate progressive social change (Morrow & Torres, 2002). Third, the Marxist contention that suggests that without access to the production and distribution of resources—the material benefits of the economy—it is impossible to sustain citizenship in political terms.

The most significant development in citizenship theory in this century undoubtedly has been linking the welfare state and its network of services with the full expression of democratic citizenship. T. H. Marshall's celebrated and much-cited 1949 article "Citizenship and Social Class" articulates, like few other works, the new postwar consensus about the notion of the liberal welfare state as a precondition for the exercise of citizenship in capitalist societies (Marshall, 1950, 1963, 1981, 1983).

For Marshall, citizenship developed over 250 years in England as three elements emerged: civil, political, and social rights. Western civil society obtained civil rights in the eighteenth century, political rights in the nineteenth century, and social rights in the twentieth century. Civil rights encompass all rights required for individual freedom (e.g., the right to own property, freedom of speech, and the right to justice). Political rights include all rights surrounding the electoral process (e.g., the right to vote, and to elect and be elected). Finally, social rights are those that appear as the most controversial of all, including not only a modicum of economic welfare and security but also what is necessary for individuals to live a full life: "To share to the full in the social heritage and to live the life of a civilized being according to the standards prevailing in society. The institutions most closely connected with welfare are the educational system and the social services" (Marshall, 1963, p. 74). Marshall's arguments on citizenship are embedded in the arguments of the ongoing democratization of society, which illustrates a central principle of the Enlightenment. Yet, as Carole Pateman (1996) points out, citizenship is not synonymous with democracy. Traditional theories of citizenship are challenged by different forms of social theory.

Feminism

Marshall along with many other scholars took for granted that all people in England during the eighteenth century were legally free and therefore enjoyed civil citizenship. A most serious challenge to this assumption, however, is the idea that adult English males had enjoyed their legal freedom and citizenship because of the commodification of women's labor and women's lack of legal power in households controlled through patriarchal practices (see Gordon, 1990). As Pateman (1996) put it:

> Despite the increasing volume and range of criticism, his commentators typically fail to appreciate the peculiar narrowness of Marshall's interest in citizenship, which runs in one direction only. . . . He fails to ask whether rights are of equal worth to all citizens, or to make the point in another way, whether citizenship means the same for all individuals. He asked about the social integration, and the material and cultural conditions of the male working class. He did not consider whether there were other citizens who might be described as second class. (pp. 7–8)

This commentary points to three interesting criticisms of Marshall: (a) that his analysis, with the drastic ideology of the (male) working class, may no longer account for changes in citizenship due to a restructured globalized capitalism; (b) that he failed to take into account the issue of ethnicity (which describes a sizable segment of what Pateman chose to call "second-class citizens"); and (c) that he obviously failed to account for the subordination of women in his analysis of citizenship. Hence it is the importance of the feminist challenge to citizenship to which I turn briefly.

Feminism has been important to the deconstruction of the prevailing inherent "maleness" of the traditional conceptions of citizenship. Let us take, as a case in point, the contribution of Chantal Mouffe's (1993) discussion on identity. Mouffe's position is that relations of subordination are multilayered, and in fact, individuals may play a dominant role in one relationship and a subordinate role in another. In part, this has to do with the material and symbolic positionality of subjects and with the fact that identity is not a fixed essence but an assemblage of positions (i.e., status/role), narratives, and discourses constructed by the subject from his or her relations (and therefore experiences) and from her or his own positionality.

The basic implication of Mouffe's analysis is that the notion of the identity of a subject should not be approached simply as the coexistence of a plurality of positions. This assertion is a most important challenge for the notion of citizenship. Since the agent cannot be singled out as formed by a basic identity, and since the notion of plurality defies easy definitions of what is a citizen, this analysis seriously challenges any simplistic definition of citizenship based on legal or territorial notions. But there is more. While a plurality of identities does exist, they cannot be simply understood as an aggregate of factors or as an amalgam of properties.

The feminist discussion highlights three rather intractable themes for the traditional liberal conception of citizenship. First, there is the notion of identity as an elusive, disputed, ever-changing assemblage of narratives and positions that will make it very difficult to speak of citizenship as a single identity correlated either with a territory, culture, or experience. Hence, Mouffe's criticisms of essentialized positions are based on the premises of "conceptualizing identities and differences as discursively constructed instead of as objectively given" (Fraser, 1989, p. 183). Second is the notion of the patriarchal foundations of liberal democracies and the indispensable criticism and changes in those foundations if all men and women are to be considered full citizens. As Pateman (1992) instructs us, "By a genuinely democratic citizen, I mean that both sexes are full citizens" (p. 28). This, in turn, invites one to criticize the political usage of the notions of the public and the private. The feminist criticism of the "public" as a male, patriarchal concept, and the need to understand democracy as method as well as content encompassing the private and public domains—a distinction that should incorporate the value of caring as related to, though not necessarily exclusive to, motherhood—are important challenges to the traditional notion of citizenship measured as voting patterns and participation rates. And third, Mouffe suggests that finding a democratic equivalence in incorporating the diverse struggles is built in the very notion of postulating alternative identities into the construction of a democratic citizenship and community. Mouffe's (1993) posture assumes the need of discussing citizenship, not as one single identity enmeshed with others, or as a sum of identities, but as an articulating principle "that affects the different subject positions of the social agent, while allowing for a plurality of specific allegiances and for the respect of individual liberty" (p. 84).

Critical feminist perspectives help in understanding the constitution of the subject as constructed through different discourses and positions. This is a view that is more adequate than the reduction of identity to one single position—such as class, race, or gender—and appears a prerequisite to understanding how relations of power are constructed and what forms of exclusion, despite the claims of liberal citizenship, prevail.

Debates within feminism, however, show the importance of the new contributions of border feminists, most predominately Chicana feminists who criticize as cultural imperialism White Eurocentric feminism for its inability to imagine the needs, desires, and rights of their women-of-color counterpart: "Feminism affects and influences Chicana writers and critics, but feminism as practiced by women of the hegemonic culture oppresses and exploits the Chicano in both subtle and open ways" (Saldivar-Hull, 1994, p. 204).

The complexity of race, gender, and class dynamics, particularly through the contributions of border feminism, needs to be situated in the life-world of globalized postcolonial societies, hence the importance of discussing the contribution of postcolonial analysis for citizenship, especially if we take into account the title of the well-known poem of Gloria Anzaldúa: "To Live in the Borderlands Means You" (1987).

Postcolonialism

As the "adult English male" subject was the citizen par excellence for Marshall, looking back at his contribution we need to recognize that the citizen he had in mind is British. But, as Pateman (1996) points out, Marshall does not draw in detail the notion of the "British subject," nor does he look at the implications of a three-staged citizenship built in England fully supported by the expansion of British imperialism in the world. For instance, Pateman notes the 1948 Act separated those acquiring British nationality by virtue of birth or naturalization in the United Kingdom from those acquiring it as part of the status of Commonwealth countries. Hence the importance of discussing postcolonialism as a challenge to citizenship.

Colonialism is linked to the expansion of control by mostly European metropolitan societies over Third World societies, a historical process that Lenin defined as *imperialism,* a superior phase of capitalism.[2] Colonialism also was an attempt to force modernization through territorial, political, and technological invasion from industrial advanced societies over less technologically developed societies. This process was not a product of authoritarian philanthropy of bringing modernity to "traditional" people but an attempt to solve some of the looming social problems of the colonial powers themselves and to exploit the untapped natural and human resources of the country being colonized.

For instance, the expansion toward "new territories"—Africa and Asia most prominently, but Latin America as well—served as a "safety valve" for Europe given the overpopulation and political crises of the last quarter of the nineteenth century and years leading up to World War I. It also addressed the superabundance of labor as well as the declining rates of return to capital in need of new markets for investments and raw materials. Finally, colonialism was based on geopolitical considerations of European nation-states and elites trying to enhance their planetary reach while trying to settle, militarily and diplomatically, their differences in European nation building.

Postcolonialism, connected with liberation movements fighting against colonialism, emerged as an attempt to criticize the rational foundations of colonialism and to decolonize "the mind," as Frantz Fanon liked to say. Postcolonial thought is, above all, criticism of the Enlightenment and its legacy of modernity. Joining the criticism of feminism, postcolonialism critiques the notion of an unqualified reason and universality, the progressive unfolding of history, ideas of national sovereignty, or the integrity of a self-identity subject that holds specific, self-reflective interests.

For postcolonialism, analysis of the various dimensions of transnationalization, of what constitutes a nation, and what role territorial spaces play in the articulation of the notion of national sovereignty are central. This also implies a serious challenge to the notions of political community and political identity. Ray Rocco (1997) claims that it is precisely the type of changes that he analyzed among nation, identity, community, territory, and state that the discourse on citizenship tries to articulate. In his study of Los Angeles Latino communities, Rocco finds that Latinos, particularly new immigrants, engage in practices that fall within the notion of citizenship building:

> They engage in practices within relational settings of civil society that under specific conditions, can be construed as in effect making claims that are about membership in the community, about having access to institutional settings, resources, and opportunities . . . about the freedom to develop and maintain culturally based associational networks, that challenge the criteria of inclusion/exclusion, and affirmations of spaces of cultural identities. [Rocco's studies] revealed a number of such practices, which although not necessarily understood nor intended by the actors to be "political," nevertheless are in effect contestations of established boundaries, rules, and constructions of citizenship. (p. 14)

"Under specific conditions"—this is the crux of theorizing citizenship from the postcolonialist perspective of hybridity, borders, and subaltern spaces. What specific conditions would facilitate that the contestations of established boundaries, rules, and the construction of citizenship can be incorporated into a discussion of how subaltern identities in multicultural societies may constitute a comprehensive, dynamic, and complex notion of citizenship?

Critical Race Theory

Despite Marshall's contribution to a theory of citizenship, a glaring omission in his analysis was the consideration of ethnicity and race. Today this is more important than ever. Race and racism continue to be central concepts in understanding the U.S. racial formation. Despite much lip service paid to discussions on race and the liberal discourse of tolerance, race and racism are perceived by critical race theorists as muted and utterly marginalized in the analysis of public policy and citizenship (Ladson-Billings & Tate, 1995).

Critical race theory was born in the United States within legal studies attempting to address the differential treatment of people of color by the courts and in prison. For many, critical race theory is the result of work by progressive legal scholars of color who see American law as permeated by racism and who make the elimination of racism in American jurisprudence a central goal in the elimination of all forms of subordination.

Critical race theory, as outlined by one of its key proponents, Derrick Bell (1995), views civil rights achievements in the United States during this century with growing skepticism: "In our era, the premier precedent of *Brown v. Board of Education* promised to be the twentieth century's Emancipation Proclamation. Both policies, however, served to advance the nation's foreign policy intent more than they provided actual aid to Blacks" (p. 2). Bell argues that, in the United States, the legal rights framework has been sacrificed on behalf of Whiteness:

> Even those Whites who lack wealth and power are sustained in their sense of racial superiority by policy decisions that sacrifice Black rights. The subordination of Blacks seems to reassure Whites of an unspoken, but no less certain, property right in their "Whiteness." (p. 7)

Critical race theory, as Daniel Solorzano and Octavio Villalpando (1998) explain, is related to five key insights: (1) the primary focus on race and racism; (2) the challenge to dominant ideology; (3) the commitment to social justice; (4) the importance of experiential knowledge; and (5) the use of an interdisciplinary perspective. Critical race theory, then, will be useful to prove that racism is endemic and deeply ingrained in American life. These culturally sanctioned beliefs, no matter how symbolically concealed, involve the defense of preestablished social, cultural, and economic advantages. Therefore, the challenge to racism entails a serious challenge to the superordinate position of Whites over racial minorities. To address this racial inequality, Gloria Ladson-Billings and William Tate (1995) claim that civil rights acts have been ineffective because, ultimately, having not challenged the basis for property subordination, Whites have, paradoxically, benefited from school desegregation. Even more, when desegregation was launched, new models of resegregation through ability grouping emerged, reproducing the conditions for a learning imbalance between Whites and colored people.[3]

A third important insight of critical race theory, one prominent in the discussion of citizenship, is that claims of neutrality, objectivity, meritocracy, and the goal of a color-blind society need to be challenged. Thus "for the critical race theorist, social reality is constructed by the formulation and exchange of stories about individual situations. These stories serve as interpretative structures by which we impose order on experience and it on us" (Ladson-Billings & Tate, 1995, pp. 55–59, especially p. 57).

For critical race theorists, racism is so deeply ingrained in the United States that a rethinking of citizenship needs to incorporate systematic challenges to the practice of racism in the legal system and, by extension, in the school system. This rethinking should challenge not only racism but also the prevalence of the logic of property rights over the logic of personal rights and the foundation of human rights as the basis for equality and justice. Given the magnitude of the task, there are no naive assumptions that antiracist positions can be easily organized in a coalition to challenge prevailing racist structures, sentiments, and values.

By putting the question of race first, critical race theorists argue that the discussion of citizenship can no longer be treated as a homogeneous identity in search of the exercise of rights and obligations. Along the same lines as critical race theorists, another important claim on the state and the constitution of citizenship is provided by old and new social movements.

New Social Movements

If we understand politics as a struggle for power, new social movements should not be interpreted exclusively in political terms, as they also represent cultural and moral practices centered on the construction of collective identities and spaces. They originate around certain demands and specific social relations, becoming increasingly autonomous from traditional institutions of political representation of interests. This is so, argues Ernesto Laclau—joining other proponents of social movement theory—because individuals no longer exclusively define their identity in relation to the means and relations of production but also as consumers, residents of a particular neighborhood, members of churches, ethnic or gender groups, and participants in the political system (Laclau, 1985; see also Garcia et al., 1981; Lechner, 1987).

New social movement theory has provided the basis for a dramatic shift in understanding the relationship between social movements and education. A distinctive characteristic of new social movements is their cognitive and ideological focus on rethinking preexisting social and cultural paradigms as part of a politics of identity. As a consequence, one of their key strategies is broadly educational, as opposed to a focus on gaining power, and its implications for citizenship are numerous. To cite just a few, consider the gains that the environmental movement has made in schools, promoting a democratic citizenship that is responsible—at a collective and even planetarian level—for the protection of endangered species, for the levels of pollution in the air and water, or for the control of dangerous substances in food. Consider the role of the Zapatista movement in Chiapas, redressing the inequality built into the interaction of Mexican aboriginal people and the postrevolutionary Mexican state, and its consistent and impetuous political program linking those ethnic and political demands to the constitution of a true radical democracy in Mexico and the constitution of a democratic citizenship without exclusions. Consider the impact of the antitobacco movement in schools, challenging the notions of the glamour of smoking and linking advertisements to the powerful tobacco lobby and multinational tobacco corporations. By challenging the consumption of tobacco, all sorts of connections between the political system, the mode of production, and the risks to the quality of life of the citizens are critically exposed. Consider the case of the racially based civil rights movement in the United States. The dismantling of segregated schools constituted, despite its obvious limitations, perhaps the most fundamental and far-reaching demands linking race and education and eventually remaining a central tenet of American citizenship (Eyerman & Jamison, 1991). Consider the growing importance of the feminist movement in affirming unequivocally the political, social, cultural, and economic equality between men and women, and drastically changing the spectrum of social relations in schools by promoting the principles and methods of feminist pedagogy and by promoting a new level of social exchange among students, teachers, and parents in defending feminist goals.

The praxis of social movements offers potentially fertile ground for a "conscientization" approach à la Paulo Freire. Social movements typically build on the knowledge base and previous struggles of people, taking into account their organizational capabilities and grievances. This allows for the building of programs *with* and *from* the communities rather than *for* them, as the late Paulo Freire illustrated in countless writings.

In short, new theories of critical modernism—including feminism, critical race theory, and subordinate social spaces theory nested within the theoretical net of postcolonialism—and the practice of new social movements have enhanced the possibilities of citizenship, particularly in multicultural democratic societies. The question, then, is how citizenship relates to the notion of democracy and education.

DEMOCRACY AND EDUCATION

The prevailing notion of democracy at the end of the twentieth century is liberal representative democracy, with its principle of the active citizen. As it is defined by David Held (1995), it constitutes "a cluster of rules, procedures and institutions permitting the broadest involvement of the majority of citizens, not in political affairs as such, but in the selection of representatives who alone can make political decisions" (p. 97).

Yet it is convenient to distinguish at the outset, as the Italian political scientist Humberto Cerroni (1976, 1992) does, between democracy as content and democracy as method. Democracy appears to be primarily a method of political representation, a cluster of rules that include elected government; free and fair elections; universal suffrage; freedom of conscience, information, and expression; the right of all adults to oppose their government and stand for office; and the right to form independent associations. As a principle, democratic governments seek to develop parliamentary and judicial systems free from the control of the executive by using a system of checks and balances. Finally, given the liberal impetus, liberal democracy upholds the belief in the predominance of individual rights over collective rights, which implies a serious recognition of the potential tyranny of majorities.

The notion of democracy as content is related to the notion of democracy as a system of political participation by the people in public affairs. It is related to the power of the people over any other regulatory institution (such as kinship), the idea of equal rights for all citizens, and, particularly in the U.S. Constitution, a political philosophy of egalitarianism. However, a notion of radical democracy goes beyond the attempt to prevent forms of exclusion that preclude political and social participation. Radical democracy postulates radical equality in racial/ethnic, class, and gender interactions, both in the public sphere and in the intimacy of the household. Thus a first important tension occurs between democratic regimes that uphold formal rules but fail dramatically to uphold democracy in terms of class, race/ethnicity, and gender interactions.

A second important tension, then, is to explain how the notion of democracy became intimately intertwined with the notion of capitalism as the most conducive mode of production for the development of democratic systems. Samuel Bowles and Herbert Gintis (1986) persuasively argue that the dynamics of democracy rely on two logics of expansion of the capitalist system: personal rights and property rights, which are often opposed. The conflict between these two logics—represented perhaps in the clash between business ideology and social movements in advanced industrial capitalism and in dependent-development capitalism—is over the use and appropriation of societal resources and also the question of setting ethical standards of social behavior. However, capitalism as an economic and social system of accumulation, production, reproduction, and distribution of commodities is intrinsically conflictual and marked by internal contradictions.

If capitalism is a conflictual system and democracy has two logics of development, then the question is why democracy and capitalism became intermingled and why this working relationship of politics and economics does not fall apart. Bowles and Gintis (1986) claim that the connection between democracy and capitalism occurred through four historical accommodations of the system: (a) in Europe, the Lockean proposal that accommodates the system by limiting the political participation of the propertied; (b) in the United States, the Jeffersonian proposal that distributing property widely among the citizenry (of Anglo-Saxon origin) reaccommodates the system in the face of increasing political strains; (c) the political proposal of James Madison to foster a sufficient heterogeneity of interest among citizens to prevent the emergence of a common political program of the nonpropertied; and (d) the Keynesian model, in which economic growth and distribution of income generate a communality of interests between the dispossessed and the wealthy.

Is there a new accommodation of the system in the face of the current crisis of democracy? What is the situation of democracy and capitalism at the end of the millennium? It can be characterized as the problem of governability of democracy in capitalist societies or, to put it in the terms of Bowles and Gintis (1986), as the lack of a new historical accommodation of the system—a risky impasse. Yet it seems that a new accommodation is emerging with the notion of citizen as consumer and the predominance of globalization from above.[4]

DEMOCRACY AND MULTICULTURALISM

The connections between democracy and multiculturalism are among the most contested polemics of our time. Let me start with the prophetic voice of Cornel West (1993), who argues that

> the new cultural politics of difference are neither simply oppositional in contesting the mainstream (or *male*stream*)* for inclusion nor transgressive in the avant-gardist sense of shocking conventional bourgeois audiences. Rather they are distinct articulations of talented (and usually privileged) contributors to culture who desire to align themselves with demoralized, demobilized, depoliticized, and disorganized people in order to empower and enable social action and, if possible, to enlist collective insurgency for the expansion of freedom, democracy and individuality. (pp. 11–12)

West sets the right tone for the discussion. Multiculturalism, in any form, shape, or color relates to the politics of difference and the emerging social struggles over racialized, gendered, and classist societies. Yet discussions on multiculturalism in the United States should start with a subtle but important differentiation among notions of multiculturalism as a social movement and a theoretical approach, multicultural education as a reform movement, and citizenship education as a curriculum-oriented specialty that, particularly given the characteristics of the U.S. racial formation, needs to take into account issues of racial identity and cultural diversity for citizenship building as an antiracist pedagogy.

As a social movement, multiculturalism is a philosophical, theoretical, and political orientation that goes beyond school reform and tackles the issues of race, gender, and class relations in society at large. As multicultural education, however, the landscape in the United States has been dominated by liberal multiculturalism.

The proponents of liberal multiculturalism will argue that it will increase fairness by representing the range and richness of America's different ethnicities and tolerance by exposing students to multiple perspectives on the meaning of history. "In this view, multiculturalism pluralizes the notion of an American identity by insisting on attention to African-Americans, Native Americans, and the like, but it leaves in place a unified concept of identity" (Scott, 1989, p. 13).

Within the pluralist framework, *identity* "is taken as the referential sign of a fixed set of customs, practices, and meanings, an enduring heritage, a readily identifiable sociological category, a set of shared traits and/or experiences" (Scott, 1989, p. 14).

From an existentialist, and not merely a sociological standpoint, identity also is related to key feelings and experiences of protection, association, and recognition. As West so forcefully claims,

> People identify themselves in certain ways in order to protect their bodies, their labor, their communities, their way of life; in order to be associated with people who ascribe values to them; and for purposes of recognition, to be acknowledged, to feel as if one actually belongs to a group, a clan, a tribe, a community. So that any time we talk about the identity of a particular group over time and space, we have to be very specific about what the credible options are for them at any given moment. (West, de Alba, & Sheris, 1996, p. 57)

In contrast, *diversity,* Joan Scott (1989) argues, "refers to the plurality of identities, and it is seen as a condition of human existence rather than as the effect of an enunciation of differences that constitute hierarchies and asymmetries of power" (p. 14). West will agree since he argued that "this historical process of naming is part of the legacy not just of white supremacy but of class supremacy" (West et al., 1996, p. 57).

Power and difference in multiculturalism narratives are always interrelated with a discussion of identity. Yet *national identity—the* most important form of territorial solidarity based on notions of a single nation-state and the experience and feeling of patriotism and a common cultural heritage—is not a fixed marker that guides citizens in their choices of loyalties and solidarities. Historically, the concept of national identity is better defined in opposition to "others" (i.e., another national identity or an enemy of the nation) rather than in reference to a set of uncontested historical properties of a nation and the national experience of its people as a homogeneous group.

Therefore, identities are constructed in a process of contestation and struggle and are subject to multiple interpretations. Identities are social constructions with material and historical bases, and indeed they are based on (or, if one allows for the Althusserian lapse, are interpellated by) perceptions of knowledge, experience, and power, particularly what knowledge is (or should be considered) legitimate and should count, what experiences should be celebrated and learned from, and how power can be negotiated among different knowledge and experiences. Yet the same notion of experience that seems to underlie the notion of identity, as Scott has so forcefully argued, is something historically, culturally, and discursively produced. Once again, as Michael Apple (1982, 1993, 1997) has so aptly argued for more than 2 decades, the connections between power and knowledge become central to any practical agenda of research and policy making in education, particularly in this new phase of the conservative restoration.

Identity, as I have argued, is not a fixed marker, an essential substance that some people share in virtue of their origin, race, religious affiliation, sexual preference, gender, or class, but a process of learning that is context dependent and, indeed, open to interpretation. As such, it also depends on the historicity of the struggles that impinge on social consciousness at a given moment in time, making experience and the consciousness of the experience a salient process of understanding and meaning making by the individuals attempting to understand the conditions of their lives.

The poet T. S. Eliot (1943/1971) said that "we had the experience but missed the meaning, / And approach to the meaning restores the experience" (p. 24). Eliot's dictum tells us that the notion of identity built on a given experience is as elusive as the notion of consciousness of identity, and this consciousness cannot be separated from processes of oppression, discrimination, and exclusion that constitute people's lives.

KEY DEMOCRATIC ISSUES
FOR A DEMOCRATIC MULTICULTURAL CITIZENSHIP

Let us take as a premise that the suffrage movement at the turn of the century, the civil rights movement in the 1960s, and affirmative action,[5] as well as the First Amendment, helped the renewal of citizenship in the United States, enhancing American democracy by creating a more level playing field and emphasizing the central role of diversity. As Walter Feinberg (1996) rightly points out, affirmative action "uses group membership to identify and correct past acts of discrimination against individuals, acts that have resulted in inadequate educational, economic, and social positioning" (p. 378).

Attacks on affirmative action and cultural diversity, particularly in higher education, may undermine the foundations of citizenship in the United States. Why? First, because affirmative action reminds us of a historical debt that needs to be repaid to specific groups. Second, and moving from the importance of race-based affirmative action to the need to be complemented with a need-based affirmative action, we should be reminded that there cannot be equality of political opportunity without equality of social opportunity.

Economic citizenship cannot be accomplished without bare essentials, as Todd Gitlin (1995) has suggested, including "the right to a job, education, medical care, housing, retraining over the course of life—these are the bare elements of an economic citizenship that ought to be universal" (p. 234). Finally, in the context of U.S. democracy, affirmative action reaffirms the importance of the critique of public policy and the history of a given social formation. Not surprisingly, many people have identified African Americans as the major subject of affirmative action despite the fact that White women have become the principal beneficiaries of these policies (Feinberg, 1996, pp. 366–367). West said it so passionately:

> One of the reasons why black people are so integral a part of American civilization is because black people have raised a lot of hell. That is very important, especially in a society in which power and pressure decide who receives visibility. By raising hell I mean organization, mobilization, chaos-producing capacity, as in rebellion. (West et al., 1996, p. 58)

The Black struggle in the United States shows that criticism and rebellion emerge as two key factors in the constitution of citizenship for a democracy of content and not merely a democracy of method.

No doubt, the capacity to generate criticism and rebellion against mainstream ideas that may represent the powers that be has long been a central component of any political democratic education for citizenship. In fact, we cannot understand citizenship without understanding the role that education, particularly higher education, plays in the constitution of the democratic pact. Moreover, we cannot understand the democratic pact without considering affirmative-action policies and cultural diversity as indissolubly linked.

Freire argued that few human encounters are exempt from oppression of one kind or another because by virtue of race, class, or gender, people tend to be victims and/or perpetrators of oppression. He stressed that racism, sexism, or class exploitation are the most salient forms of dominance, but he also recognized that oppression exists also based on religious beliefs, political affiliation, national origin, age, size, and physical and intellectual handicaps. Starting from a psychology of oppression, influenced by the works of psychotherapists such as Freud, Jung, Adler, Fanon, and Fromm, Freire developed a "pedagogy of the oppressed." He believed that education could improve the human condition, counteracting the effects of a psychology of oppression and ultimately contributing to what he considered the "ontological vocation of mankind": humanization. In the introduction to his widely acclaimed *Pedagogy of the Oppressed*, he wrote, "From these pages I hope at least the following will endure: my trust in the people, and my faith in men and women and in the creation of a world in which it will be easier to love" (Freire, 1972; see also Torres, 1998b).

Following Freire, one may argue that the central question of education today is what role, if any, educational institutions and practices should play in the constitution of the social pact that articulates democracy. This brings us to the dilemma of a democratic culture: the construction of a democratic citizen. To put it simply, democracy implies a process of participation in which all are considered equal. However, education involves a process whereby the "immature" are brought to identify with the principles and forms of life of the "mature" members of society. Thus construction of the democratic citizen is a process of cultural nurturing, but also it involves articulating principles of pedagogic and democratic socialization in individuals who are neither tabula rasa in cognitive or ethical terms nor fully equipped for the exercise of their democratic rights and obligations.

This central problem of education—how to contribute to the democratic pact—is compounded by the fact that teachers relate to the demands of a common public school increasingly segregated by race and class, in a society with a growing gap between the haves and have-nots, and in which gender distinctions continue to be central to school discrimination. In this context, several issues stand out clearly as central themes in the discussion on public policy in the minds of policy makers, teachers, researchers, and citizens, among them diversity and multiculturalism.

Citizenship can be predicated in terms of civic virtues or legal status. Civic virtues point to a sense of solidarity that unites individuals around common goals. These goals are, at the very least, how to survive and live together in our contemporary diverse society; but they also can be accomplished with a more ambitious agenda: how to thrive as a community of communities, as a culture of cultures, drawing from our cultural diversity as a cultural strength and from affirmative action, broadly understood, as a useful policy.

Yet as Gitlin (1995) cautions us:

> The question is how to cultivate the spirit of solidarity across the lines of difference—solidarity with "anyone who suffers." For surely that spirit cannot be expected to generate spontaneously inside fortified groups, each preoccupied with refining its differences from other groups. (p. 217)

For a framework of solidarity and common ground across cultures, ethnicities, classes, and gender, the goals of cultural diversity are central. We need to develop flexible frameworks for solidarity in schools that take seriously the need for democratic reform. Cultural diversity is a major by-product of the growing process of economic, cultural, and political globalization that has no parallel in history. Globalization has produced all sorts of implications for the multicultural, multilingual, and multiethnic configurations of local communities in the United States and elsewhere. In terms of the social covenant, not surprisingly, diversity is a key challenge for any institution of higher education in complying with federal and state statutes for affirmative action and in facing the growing social and educational demands.

Higher education institutions are at the center of the storm in terms of diversity and affirmative action and, I must say, in terms of promoting

a renewal of citizenship. A commitment to diversity and multiculturalism implies a commitment to diversify the faculty resembling, to the extent possible and given the available resources, the demographic traits of
schools and universities in the United States. Diversity also implies the
diversification of the student body, so demands from different intellectual,
ethnic, gender, and underrepresented groups and constituencies will be
appropriately addressed in the classroom. To achieve the goals of diversity and multiculturalism, universities should be able to attract the best
and brightest, the most qualified scholars, undergraduates, and gradu-
ates who can explore in their teaching, research, and outreach the frontiers
of knowledge without prejudice, approaching their work with creativity,
with joy, with enthusiasm and dedication, with a sense of utopian hope.

Achieving such goals is not easy. Tensions will always arise between
growing social and intellectual demands and diminishing fiscal resources.
There will also be tensions among diverse intellectual, ethnic, and social
constituencies and among faculty desires to serve the ideals of equity
coupled with the imperatives of equality in the context of the perennial
academic quest for excellence and community. There will be serious criticisms of policies oriented to equity and equality in education, including
affirmative action policies. Affirmative action should not be considered as
a moral absolute, but it should be included in a democratic conversation
of how affirmative action and cultural diversity enhance citizenship and
what role higher education institutions should play in this respect.

I believe that in order to achieve the missions of higher education, the
construction of an academic consensus based on diversity is essential.
This consensus building, however, should begin with a recognition of the
importance of these tensions, should take into account the precariousness
of many of the managerial solutions available, and should recognize the
limitations of the many intellectual paradigms in vogue. These are some
of the intellectual challenges of discussing citizenship, cultural diversity,
and affirmative action in higher education. This, in turn, brings us to the
question of canon versus culture in the construction of a democratic multicultural citizenship.

CANON, CULTURE, AND
DEMOCRATIC MULTICULTURAL CITIZENSHIP: CONCLUSIONS

The impossibility of an uncontested canon results from the impossibility
of defining a single, integrated, nonproblematic, and descriptive social
and pedagogical identity in the culture of the West. (R. A. Morrow & C. A.
Torres, 2002, p. 428)

In a sense, this is a game of never-ending mirrors. (I. Wallerstein, 1997, p. 1254)

Canons and cultures are not, in principle, opposed, but they have a difficult time in cohabitation. This is especially true when a given canon—which is, in principle, a social construction accepted as the foundation of a given identity, be it national, cultural, or otherwise—is made as a set of metaphysical principles that cannot be historically examined, and therefore changed, or that should be preserved at any cost without accepting challenges, negotiations, or changes. Metaphysical canons become, in principle, opposed to cultural negotiation.

Foundational canons, however, are ongoing processes of cultural negotiations, taking as their precedents key foundations for dialogue and open-ended interpretations of history and community experiences. They also enjoy what Freire would like to term an "epistemology of curiosity": an endless need to define what cultural principles make the life of people more harmonious, the cultural exchanges more self-reflective, and the ethical underpinnings of the culture closer to the cultural imperatives of social justice, individual responsibility, and caring.

Foundational canons are changed through cultural negotiation:

> Negotiation may take place—does take place—on the edges of a canon, so that Whitman was brought in in the '40s, while Whittier was booted out (Leo Marx has made that point), and during recent years Ellison's Invisible Man is effectively canonized. In other words, once a foundation is clear, there's plenty of room for divergences and plurality. (T. Gitlin, personal communication, 1998)

Any cultural canon, as long as it is made into a metaphysical condition of being, is in principle opposed to cultural negotiation. As such, a metaphysical cultural canon—a canon revered as the encapsulation of virtue, wisdom, and truth—must have several authority sources or legitimacy claims, which may include, for instance, the sheer power of a given group establishing legal restrictions that become the law of the land (e.g., the South African White power before the establishment of a racial democracy in 1994 or the legislation of slavery in the American South); claims to enjoy racial purity (e.g., Nazism); claims to being the original founding fathers of the nation (e.g., Caucasian and Eurocentric immigrant-bashing groups); claims to control the language that constitutes identity and make social, political, and economic exchanges possible (i.e., English-only movements); or claims to moral or ethical superiority based on a religious mandate (e.g., Christian bigotry, movements to establish the biblical superiority of men over women, and homosexual-bashing movements based on Christian faith).

The liberal pluralist call to recognize the richness of "otherness" and diversity in a society otherwise characterized by shared historical foundations based on cultural consensus (e.g., the notion of "togetherness" as an essential pragmatic principle for the social pact to work) can be confronted with a more radical perception of multiculturalism, a historically nuanced vision of multiculturalism.

> Oddly enough, given the charges of incoherence and anarchy made against multicultural approaches, historicizing the question of identity also offers the possibility of a more unified view than that of the liberal pluralists. . . . An alternative to pluralism is to make difference and conflict the center of a history "we" all share. (Scott, 1989, p. 16)

Now, if national identity is not a fixed marker but a process of learning as I have defended, this creates another conundrum. The first question is to consider whether it is possible that exposure to similar processes of learning creates different conclusions. This is certainly the drama of democratic education and democratic life. What we pursue in democracy is to allow the process of learning to go on and, at the same time, to accept that the conclusions could, and indeed will, be divergent. People will have different views, and political disagreements will be the bread and butter for education as much as coalition and alliance politics is for democratic governance.

This has implications at the level of the knowledge base of the society and the democratization of knowledge. The next question is whether some explanations are more powerful than others. In other terms, is one type of social science more useful (I am tempted to say more truthful) than others? Discussing the impact of deconstructionism in the social sciences, Immanuel Wallerstein (1997) warns us that "we are clearly involved here in a very complex activity, one in which equilibria (canons) are at best transient and one in which there can be no determinate future, since the aleatory elements are too vast" (p. 1253).

The problem, it seems, is the consideration that, because reality is a social construction, everything goes, and therefore that every explanation is as valuable as the next, that there are no particular criteria from which to ascertain which explanation is more truthful or powerful or which is a better approach to understand and explain the complexity of the real. Wallerstein (1997) is very clear in this respect:

> The role of the scholars is not to construct reality but to figure out how it has been constructed and to test the multiple social constructions of reality against each other. In a sense, this is a game of never-ending mirrors.

We seek to discover the reality on the basis of which we have constructed reality. And when we find this, we seek to understand how this underlying reality has in turn been socially constructed. In this navigation amidst the mirrors, however, there are more correct and less correct scholarly analyses. Those scholarly analyses that are more correct are more socially useful in that they aid the world to construct a substantively more rational reality. Hence the search for truth and the search for goodness are inextricably linked to each other. We are all involved, and involved simultaneously, in both. (p. 1254)

Three points should be retained here. First, despite the deconstructionist storm and the fact that we can think of reality as a social construction, this social construction is not just the product of our imagination but the product of real people interacting in complex ways, and hence not all explanations have the same quality (i.e., logical coherence, analytical insights, empirical documentation), explanatory power, or truthfulness. Second, even if all explanations, by their very nature, are transient—that is, they are works in progress until a better explanation is constructed— they are all to be judged against their ability to explain, and in turn, their ability to help the construction of a more rational society. Hence there is an element of usefulness in each validity construct that cannot be overlooked. While the previous comment can be read as overtly pragmatic, it, in itself, points to the third implication of Wallerstein's analysis—that the notion of the truth and the goodness in society are intimately and inextricably intertwined. Hence a more constructive, useful rational society refers to Wallerstein's suggestion of looking at the social sciences as part of the quest for a just society. Wallerstein thus is proposing a categorical imperative of justice and goodness to inspire, if not to guide, the analytical endeavor.

In politics and social struggles, however, disagreements could be even more drastic than the implications of debates in the social sciences about causality or explanatory validity. Consider, for instance, the situation in Algeria. If democratic elections are granted (as happened in 1992), fundamentalist Islamic movements are likely to win. Considering their platform of basing the social order in a peculiar vision of strict literal adherence to the Koran and their practice of intimidation of citizens (the death toll from massacres in small towns has been estimated to be at least 100,000 in the last 5 years) this victory not only would result in many people losing their civil liberties—particularly women, as demonstrated in the Taliban government in Afghanistan—but would also put the democratic structure at peril. Here the government of the majority that could be achieved through democracy as a method will undoubtedly destroy democracy as practice and content. The constitution of a democratic political culture is then a foundational premise for the continuation of democracy and the exercise of democratic life.

The idea of democracy is to learn to live with challenges and tensions and to learn about the process of learning about democratic differences. Democratic disagreements will take place everywhere, from dinner-table discussions in which families disagree passionately over public and private issues to political pulpits in which leaders and coalitions try to capture the imagination of most people and to constitute electoral majorities. These coalitions, however, will always be temporary, fragile, and subject to disintegration—in one word, ephemeral.

The notion of democracy as a method facilitates the process of differential representation and participation in which some conclusions through the voting process, alliance making, and the notion of majority coalitions may prevail in a particular moment of time. Thus some majorities may push for a particular vision that is not, by definition, shared by all the inhabitants of the given polity. As I have argued, however, democracy as a method does not and cannot totally encapsulate the notion of democracy as content.

The notion of democracy as content, however, places some limits on what is expected and acceptable for democratic behavior and highlights civil minimums that go beyond the formalities of the democratic methodology, reaching a more radical understanding of democratic representation and participation—in short, of democratic interactions in the public and private spheres. Thus, considering identity as a process of learning, we are back to the unpleasant question of how to establish that some views are more plausible than others. This question is made even more uncomfortable if, as I have discussed elsewhere (Torres, 1998a, chap. 7), science can be related to power and therefore cannot be used, without qualifications, to settle the disputes. There is no metaphysical answer to this question, but there are procedural and methodical answers as well as historical answers. The procedural and methodical answers attempt to expand, to push the democratic envelope to its limits but to respect the rules of confrontation and negotiation, to try to understand how democratic life may accommodate a diversity of interests, a diversity of identities and experiences, and a diversity of ideologies without damaging the fabric of the democratic discourse and without accepting the premise that a final solution for a problem will be arrived at in the deliberations. We know what the implications of metaphysical notions such as a "final solution" are.

The historical answer is partly what we have defined as historical accommodations between capitalism and democracy. The period in which we are living shows that the process of globalization may in fact be creating the conditions for a new historical accommodation. Yet, as has been clear in the past with the previous historical accommodations, the viability of the social pact is always suspect with sizable segments of the population. Tensions and conflicts will continue to arise, more prominently where the ability to redistribute resources diminishes. Consensus building and consensus politics are always fragile, and democracy continues to be a dream as much as a system of radical political representation and participation.

The notion of consensus should be differentiated from the notion of the democratic social pact. Social pacts are more enduring than historical consensuses, which are by nature ephemeral. The paradox is that social pacts are made up of historically consensual agreements that generations create, sustain, and transform into laws, routines, customs, practices, habits, regulations, and even cultures. What cannot be changed, unless we are willing to do away with the notion of democracy, is the notion of a prevailing social pact that, by its mere existence, in the long run, will prevent the polity from falling into chaos or authoritarianism. A social pact that strives to accommodate diversity and sameness as the keystone of the government of the people, by the people, and for the people. Or as Freire so often reminded us, the ability to agree to disagree is fundamental for a politics of democratic dialogue as much as the ability to live with tensions and contradictions is fundamental for democratic politics.

Another important question falls squarely in the domain of education: Is there an opposition between identity formation (which should be a remarkable part of the educational agenda) and the formation of citizenship through the establishing of a knowledge floor? Identity formation has always been part of the liberal state ideology, the first duty of the state—as historian Ted Mitchell reminds us and as governor DeWitt Clinton told his constituency in 1882 (Mitchell, 1998). Paradoxically, identity building has always been, consciously or unconsciously, blended in educational policy with the notion of citizenship building, as if identity and citizenship are fixed markers and, moreover, both will always coincide, assuming that citizenship can be predicated as a cultural representation with an acute degree of homogeneity and historical accuracy.

Toward the end of the millennium, it is clear that identity formation takes place in many diverse spheres, including education, but that formally citizenship building has been confined mostly to the educational domain. The question, which certainly goes beyond the limits of this chapter, is whether they should both—identity and citizenship—be treated as processes of lifelong learning (with potential divergent conclusions), whether both should be treated as discrete theoretical entities, which may intersect at some point (and hence the need to rethink their contradictions and correspondences), and whether this interaction (between identity and citizenship) can be accomplished at all in the context of late capitalism and the criticism of democratic ingovernability.

Thus identity is a never-secured effect of a process of enunciation of cultural difference. Taken to the extreme, however, this epistemological premise may seem impractical for pedagogy or political mobilization. Yet, from a progressive perspective, it would be simplistic to think of cultural difference as the difference between dominant and subordinate cultures. The fact is that critical multiculturalism also should address the ideological cleavages and differences within subordinate cultures, not only as the negotiation between peoples of color and the oppressive networks of power, but also among people of color themselves. Here, the words of critical race theorists resonate with peculiar force: "Unfortunately, the tensions between and among these differences are rarely interrogated, presuming a 'unity of difference'—that is, that all difference is both analogous and equivalent" (Ladson-Billings & Tate, 1995, p. 62).

Membership and experience in a given identity does not guarantee the accurate recollection of the experience—for instance, using the analytical tools of social sciences and humanities—and hence the political risks are many, including the fact that in many multiculturalist quarters

> personal testimony of oppression replaces analysis, and this testimony comes to stand for the experience of the whole group. The fact of belonging to an identity group is taken as authority enough for one's speech; the direct experience of a group or culture—that is, membership in it—becomes the only test of true knowledge. (Scott, 1989, p. 18)

Despite the growing literature on multiculturalism, only recently has the discussion shifted to address the connections between multiculturalism and citizenship, exploring the limits and possibilities of multiculturalism in democratic societies. Perhaps it is fair to argue that the multitude of tasks confronting multiculturalism is overwhelming. They include the attempt to develop a sensible, theoretically refined, and defensible new metatheoretical and theoretical territory that would create the foundations for multiculturalism as a paradigm; the attempt to establish its epistemological and logical premises around the notions of experience, narrative, voice, agency, and identity; the attempt to pursue empirical research linking culture/power/knowledge with equality/inequality/discrimination; and the need to defend multiculturalism from the conservative Right that has demonized multiculturalism as an antipatriotic movement, opposing the need for a canon that can regulate the cultural exchanges from a principle of order. These multifaceted tasks and the concrete political experience of the 1980s and 1990s in the United States have forced the different proponents of multiculturalism onto the defensive, both in theoretical and political terms. This means that they have been so far unable to fully address the need for a theory of multicultural citizenship, a theory that should be instrumental in advancing democratic goals in the context of theories of democracy, despite the fact that they operate within the capitalist framework. Yet a final dilemma for multiculturalism is the understanding of the connections between diversity and the commons, that is, the question of unity in diversity.

There are certainly many analytical and political alternatives in confronting the dilemma of unity in diversity. First and foremost is the need to explore the degree of hybridization of cultures and the notion that every social subject is constituted by multiple identities and multiple affiliations. Recognition of the complexities posed by the process of hybridization, and the notion of multiple identities in the social and psychological construction of the pedagogical subject should challenge any attempt to essentialize differences based on race, gender, class, nationality, ethnicity, religion, or sexual preference. Second, rather than dealing with differences in ethical and political commitments as primary contradictions, one may see them as secondary contradictions, or as conflicting loyalties in the social construction of identity. This opens up areas of negotiation in the context of progressive alliances based on multiple identities and learning communities. A fundamental premise is the avoidance of any essentialization of cultural struggles. Yet it is also important to recognize that there are a number of insights in neoconservative and neoliberal arguments. For instance, West (1993) and a number of Black intellectuals are concerned with the "cultural breakdown and escalating self-destructive nihilism among the poor and very poor" (p. 196). Nihilism offers certainly poor foundations for the advancement of democracy and the attainment of citizenship.

West has said that people do not live on arguments, although they might be influenced by arguments. Reading his *Prophetic Thought in Postmodern Times* (1993) helped me to revisit, once again, why we all conduct educational research, or at least why we should, and why we should take seriously the contradictions among education, citizenship, and democracy. West argues that there is an undeniable cultural decay in America that frightens him more than anything else: "By unprecedented cultural decay I mean the social breakdown of the nurturing system for children. The inability to transmit meaning, value, purpose, dignity, and decency to children" (p. 16).

While historically situated, his remarks, I believe, apply to many societies. Facilitating the nurturing and learning of children, youths, and adults is what public education—jointly with the family and a few other societal institutions—is supposed to do. That is what educational research should be about: understanding the indissoluble linkages of theory and practice. This is another practical reason that, periodically, we should revisit theoretically the relationship among state, education, citizenship, democracy, and multiculturalism and why we should strive, as Freire has told us on innumerable occasions, to build a world that is "less ugly, less cruel and less inhumane."

Democracy is a messy system, but it has survived because there is a sphere for debates and a set of rules that people follow even if they do not benefit from them. Schools and universities within democratic communities cannot be less committed to expanding the democratic discourse. Without a serious exploration of the intersections among cultural diversity, affirmative action, and citizenship, the plural bases of democracy and the democratic discourse per se are at risk. Without a technically competent, ethically sound, spiritually engaging, and politically feasible theory and practice of democratic multicultural citizenship, the people will perish.

Where there is no vision, the people perish. (Prov. 29:18, AV)

NOTES

1. While I am aware that the "classics" of political philosophy reflect primarily male, European, and heterosexual views, thus making it impossible to uncritically accept them as a cultural canon, I do contend that—properly deconstructed and analyzed with a nuanced historical sense—they continue to be an invaluable source for thinking and praxis. A similar argument is made by Carole Pateman (1986) discussing the pertinence of these works for feminist political science: "It is impossible to completely turn our backs on the classics or on contemporary methodology, because all modes of discourse reflect and are implicated in the past to a greater or lesser degree. Moreover, there are valuable insights to be gained and lessons learned from male-stream theory" (p. 3).

2. Discussions of colonialism also must include the United States and its experiences in the Philippines, Cuba, and Puerto Rico and the former Soviet Union and its relationship with Eastern Europe and Afghanistan. To the dismay of many conservative analysts, and given its historical peculiarities, socialist Cuba continues to be an exception to colonialist doctrine.

3. The classic text of how ability grouping structures inequality continues to be J. Oakes's *Keeping track* (1995).

4. *Globalization* has been defined as "the intensification of social relations which link distant localities in such a way that local happenings are shaped by events occurring many miles away" (Held, 1991, p. 9). Held suggests, among other things, that globalization is the product of the emergence of a global economy, expansion of transnational linkages between economic units creating new forms of collective decision making, development of intergovernmental and quasi-supranational

institutions, intensification of transnational communications, and the creation of new military orders. I have suggested elsewhere that globalization puts limits to state autonomy and national sovereignty. These limits are expressed in the tension between global and local dynamics in virtually every decision and policy domain in the social, cultural, and economic spheres (see Torres,1998a). Globalization therefore not only blurs national boundaries but also shifts solidarities within and outside the national state. Globalization cannot be defined exclusively by the post-Fordist organization of production but emerges as a major characteristic of a global world economy. Issues of human rights, regional states, and cosmopolitan democracy play a major role affecting civic minimums at the state level, the performance of capital and labor in different domains, and particularly the dynamics of citizenship, democracy, and multiculturalism in the modern state.

5. "Affirmative action began with Title VII of the Civil Rights Act of 1964, which prohibited discrimination on the basis of race and sex and which was later augmented by a number of executive orders that regulate federal contracts and set goals and timetables for hiring minorities" (Feinberg, 1996, p. 363).

CHAPTER 4

Globalization, Education, and Citizenship

Solidarity Versus Markets?

Education has in modern times been situated within the nation-state. It has been shaped by the demands within the state to prepare labor for participation in its economy and to prepare citizens to participate in the polity. This approximate congruence of nation-state and formalized education becomes problematic as globalization blurs national sovereignty and puts limits on state autonomy. If our contemporary discussion of education is to have meaning, it must move beyond assumptions about national boundaries and goals internal to national agendas. It must address the questions raised by the globalization of the two traditional bases of formalized educational systems: governance and economies. These questions are very straightforward: Will globalization make human rights and democratic participation more universal, or will globalization redefine human enterprise as market exchanges invulnerable to traditional civic forms of governance? Whether education as a publicly shared invention, contributing to civic life and human rights, can thrive depends on the future of globalization—a future that may offer the internationalization of the ideals of a democratic education or may reduce education, and civic participation, to narrow instruments of remote and seemingly ungovernable market forces.

This chapter suggests that the phenomenon of globalization does place limits on state autonomy and national sovereignty. These limits are expressed in tension between global and local dynamics in virtually every decision and policy domain in the social, cultural, and economic spheres. Globalization therefore not only blurs national boundaries but also shifts solidarities within and outside the national state. Globalization cannot be defined exclusively by the post-Fordist organization of production, but emerges as a major characteristic of a global world economy. Issues of human rights, regional states, and cosmopolitan democracy will play a major role affecting civic minimums at the state level, the performance of capital and labor in different domains, and particularly the dynamics of citizenship, democracy, and multiculturalism in the modern state. To understand the issues at stake in education, we have to consider these tensions within globalization and their implications for reshaping the limits on or potential for civil society.

THE PHENOMENON OF GLOBALIZATION

Increasing globalization is a two-edged sword. On the one hand it is quite obvious that it removes competence from the national context and that it undermines the institutions which civil society and the democratic public hitherto have used for communication. On the other hand globalization opens up new possibilities for democratic influence on essential common issues which by their nature are about the notion of the nation state. Attempts to democratize are, therefore, forced to work for the establishment of democratic global structures, including international organs for civil society. (O. Korsgaard, cited in Mayo, 1999, pp. 175–176)

Globalization has been defined as "the intensification of worldwide social relations which link distant localities in such a way that local happenings are shaped by events occurring many miles away and vice versa" (Held, 1991, p. 9). Held suggests that globalization is the product of the emergence of a global economy, expansion of transnational linkages between economic units creating new forms of collective decision making, development of intergovernmental and quasi-supranational institutions, intensification of transnational communications, and the creation of new regional and military orders.

The process of globalization is seen as blurring national boundaries, shifting solidarities within and between nation-states, and deeply affecting the constitutions of national and interest-group identities. Neil Smelser (1994) captures this theme quite well:

A convenient starting-point for depicting the world situation is to consider the status of the nation-state. Once commonly supposed to be the natural and sovereign focus of the loyalty and solidarity of its citizens, this idea of the state has recently been challenged with respect to all of these constituent elements. The international boundaries of the state have become permeable through the greater globalization of production, trade, finance, and culture with a resultant loss of control of all states over their own fortunes. The sovereignty of states has been further compromised through shifting patterns of regional political federations and alliances. At the subnational level, the state has found itself challenged by the efflorescence and

revitalization of solidarity groupings with multiple bases—regional, linguistic, religious, ethnic, gender, and life-style—as well as a bewildering
array of novel social movements that generate their own solidarity. All of
these compete with the state for the loyalties of peoples and sometimes
for jurisdiction over territory. In a word, the contemporary state has been
pressured from both above and below by contested boundaries and shifting solidarities.[1]

Globalization is indeed a social construct that, as Douglas Kellner (1997)
has suggested, needs to be considered critically from the perspective of
critical theory. Kellner suggests that the concept of globalization is ubiqui-
tous, and entails from the Westernization of the world to the ascendancy
of capitalism. Some people see globalization as increasing the homogeneity of societies, whereas others see it as increasing the hybridization of cultures and diversity. For still others, globalization is an evolving operation
of power by multinational corporations and state power, or the linchpin
for environmental action, democratization, and humanization. Some see
the concept of globalization as a contemporary ruse to describe the effects
of imperialism or modernization; some claim that modernization would
open a new "global age" that differs from the "modern age." Moreover,
whereas some theorists claim that globalization is the defining concept of
a new epoch in the history of humankind, others claim that the novelty
and centrality of globalization has been exaggerated (Kellner, 1997, p. 2).
Kellner concludes that globalization is all of the above and that, in many
ways, the discourse of globalization can be articulated with modern and
postmodern theories. In fact, for Kellner, we are in an "interregnum period between an aging modern and an emerging postmodern era" (p. 3).

What is important about Kellner's analysis is that he has captured very
well the spirit of the epoch as far as social theory is concerned: Globalization cannot be analyzed only in terms of polar discrete opposites but
should be seen as a borderline situation between two historical epochs. As
such, it is a complex, multidimensional phenomenon "that involves different levels, flows, tensions, and conflicts, such that a transdisciplinary
social theory is necessary to capture its contours, dynamics, trajectories,
problems, and possible futures" (Kellner, 1997, p. 4).

Kellner is skeptical that historical epochs rise and fall with neatly defined chronological boundaries. He sees the current epoch as a period that
is parallel in many ways to the Renaissance, a transitional period between
historical eras. In fact, Kellner (1997), despite his mild defense of postmodernism as more than a historical fad, does not see globalization as
responding to clear "postmodern" conditions because "capitalist relations
of production still structure most social orders and the hegemony of capital is still the structuring force of most dimensions of social life" (p. 31).

From the perspective of critical modernism—that is, a position that sees the interplay of class, race, and gender as distinct and autonomous modes of domination, which nevertheless have interactions that are systemic and deserve to be studied from interdisciplinary perspectives (Morrow & Torres, 1995)—I turn now to analyze the globalization of capitalism and economic restructuring worldwide.

CITIZENSHIP: SOVEREIGNTY, MARKETS, AND HUMAN RIGHTS

The irony of this postmodern world is that everything has been deconstructed but computer-aided capitalism. (DiFazio, 1998, p. 151)

Changes in the conditions of production; in the domains of politics, information technology, consumer taste, capital flows, and the economy overall; and most important, in the politics of culture worldwide, have implied theoretical and practical challenges to the notion of citizenship as predicated by most political philosophy traditions. Here I would like to consider the connections of globalization with the concerns with worldwide markets and free trade, and how market competition in the context of neoliberalism affects the notion of citizenship and democracy at a global level. In the same vein but from the very different political-ideological standpoint of universal human rights, I would like to offer a systematic appraisal of the limits of citizenship given the growing awareness of—and the globalization of the discourse and institutions of—universal human rights. These two paradoxically similar arguments from disparate, even antinomical, political-philosophical perspectives underscore the complexities associated with globalization and its cultural implications for citizenship. Each carries enormous implications for the future shape of a public education.

CITIZENS AND MARKETS

Nation states are political organisms, and in their economic bloodstreams cholesterol steadily builds up. Over time, arteries harden and the organism's vitality decays. (Kenichi Ohmae, 1995, p. 142)

Kenichi Ohmae (1995), a respected Japanese business strategist, advances the thesis in his work *The End of the Nation State* that the nation-state is economically sclerotic. He asserts that, although still a player in the world system, the nation-state has lost its capacity to control its national economy, especially to control exchange rates and protect its currency. Moreover, the nation-state can no longer generate real economic activity. It has lost its role as a critical participant in the global economy. Instead, the four I's (investment, industry, information technology, and individual consumers) that Ohmae says drive the expansion and operation of the global economy have taken over the economic power once held by the nation-state.[2] The result of this economic process is the rise of the region-state, defined simply as an area that often comprises communities situated across borders, centered around a regional economic center having a population with a range from a few million to 20 million people (Ohmae, 1995, p. 143).

Thus the nation-state has lost its ability to cope with its own economic dynamics and political tensions because, as Ohmae (1995) argues,

> Buffeted by sudden changes in industry dynamics, available information, consumer preferences, and flows of capital; burdened by demands for the civil minimum and for open-ended subsidies in the name of national interest; and hog-tied by political systems that prove ever-less responsive to new challenges, [the nation-state] no longer makes compelling sense as discrete, meaningful units on an up-to-date map of economic activity. (p. 79)

For Ohmae the nation-state has become a dysfunctional unit in terms of economic organization. As the creation of an earlier stage of industrial history, it lacks incentive, credibility, tools, legitimacy, and even the political will to play a central role in today's borderless economy in terms of real flows of economic activity:

> As the workings of genuinely global capital markets dwarf their ability to control exchange rates or protect their currency, nation-states have become inescapably vulnerable to the discipline imposed by economic choices made elsewhere by people and institutions over which they have no practical control. (Ohmae, 1995, p. 12)

These changes, resulting from the "new discipline" imposed by the process of globalization over the nation-states, will write the obituary of what Ohmae considers a long-dead body of thought: liberalism—and, by implication, liberal democracy. For Ohmae, the central tenet of the liberal ideal in civic life is the importance of sustaining extensive public investments in education, to facilitate the action of responsible individuals, fostering, at the same time, cultural diversity. Liberalism will promote these twin aims except where either goal may conflict with the perceived *volunté general* or public good (Ohmae, 1995, p. 75).

Yet for liberalism to work, Ohmae argues, mutual respect among citizens is necessary. Differences in choices, lifestyles, or consumer preferences are not interpreted as challenging to the social order or to specific individual interests. In addition, to sustain the liberal edifice there must be mutual trust among citizens in such a way that state actions are legitimated as necessary for the social pact and not seen as mere imposition or caprice. A further requirement is transparency in the actions of the state and in the ability to produce and disseminate information, so that every member of the society can be confident that the decisions reached after a broad debate are fair, even if he or she does not particularly like them or obtain benefits from them.

For Ohmae, neither the behavior of individuals nor the behavior of the governments in today's liberal democracies meets these three criteria. In contemporary capitalist democracies there is almost no civic participation apart from voting, and even voting turnout is low. There is increased competitive self-interest rather than increased solidarity. And, in turn, governmental information has become opaque rather than transparent, leading to what Ohmae (1995, pp. 75–76) calls the "Iron Triangle" of decision making, in which lawmakers, bureaucrats, and special interest groups dominate the process. Thus, for Ohmae, the state is a nostalgic fiction because managers in the public enterprise or in private enterprises cannot any longer be treated as part of discrete national units. Moreover, the production of goods and services cannot easily be attached to a particular national label.

Therefore, growing desires for low-cost products override traditional choice for nationally made products. This new culture is embedded in a new form of international cultural taste that Ohmae calls the "Californianization" of taste. This seems to be particularly relevant in the world of teenagers, who show a fundamental process of convergence in taste worldwide (e.g., consider the dominance of rap music, Levi's jeans, and Nike shoes). A growing convergence of worldviews, mind-sets, even thought processes, and a commodity consciousness—all multimedia driven—are creating a serious generational rift between the "Nintendo kids" generation and their predecessors (Ohmae, 1995, pp. 15–16; Barnet & Cavanagh, 1996b, pp. 72–73).

Technology plays a central role in this globalization of information and culture, particularly because at a macroeconomic level, technological change has made it possible for capital to be shifted anywhere in the world with virtually no restrictions. Thus capital flows, which have increased dramatically worldwide, need not be tied to any physical movement of goods or services.[3] By extension, traditional forms of trade represent only a fraction of trade across borders and of the borderless economy. Not only capital but, at the level of companies, information technologies have changed the ways that managers can achieve quick, effective, and interactive information about their customers, markets, products, and organizational processes. This, in turn, permits managers to be more responsive to customers and more flexible in organizing their provision of services worldwide. Finally, at the market level, technological changes (and particularly exposure to mass media) have changed the ways that customers learn and appreciate how other people live, what kinds of goods and service are available to them, and the relative value of those goods worldwide. In these circumstances, traditional notions of economic nationalism will have only a small influence on purchase decisions (Ohmae, 1995, pp. 27–28).

Not only do the nation-states lose their prestigious position in the world of trade, facing the emergence of regional states, but as their economic position weakens their political position follows suit, facing growing demands for the civil minimum:

> Adding to these burdens, of course, is the steady growing share of the civil minimum demanded of government in the form of broad-based social programs—welfare, unemployment compensation, public education, old-age pensions, health insurance, and the like. (Ohmae, 1995, p. 55)

This demand for the civil minimum shows an important schizophrenia in liberal democracies: Citizens do not want these benefits reduced, but neither do they want to pay for them. Ohmae (1995) discusses in some detail the responses that a nation-state may make to civil discontent and to the conflicting demands of private and public interests within the new globalized economy. Essentially, he argues that economic and political problems are mostly organizational problems, not fundamental questions of ideology. Therefore, these problems cannot be answered by imposing any ideological answer in the nation-states, be it that of liberal democracy, market economy, socialism, or communism:

> The goal, after all, is not to legitimize this or that political establishment or power arrangement. It is to improve the quality of life of people, regular people—us, no matter where they live. People come first; borders came afterwards. It is time for economic policy to remember this simple fact. (p. 148)

In short, in today's borderless economy, with the growing mobility of investment, industry, information technology, and individual consumers, central governments have only one option in their efforts to avoid economic sclerosis and to restore sustainable and self-reinforcing vitality to their economies without mortgaging the long-term prospects of their citizens. That solution is to put global logic first, entering the global economy. To do this, nation-states should allow full operational autonomy to the region-states that emerge within or across their borders: "The only hope is to reverse the postfeudal, centralizing tendencies of the modern era and allow—or better encourage—the economic pendulum to swing away from nations and back toward regions" (Ohmae, 1995, p. 142).

Ohmae, both in his 1995 book *The End of the Nation State* and in his earlier and more popular book *The Borderless World: Power and Strategy in the Interlinked World Economy* (1990), seems to advance the idea of global citizenship as consumer and producer in region-states. Briefly, his argument rests on the assumption that the market discriminates (that is to say, determines) who belongs to, and who has fallen out of, the realm of citizenship. In fact, for Ohmae, corporations, some state institutions, and some citizens have found perfect niches in science, technology, capital, or labor from which they can compete favorably in the world system of commodity production and exchange. These regional niches—whose only legitimacy rests on their ability to compete successfully in a world dominated by free trade, and on their status of comparative advantage in the allocation of resources and endowments—are in fact the only productive units that can build the polity around them with all its philosophical, economic, and political implications.

A natural corollary of this analysis is that the nineteenth-century notions of the nation-state are totally obsolete today. Nation-states have allowed regional trading blocs to flourish without controlling them, and sometimes even without levying taxes on them. Therefore, at a global level, worldwide competitive activities of state institutions, capital, labor, and corporations constitute the only viable sense of organized community, of economic citizenship. As such, they override any sense of political citizenship, and even any viable sense of cultural-national homogeneity. This is particularly so when popular mass culture has become the norm worldwide, and the mass media is stimulating and even regulating consumption as well as values worldwide.

For Ohmae (1990, 1995), there is certainly no reason to strive for any notion of citizenship's rights or obligations, or to substantiate any needs for citizen virtues, given the facts that the state has little, if any, power to regulate exchanges between "trading states" and that pressures for the civil minimum in liberalism have had disastrous results. Therefore, the notion of citizenship without market sponsorship is meaningless.

ORGANIZED SOLIDARITY
AND HUMAN RIGHTS AGAINST THE MARKETS?

Preconceptions obfuscate the reality within which we speak. . . . They make us became myopic, which creates difficulty in seeing the reality for what it is. (Carlos Alberto Torres, quoted in Freire, 1993, p. 119)

The precisely opposite political-philosophical view is that, whereas the limits of citizenship as described by Ohmae can be substantiated in the experience of industrialized advanced nations, the real basis for those limits is not merely or exclusively economic but the predominance of human rights, which creates a new and more universal concept of citizenship. The movement of human rights has unfolded in the postwar era and is, for instance, clearly represented in the human rights policies developed for guest workers in Europe. It is the predominance of universal human rights, rather than simply the predominance of market rules, that underscores the new demands for citizenship but also the limits of citizenship within the nation-states.[4]

Personal rights, through the universal extension of the notion of human rights, are becoming available to individuals who fall outside the status of national citizenship. Human rights appear as a new normative framework and a new transnational discourse and structure that not only celebrates but also actively promotes human rights as a world-level organizing principle. Thus the predominance of universal personhood over national status undermines the national order of citizenship. Yasemin Nuhoglu Soysal (1994) challenges the popular notion, well-entrenched in the tradition of political philosophy, that national citizenship is an imperative for acquiring membership in the polity. She claims:

> Incorporation into a system of membership rights does not inevitably require incorporation into the national collectivity. . . . [In Europe] the guest worker experience attests to a shift in global discourse and models of citizenship across two phases of immigration in the twentieth century. The model of national citizenship, anchored in territorialized notions of cultural belonging, was dominant during the period of massive migration at the turn of the century when immigrants were expected to be molded into national citizens. The recent guest worker experience reflects a time when national citizenship is losing ground to a more universal model of membership, anchored in deterritorialized notions of persons' rights. (p. 3)

Nuhoglu Soysal (1994) describes this new model, in which rights are institutionalized on the basis of personhood, as "postnational citizenship":

> Postnational citizenship confers upon every person the right and duty of participation in the authority structures and public life of polity, regardless of their historical or cultural ties to that community. (p. 3)

Her analysis is based not only on a faithful acceptance of human rights as a preordained normative framework superseding national, regional, or local cultures (and the politics of identity per se) but also on the preponderance of a new institutionalism and organizational rules that are the result of the consolidation of a new world order—with education playing a central role in the world system.

Institutions are built around routines, rules, norms, and structures. Within certain limits and frames of behavior, they can guide the transformation of social action. For this new institutionalism, changes in the relationships among economy (deindustrialization, export-oriented models, globalization), politics (diminishing roles of the state and private sectors, withdrawal of public investment, shrinking state employment), and education (higher user fees, privatization, decentralization, and problems in quality of education) challenge the role of education in development.

Compulsory schooling has been associated with the processes of Westernization, modernization, social control, and status group competition. The early institutionalist approach represented by the work of J. Meyer (1977) and of J. Boli and F. Ramirez (1992), among others, argues that educational development is not the result of domestic (internal) processes that result from economic and social differentiation, especially industrialization and urbanization. Thus mass schooling did not develop as a deliberate attempt to establish social control (over the lower classes or immigrants) or to reorient traditional attitudes of populations. Boli and Ramirez argue, instead, that mass schooling "is a prominent consequence of the development of the cultural framework of the West as a whole" (p. 28). Undoubtedly, the politics and discourse of universal human rights appears as a cornerstone of this new cultural framework of the West.

This Western framework implies developing the notion of the nation-state and a modern conception of citizenship that is seen as a source of compulsory mass schooling. It also implies, as Boli and Ramirez (1992) put it, that schooling serves as a ceremonial induction into modern society, as

> an extended initiation rite that symbolically transforms unformed children into enhanced individuals authorized to participate in the modern economy, polity, and society, and it does so by definition. (p. 30)

For these purposes, the role of the state as a modernizer is paramount. And increasingly, even with the pressures of globalization, the state is beginning to reassert itself in the face of terrorist threats after September 11, 2001. The state must acquire material capital and technical know-how as it fights for the legitimation and organizational efficacy required for its own survival. Thus the states' fragility in developing societies and the contradictions they face have more to do with states' competing with other modernizing institutions than with external and internal forces that erode state autonomy, particularly in the context of the globalization of world economies. Similarly, the state's inability to govern (including the ungovernability of democratic systems) occurs when it provides conflicting signals to communities.

There are obvious problems with this approach that cannot be explored in detail here. However, posing the question of the global paradoxes of membership, Nuhoglu Soysal (1994) hints at some of the most intractable questions in the analyses of the new institutionalists:

> In the postwar era, if one facet of the discourse and praxis of immigration is the closure of national polity, the other is the expansion of the same polity beyond national closure. While the first involves boundary construction through restrictive policy measures and national(ist) narratives, the other is about "border crossing" . . . a constant flux of people, the extension of rights of membership to foreigners, and narratives of multiplicity. This apparent paradox is only intelligible if world-level institutional frameworks and processes are taken into consideration. (p. 6)

Two principles then become antagonistic, namely, national sovereignty and universal human rights. For Nuhoglu Soysal (1994), "these two global precepts simultaneously constrain and enhance the nation-state's scope of action" (pp. 7–8). This creates an incongruity between the normative and the organizational bases of rights, as well as between constitutional prescriptions and laws. There is incoherence, also, in the factual application of those laws in disputed social contexts. In short, in the context of disputes about identity and the politics of culture as performed in social formations, one cannot ignore racism and ethnic tensions, sexism and patriarchy, and class exploitation and patrimonialism as constitutive of the daily experience of people, both at the level of the elites and in the socially subordinated sectors.

Challenging traditional assumptions about access to citizenship and exercise of membership rights in a polity, Nuhoglu Soysal (1994) departs from key assumptions of the early institutionalist theory, arguing that

> the state is no longer an autonomous and independent organization closed over a nationally defined population. Instead, we have a system of constitutionally interconnected states with a multiplicity of membership. [Hence] . . . the logic of personhood supersedes the logic of national citizenship, [and] individual rights and obligations, which were historically located in the nation-state, have increasingly moved to an universalistic plane, transcending the boundaries of particular nation-states. (pp. 164–165)

Yet, in the name of preserving universal human rights in the face of deteriorating societal and state conditions, atrocities have been committed, evidenced, for instance, by revelations of human rights abuses by the peacekeeping mission in Somalia in 1991. In that case Canadian and Italian soldiers are charged with torturing and killing Somali teenagers (Fox, 1997). Nuhoglu Soysal's (1994) analysis of the limits of citizenship has implications at three levels. First is the level of citizenship, where notions of identity and rights are decoupled. Second is the level of the politics of identity and multiculturalism, where the emergence of membership in the polity "is multiple in the sense of spanning local, regional, and global identities, and . . . accommodates intersecting complexes of rights, duties and loyalties" (p. 166). Third is the level of what could be termed *cosmopolitan democracies,* which Soysal highlights as emerging from the importance of the international system for the attainment of democracy worldwide. The cosmopolitan democracies constitute a system relatively divorced in its origins and constitutive dynamics from codes of the nation-states.

Citizenship has always been associated with the constitution and operation of the modern nation-state. The question facing us in the process of increased globalization is whether the nation-state and citizenship are withering away. Paradoxically, these questions are related to the postmodernist gaze.

Postmodernism argues that nation-states are losing importance in the context of an increasingly interdependent world and in the context of more local struggles. Yet, as Immanuel Wallerstein (1997) argues, the history of the (capitalist) world system has been a trend toward cultural heterogeneity rather than cultural homogenization. Thus the fragmentation of the nation in the world system is happening at the same time that there is a tendency toward cultural differentiation or cultural complexity, that is, globalization. Globalization and regionalization seem to be dual processes occurring simultaneously. This fact has not been overlooked by certain strands of postmodernism, providing an avenue to understanding globalization and the rise of ethnicity and nationalisms, which emerged simultaneously with globalization, as not necessarily contradictory but, rather, related phenomena.

Held (1991) has persuasively argued that there is a New World Order associated with the globalization of capitalism,

> an international order involving the conjuncture of a global system of production and exchange which is beyond the control of any single nation-state (even of the most powerful); extensive network of transnational interaction and communication which transcend national societies and evade most forms of national regulation; the power and activities of a vast array of international regimes and organizations, many of which reduce the scope for action of even leading states; and the internationalization of security structures which limit the scope for the independent use of military force by states. (p. 101)

Held's general argument overlaps with Ohmae's arguments on regional states and rests on the assumption that, in the past, trade routes and
empires linked distant populations together with networks of interaction
of limited sophistication. The present social order, however, is defined by
multiple systems of transaction and coordination linking people, communities, and societies in a complex way that renders territorial boundaries
virtually useless in controlling economic, cultural, and political activities.
Needless to say, this situation generates new political uncertainties.

EDUCATION IN A GLOBAL ERA: QUESTIONS AND QUERIES

> The invention of universal compulsory publicly funded education was
> mankind's greatest social invention. (Lester Thurow, 1999, p. 130)

In this historical context of political and economic uncertainties, what are
the implications of globalization for citizenship, democracy, and education? Any redefinition of the notion of democracy situates public schooling at the center of the modernist-enlightenment project. Postmodernists
would argue, however, that the ethical, substantive, and procedural elements of democratic theory should be reexamined considering postmodern culture. Globalization makes problematic all of these—the ethical, the
substantive, the procedural—as they relate to education because, as we
have seen, the erosion of traditional boundaries makes it less certain who
governs, and who is served by, educational systems and practices.

In my view, the challenge for educators, parents, students, and policy makers is to think critically about the failures of the past and about
the myriad of exclusionary practices that still pervade the process of
schooling—hence bringing to the forefront issues of power and domination, class, race, and gender. Yet this attempt will be confronted by the
logic-in-use in educational policy and reform.

The guiding rationale of educational reform is the notion of instrumental rationality because it gives attention to administration, procedures,
and efficiency as the prime criteria for change and progress and because
it assumes that there is a common framework structuring the experience
of all people.[5]

Yet instrumental rationality cannot account for some of the most compelling paradoxes of contemporary life. Let us take as an example the ideology of human rights, emerging as the most comprehensive narrative
of the Enlightenment today. The paradox is that without human rights, a
number of the key tenets related to postmodernist politics will not survive

close analytical scrutiny. The ideology of human rights, in fact, constitutes the basis for identity politics, and the notion of tolerance appears as a central foundation for diversity and citizenship premised on human rights. Todd Gitlin (1995) explains:

> A humane respect for difference, an understanding that one aspect of the human condition is to live in a distinct milieu, an acknowledgment of the limits of what anyone can know—these remain the basis for common human rights. The Enlightenment's enduring ideal of universal rights, once extended logically, guarantees the right to be different—although it is also a reminder that human beings have good reason not to differ about one elementary right: the right to be who one wishes to be. (p. 215)

As has become clear in the analysis so far, opposing forces—those of the marketplace and those of the ideology of human rights—are making the discussion on democracy and citizenship even more complex and convoluted. Not surprisingly, education is caught in the storm.

In the recent past, fueled by the winds of modernization, the role of education was considered a very simple question. From an economicist perspective, the question was how schooling should make labor highly skilled and therefore more competitive. Facing the changes in the world system, the model was slightly modified to acknowledge that if people are educated to think more analytically rather than through a pedagogy of drills on skills and if, at the same time, people learn how to work on problem solving more collaboratively (teamwork), then education will fulfill its role. It is exactly this reasoning that is behind an agenda for educational change "that includes developing national standards for curriculum, student achievement, and teacher certification, and Europeanizing the school-to-career transition" (Weiner, 1998, p. 185).

The question of linking this educational reform with the workings of democracy was simply stated as promoting a model of citizenship that will allow the educational system to meet the challenges posed to it by a democratic system based on citizenship demands and the demands of institutional capitalism. What was subtly understood in that model is that there is a perpetual tension between capitalism and democracy, which in turn affects the role of education. However, that tension will go through a constant process of accommodation (Bowles & Gintis, 1986), and a new resolution of this tension will emerge—in itself subject to further changes in the future given the notion of unstable equilibrium.

In neoliberal times the main questions are how globalization is affecting organized solidarity, how citizenship is being checked by market forces and globalization dynamics, and how democracy could be effective despite its ungovernability. The unstable linkage between democracy and capitalism has been blurred to levels rarely seen before. Since capitalism has no alternative system to compete for recognition in terms of social organization of production and distribution worldwide, the democratic requirements for the operation of the capitalist system are being seriously criticized, particularly by neoconservatives who find democracy expensive and ungovernable. One may argue, however, that "when social movements press schools to live up to their democratic purposes, the struggles alter the relationship of social forces, exciting forces that can weaken capitalism's social and political hegemony" (Weiner, 1998, p. 194).

This is truth: The antiglobalization movement met its first known activist death in the old port of Genoa, Italy. On July 20, 2001, in Piazza Alimonda, blood and violence marked the last summit of the G-8 leaders, changing forever the way that neoliberalism and globalization proponents broadcast their arguments to the world through annual G-8 summits. Social movements have, increasingly, a more powerful voice in arguing against "Globalization Without Representation," the banner of the Seattle protest. Yet one may wonder to what extent a comprehensive agenda for social and political reform with an emphasis on social justice and democracy could be accomplished in neoliberal times, including an educational agenda. Resistance by social movements and their increased capacity to veto political initiatives does not guarantee the ability to create a lasting, long-term, comprehensive political agenda for reform.

Clearly, the challenges to education have been magnified. How can education contribute to democratic citizenship? Will Thurow's view of universal, compulsory, publicly funded education as "mankind's greatest social invention" survive as a fundamental part of the democratic pact?

We use the term "children at risk" in our academic deliberations to refer to those who need the most assistance and consideration from educational policy. I am afraid that we are now going to coin a new slogan: "human rights at risk." With terrorism as the new evil of Western civilization (as portrayed in the "axis of evil" metaphor used by the U.S. president George W. Bush), what is at stake are the very foundations of respect for human rights in the United States and worldwide. In a perverse way, not only are globalization pressures pushing for a radical market orientation (an expression of instrumental rationality) as the logic guiding social policy, including education policy, but also, with the broad new antiterrorist legislation in the United States, the very foundations of tolerance, conviviality, and respect for the integrity of human rights are at risk.

In light of all these forces and challenges, to ask how educational policies could contribute to a democratic multicultural citizenship poses a formidable challenge to the theoretical imagination and to any political model that strives to go beyond the logic of instrumental rationality or, worse, beyond the logic of fear.

NOTES

The arguments presented in this article are elaborated more extensively in my book *Education, Democracy, and Multiculturalism: Dilemmas of Citizenship in a Global World* (1998a) and in a book that Nicholas Burbules and I edited, *Education and Globalization: Critical Concepts* (2000).

1. This is well documented in the sociological literature. The 12th World Congress of Sociology, which took place in Bielefeld, Germany (July 18–23, 1994), had as its central theme "Contested Boundaries and Shifting Solidarities" (see Smelser, 1994, p. 5).

2. The theoretical notion of the state covers federal and state governance. Yet the presence of "provincial" or single states with premier economies makes matters more complicated. For instance, in Canada there is a clear division of labor between federal and provincial states. The federal state is charged with key symbolic processes to increase the legitimacy of the political system, including, for instance, immigration and constitutionalism; the provincial state is primarily in charge of specific roles in promoting capital accumulation. Hence education is fundamentally a provincial responsibility. Another example is the differential might of single states in a union, such as California in the United States. Journalistic reports remind us periodically that California's output ranks seventh among all nations and provincial states in the world (above Canada and following Great Britain very closely), with an annual output of $1,037 billion. California's productivity is based on its position at the crossroads of one of the busiest trade routes in the world, linking Asia and Latin America; and the state is a powerhouse in agricultural products, entertainment, computers, and electronics, among other things. The top G-7 countries are the United States (GNP $6,773 billion), Japan ($4,321 billion), Germany ($2,075 billion), France ($1,355 billion), Italy ($1,101 billion), Great Britain ($1,069 billion), and Canada ($900 billion). Russia's inclusion in the G-8 is based on politics more than economics (*Los Angeles Times*, January 8, 1998, p. A22).

3. Goldsmith (1996, p. 502) asserts that since World War II the global GNP has increased fivefold and world trade, twelvefold. Money itself, Barnet & Cavanagh (1996a, p. 368) tell us, has become a global product. For instance, the total sum of Eurocurrency accounts worldwide in 1973 was $315 billion; by 1987, it was nearly $4 trillion.

4. For a compelling analysis of the limits of citizenship given the predominance of human rights, see Nuhoglu Soysal (1994).

5. The notion of *instrumental rationality* is central to critical theory. It is defined here as combining the Weberian notion of rationality as purposive-instrumental action and Habermas's notion of instrumental action. For Max

Weber, purposive-instrumental action is "determined by expectations as to the behavior of external objects and of other men, and making use of these expectations as 'conditions' or 'means' for the rational success-oriented pursuit of the agent's own rationally considered ends" (Weber, quoted in McCarthy, 1979, p. 28). The notion of instrumental action in Habermas "is governed by technical rules based on empirical knowledge. In every case they imply empirical predictions about observable events, physical or social" (McCarthy, 1979, p. 391). I should add, following Marcuse's criticism of technical reason, that every form of instrumental rationality, insofar as it represents an adequate means to a given end, is governed by technical rules based on empirical knowledge seeking to forecast and control social and physical events. It involves a substantive purpose of domination, yet is exercised through methodical, scientific, calculating, and calculated control. This certainly challenges some key postmodernist approaches.

CHAPTER 5

Education and the Archeology of Consciousness

Freire and Hegel

The political philosophy of education of Paulo Freire has been very in-fluential in the constitution of many of the more innovative aspects of critical pedagogies, not only in Latin America but worldwide. Freire has masterfully bridged the levels of totalities and individualities in linking structures and action in a sociology of knowledge and education. He has always worked on two different lines of theoretical development: an evolving theory of agency and a historical perspective that emphasizes the dialectics of individuals and structures in producing the material and symbolic layers of social life.

As Freire himself recognizes, his understanding of the relationship be-tween subjectivity and power bears some resemblance to certain strains of poststructuralist thought (Freire, 1992a; McLaren & Lankshear, 1994). For Freire, knowledge is a social construct, a process and not merely a product. Thus knowledge seen in terms of a dialectic of oppositions is fundamentally at odds with traditional idealist and positivist epistemol-ogy.[1] Correspondingly, Freire's pedagogy emerged in Latin America as a critique of both the traditional (authoritarian) educational paradigm and its challenger in the region, positivist pedagogy, which was gaining ground in Latin America in the 1950s and 1960s.[2]

Insofar as the state and public schools constitute institutions of media-tion and control, pedagogues of liberation have developed—paraphrasing Paul Ricoeur—a hermeneutics of suspicion of schooling. More than 30 years of implementation of Freirean pedagogical and political approaches in Latin America and elsewhere have generally led more to the design of educational ventures sponsored by nonformal and nongovernment orga-nization (NGO) than to working within schools or other state-sponsored institutions. It is only recently that the notion of *public popular schooling* has been advanced by Freirean pedagogues in the context of Brazilian debates concerning school autonomy (Freire, 1993; Gadotti, 1990). Similarly, the reception of Freire in the United States has resulted in serious questions about the limits and possibilities of Freirean models in public schooling (Giroux, 1984; Macedo & Freire, 1987; McLaren & Lankshear, 1994; McLaren & Leonard, 1992; Shor, 1987a, 1992).

Not surprisingly, many of the representatives of this pedagogy have worked, politically and professionally, within political parties, universities, and research centers, as well as with organizations originating in, or linked to, churches. Freire's overall proposal was defined, 3 decades ago, by the Portuguese word *conscientização*. This term, popularized by Freire in educational environments, has been translated as "conscientization" or "critical consciousness" in English. It was defined by Freire as follows:

> The French "prise de conscience," to take consciousness of, is a normal way of being a human being. Conscientization is something which goes beyond the "prise de conscience." It is something which is starting from the ability of getting, of taking the "prise de conscience." Something which implies to analyze. It is a kind of reading the world rigorously or almost rigorously. It is the way of reading how society works. It is the way to understand better the problem of interests, the question of power. How to get power, what it means not to have power. Finally, conscientizing implies a deeper reading of reality, [and] the common sense goes beyond the common sense. (Freire, 1990; See also Torres, 1992b)

The implications of Freire's proposal for schooling are vast. Consider for example the idea of drawing from the needs of the community as the prime material for the design of a vocabulary for literacy programs. To implement this community-based curriculum in the classroom, or to practice pedagogy as cultural politics, will simultaneously undermine the power of "curriculum experts," school administrators, and the state bureaucracy, by giving back to the individual teacher traditional craft control over what goes on in the classroom (Apple, 1993; Giroux, 1991; Giroux & McLaren, 1994; McLaren, 1993; Popkewitz, 1991; Torres Santome, 1992). However, because teachers' control will be in contradiction with the attempts to control curriculum and school practices by other segments of civil society (interest groups, business groups, social movements) or by bureaucratic categories in the state, the promotion of teachers' autonomy and their control over curriculum will eventually require an overhaul in school organization and administration. Furthermore, in the context of debates between school excellence for international competitiveness versus equality of educational opportunity, or proposals stressing adapting schools to the needs of industry and the market-place, the agenda of liberating pedagogy will be disruptive of any school "ethos" based on the premises of corporate culture and the technical discourse of managerialism.

The preceding discussion highlights the importance of understanding the political philosophy of education developed by Freire, and particularly its theoretical roots. What has made Freire's political philosophy of education so current and universal, placing him and some of the "generative themes" suggested by his method at the center of educational debates in critical pedagogy for the last three decades?

Influenced by the work of psychotherapists such as Franz Fanon and Erich Fromm, Freire in his *Pedagogy of the Oppressed* (1970b) argues that few human interpersonal relations are exempt from oppression of one kind or another; by reason of race, class, or gender, people tend to be perpetrators and/or victims of oppression. He points out that class exploitation, racism, and sexism are the most conspicuous forms of dominance and oppression, but he recognizes that there exists oppression on other grounds such as religious beliefs or political affiliation. Freire's *Pedagogy of the Oppressed* was influenced by a myriad of philosophical currents including phenomenology, existentialism, Christian personalism, and humanist Hegelism. This new philosophical synthesis called for dialogue and ultimately social awareness as a way to overcome domination and oppression among and between human beings.

A key influence in Freire's philosophy is that of G. W. F. Hegel. This chapter will analyze the links between Hegelian thought and the political philosophy of education developed by Freire, especially in his seminal work *Pedagogy of the Oppressed*. It will look at the key themes constituting both Hegel's and Freire's dialectics, such as the relationships between subject and object, the notion of self-consciousness, the relationships between theoretical and practical consciousness, and the link between ego and desire in Hegel, an insight that helped Freire to recognize the struggle of opposed consciousness (Torres, 1976a, 1976b). Other key Hegelian concepts, such as the notion of dominion, fear, and cultural formation, also become incorporated as central elements of Freire's political philosophy of education (Torres, 1998a).

The main thesis advanced in this chapter is that the dialectics of *Pedagogy of the Oppressed* have been deeply influenced by the logical structure of Hegel's dialectics. However, Freire's pedagogical and political utopia has transformed the epistemological principles in Hegel's logical structure, producing Freire's pedagogical *aufhebung* of Hegelian dialectics.[3] The article is divided into three parts. In the first part, I will analyze the premises of Hegel's dialectic of the Master and the Slave. In the second part, I will discuss the premises of Freire's dialectic of the Oppressor and Oppressed. In the third part, I will offer a comparison between Hegelian and Freirean dialectics.

THE DIALECTIC OF THE MASTER AND THE SLAVE

Hegel begins by establishing the situation of a subject with respect to an object. This situation generates two movements: (1) the movement of knowledge (the subject), which he denominates as "concept"; and (2) the movement of the "object," which he denominates as the "object of knowledge." In other words, "concept" is the object *"in itself"* as opposed to the object as it is *"for another."* Thus he establishes two possibilities of consciousness: to be in itself or for another.

Self-Consciousness in Itself

Hegel says, "Self-consciousness is reflection out of the bare being that belongs to the world of sense and perception, and is essentially the return out of otherness" (*PM*, p. 219).[4] Consciousness is of itself an active consciousness. Its activity consists of a certain negativity. Its negative force is expressed in the act of examining things that may appear in front of it (in its conceptual and objectual field of relations), as if the "notion" that it has of these things is not the same as their "truth"; as if what they show (what it negates immediately) will not express what they are (the truth of things which will appear as a negation of the negation in consciousness).

Self-consciousness is no longer a sensible, theoretical consciousness, it is a practical consciousness. Now, what is the motive of its activity? To satisfy a desire. Hegel tells us, "This opposition of its appearance and its truth finds its real essence . . . only in the truth—in the unity of self-consciousness with itself. This must become essential to self-consciousness; in other words, self-consciousness is the state of *Desire* in general" (*PM*, p. 220). Consciousness has become self-consciousness; therefore, it has not only as its aim the contemplation of things (theoretical consciousness) but the apprehension of true essence, which is itself (by which it enters into absolute opposition with the first aim, the contemplation of things).

Life

Hegel tells us that the object of desire and what is perceived in sense-certainty is something "living." Here he again touches on a concept that is central to the understanding of his thought: the concept of "Life," which he elaborated in his early theological writings in Tübinga. Just as the Mind is the Whole, Life is Unity, the unity in the fluent condition of the mobility of the self. In its simplest form, it is presented to us as a factual event, one and undivided, in which self-consciousness lives the experience of need (desire) and of freedom (satisfaction or completion); that is, it became unbalanced psychologically and sought to restore that unbalance. Here Hegel describes a double independence: that of self-consciousness which is "for itself" and which executes negative activity toward objects, and that of those very objects which appear as truly independent of self-consciousness. At this point, Hegel attempts to clarify three fundamental categories in the understanding of the relationship that exists between this self-consciousness (the Ego) and its craving (desire): the *for itself*, which he defines as true independence, the *in itself*, which he defines as simple and universal fluidity (life itself), and finally the *other*, the difference between successive configurations that objects or consciousnesses can take, with respect to the first self-consciousness.

The Ego and Desire

Hegel also discovers that self-consciousness, which knows its own truth unto itself, is surprised upon seeing that it is not the only independence that exists in life, that other independent objects appear, and that it can only arrive at having the true certainty of its truth if, by exercising its negative activity (as indicated above), it seeks to cancel them in such a way that "its truth" is no longer known only by a subjective condition, but can be expressed in objective facts.

Now this satisfaction of self-consciousness goes through the experience of defining the object as the essence of its craving (desire) of self-consciousness, but at the same time recognizing it as independent. But the paradox is that consciousness discovers that upon seeking to negate the object, it understands that it can only obtain satisfaction when the object itself fulfills this negation in it. In the words of Hegel, "Since the object is in its very self negation, and in being so is at the same time independent, it is Consciousness" (*PM*, p. 226). Thus begins the road along which self-consciousness realizes that it will only manage to attain the satisfaction of its desire in another self-consciousness.

The Recognition of Self-Consciousness

Hegel notes that "Self-consciousness exists in itself and for itself, in that, and by the fact that it exists for another self-consciousness; that is to say, it *is* only by being acknowledged or 'recognized'" (*PM*, p. 229). The self-consciousness lives a double effect. On the one hand, it has lost itself, and finds itself with another essence (whence its surprise); on the other hand, it feels it has transcended the other, because it sees itself in the other. Hence at the beginning of this subjective experience, it may seek to be recognized without recognizing. What is curious about this case is that this movement is not exclusive to one self-consciousness but that both self-consciousnesses put it into effect. In this duplicated movement, both seek that one of them behave as subject while the other behave as object of the craving.

In the words of Hegel, the play of forces between self-consciousnesses is expressed as: "The middle term is self-consciousness which breaks itself up into the extremes; and each extreme is this interchange of its own determinateness, and complete transition into the opposite" (PM, pp. 230–231). Hence they oppose one another mutually; while one wants the other to be for it (while it is for itself), the other attempts not to be for the first "other," but to continue to be for itself; thus in this double relationship both try to continue to be in themselves: "They recognize themselves as mutually recognizing one another" (PM, p. 231). In sum, each self-consciousness affirms its Ego in an absolute and exclusive fashion, and tries to attain universal recognition. There is, then, a plurality of desires, but at the same time, the patency that only one of them ought to impose itself; for that reason, a struggle into death ensues.

The Struggle of Opposed Consciousnesses

Hegel says that "The relation of both self-consciousnesses is in this way so constituted that they prove themselves and each other through a life-and-death struggle" (PM, p. 232). Only by risking life to obtain recognition and freedom, according to Hegel, does one manage to become a human being. The individual who is not able to risk death in order to live as a human being will be able to be a person, but will not be recognized as such. The human being risks life to uphold freedom.

Now, each individual must tend toward the death of the others, for the other is not worth to him more than he is worth to himself. Nevertheless, if one of the two contenders were to actually die, although the winning self-consciousness would be sure of itself and of its own truth (expressed in its power over the vanquished self-consciousness):

This trial by death, however, cancels both the truth which was to result from it, and therewith the certainty of self altogether. . . . Through death, doubtless, there has arisen the certainty that both did stake their life, and held it lightly both in their own case and in the case of the other; but that is not for those who underwent this struggle. (PM, p. 233)

If all the selves in the process of constituting themselves into human beings were to proceed in the same fashion—carrying the struggle to the end—there would only be one victor, whose desire at the same time would be frustrated because nobody would remain alive to recognize him. Finally, nobody wants to be recognized only by himself after carrying out a struggle based on pure prestige. Therefore, in order that human reality continues to shape itself, it is necessary that both adversaries remain alive after the struggle; still, this can only be accomplished if both have different behaviors in the struggle. What is the negative act of the self-consciousness ready for battle like? Hegel tells us: "Their act is abstract negation, not the negation characteristic of consciousness, which cancels in such a way that it preserves and maintains what is sublated, and thereby survives its being sublated" (*PM*, p. 234).[5]

From this experience, Hegel draws one sole but very important consequence: life for self-consciousness is as essential as perceiving itself as pure self-consciousness (recognized self-consciousness). In this struggle, then, one self-consciousness will assume the role of subjectivity known by History as the Master, while the other will assume the role of pure thinghood, which Hegel denominates the Servant, Slave, or bondsman. The Master is consciousness that is for itself (to be for itself), the Slave is dependent consciousness (to be for the other).

Dominion

Here Hegel tries to show Servitude from the point of view of the Master. The Master is mediation with himself through another consciousness. There is a biological recognition of the Master on the part of the Servant. Every human being has two basic relationships in his life; in the case of the Master we find ourselves with his relationship with Nature (things) and his relationship with other human beings (servants). Hegel says that "the Master relates himself to the bondsman mediately through independent existence" (*PM*, p. 235). The Slave works for a Master, hence the Master is seen through the eyes of the Slave with respect to his relationship with things (nature): "In the same way the Master relates himself to the thing mediately through the bondsman" (*PM*, p. 235).

The Master has shown himself to be a good warrior; he won in the struggle, fought for his recognition, but consumes without working, like an animal:

> Desire alone did not get the length of this, because of the independence of the thing. The Master, however, who has interposed the bondsman between it and himself, thereby relates himself merely to the dependence of

the thing, and enjoys it without qualification and without reserve. The aspect of its independence he leaves to the bondsman, who labours upon it. (*PM,* pp. 235–236)

On the other hand, the Master has no way out. Hegel says:

He is thus not assured of self-existence as his truth; he finds that his truth is rather the unessential consciousness, and the fortuitous unessential action of that consciousness. The truth of the independent consciousness is accordingly the consciousness of the bondsman. (*PM,* p. 237)

What kind of victory is this? If he who recognizes the Master is a quasi human being (since he is a Slave, not a free human being), what value does his triumph hold for him? Where is the richness of intersubjectivity, of communication, if the essential consciousness considers the other one as unessential, spurns it, relegates it, at the same time that it perceives itself as a human being in the living of its possessions (the possession of the fearful Slave who has given in and the possession of things that the Slave works for him)? The Master is not the true human being; he is merely one phase in the movement toward the real configuration of humanity.

Fear

From the point of view of the Slave, Hegel says that servitude is self-consciousness. Consciousness feels that its essence, as Servitude, is to serve the Master, but, in the same fashion, its truth will be for it this essence (imposed on it by the circumstances of the struggle). Nevertheless, Hegel clarifies that "this truth is not taken yet as inherent in bondage itself" (*PM,* p. 237). It is a Slave because it has been afraid of death. This experience can be commented upon as a certain anxiety before the possible living of an ultimate feeling—ceasing to exist—and this certain anxiety causing the Slave to experience Nothingness. In this experience of nothingness he begins to experience as a human being; since nothing remains fixed upon his consciousness, the only thing left for him is that ultimate experience, through which the Master does not pass because he always perceives himself as victorious, safe, tranquil.

The Slave underwent the experience of the struggle. He was vanquished; still this situation leads him to discover and appreciate new dimensions of his life. After this experience of the struggle comes the experience of work: and by means of work, the Slave overcomes his fear and powerlessness with respect to nature, which was oppressing him. The Slave eliminates, Hegel adds, by means of work, his subordination to natural existence. Now, is work so important? If it is, we would find here the prime difference between the Master and the Slave, since the Master consumes without working. He does not hold the experience of labor since the Slave holds it on his behalf.

Cultural Formation

Hegel explains that "albeit the fear of the lord is the beginning of wisdom, consciousness is not therein aware of being self-existent. Through work and labor, however, this consciousness of the bondsman comes to itself" (*PM*, p. 238). Fear of the Master is the beginning of philosophy (as the wisdom of life and the love of wisdom), but philosophizing in this consciousness which, still not yet fully for itself, completes itself with self-understanding as a generous being; and so, through work, through the formative and educational quality of work, it can satiate its desires qua self-consciousness. Hegel is concrete on this point: "The consciousness that toils and serves accordingly attains this means to the direct apprehension of that independent being as its self" (*PM*, p. 238).

Only the consciousness formed by toil (the Servant) can attain the intuition of generic being and build a true community of equal human beings, where intersubjectivity will not provoke conflict, but where this will come to be true collaboration. But for this, the Slave must experience: *fear* (fear of dying); *service* as a general way of being a universal sentiment, through obedience; and *work* as forming agency, as something educative. By this threefold experience the Servant is liberated from Nature (as opposed to the Master, for whom things continue to be independent of himself) and, when he becomes aware of his own situation, he will free himself from the Master.[6]

To summarize, Hegel distinguishes four situations. In the first of these, the subject (understood as Reason) finds that it affirms itself as the Universal Abstract (the situation of the Mind before it comes out of itself), but since it will only come to full possession of itself through the objective world, it effects a coming out of itself, a flexion toward the object (nature). This flexion or exteriorization causes the mind to deny itself as such, and it loses itself in the world of objects (specific and concrete), which, in turn, cause the first situation to be modified into the second one, by which the denial of the Universal Abstract through the exteriorization of the subject in Nature brings on an estrangement unto itself. Here the moment is generated where the consciousness of the subject, outside of itself, recognizes others who are not itself. The third situation is the existential risk of the subject. Estrangement implies a risk not indispensable in itself: alienation, remaining lost, in the world of objects, having become a thing. This alienation (the German term used by Hegel is *entfremdung*) is the opposite of its appropriation. In the fourth situation, the consciousness makes an effort of re-flexion, of turning toward itself, denying in its turn the situation of exteriority and even of becoming a thing. But now the Subject that returns from the world of things (in principle, the world of concrete particulars) does not revert into the abstraction of its initial affirmation, but as Universal (attribute of the Subject, communicable) though Concrete (the Universal Concrete).

Hence the Hegelian dialectic is the rational construction of reality by which the subject assimilates its vital experience in an ongoing fashion until it finds itself again with itself through the positivity of the determinate negation. Hegel foresaw that the subject would not only appropriate things (basic property) but that it was trying to appropriate subjects as well (the struggle of opposed consciousnesses). When the conflict of two self-consciousnesses is brought to bear (that of each consciousness that has gone out of itself and is for itself), both fighting to appropriate the same good, a road toward a solution is being established. This road is the pact; a pact in which one of the two consciousnesses submits to the other so as not to die. In this way, there comes to light an independent consciousness and a dependent consciousness (dependent on the first one); in classical terms, the Master (Lord) and the Slave (Servant). In this dialectic we see the origins of one of Freire's basic insights about oppression and education.

THE DIALECTIC OF THE PEDAGOGY OF THE OPPRESSED

Every educator, upon pondering human learning, tends to place in the two extremes of the teaching-learning process an object (object of learning, knowledge, habits, abilities) and a cognizant subject. The teaching-learning process, therefore, happens between a subject who relates itself to one or several objects, and vice versa. Freire, upon studying this relationship between subject and object, concludes the following: (1) Knowledge is possible, and is, at the same time, part of the greater process of human liberation. For Freire, it is possible to know the thing in itself, thereby overcoming the simple empiricist and neopositivist conceptions of experience and the relation of Kantian categories. (2) The consciousness (of the cognizant subject) and the world (the cognizable object) mutually constitute themselves; one implies the other, but at the same time they imply difference. There exists a certain distance between the cognizant subject and objective reality. (3) To bridge this distance, an effort toward mutual reconciliation must be made. Such an effort implies an action, a sense, and an outcome. The action is the elaboration of lines of thought based upon certain laws of logic. The sense is not a mere contemplative cognizance but constitutes itself into a contribution to the transformation of that objective reality, a transformation that can only be carried out through its humanization—that is to say, the identity of human beings in the world by means of a compromise, through their praxis with that world, and an outcome, which would be the creation of new knowledge, but at the same time a new social practice.

Freire starts from a dialectical unity in which consciousness and world cannot be dichotomized. Hence there is always a unity between theory and praxis, between content and method, between thought and being, and between objectivity and subjectivity. Freire (1975a) elaborates on this premise of dialectical unity in the following words:

> This question brings us to the very center of a fundamental problem that has always preoccupied modern philosophy. I refer to the relationship between subject and object, consciousness and reality, thought and being, theory and practice. Any attempt to treat the relationship based upon the duality of subject and object, thus negating its dialectical unity will not explain this relationship in a satisfactory manner. Upon destroying the dialectical unity subject-object, the dualist view implies negation, as much of objectivity (submitting it to the power of a capricious consciousness) as of the reality of consciousness, a consciousness thus transformed into a simple copy of objectivity. In this first hypothesis we have the subjectivist error, the expression of an anti-dialectic and pre-Hegelian idealism. In the second one we are dealing with the objectivist mechanicist error, equally anti-dialectic. (pp. 29–30)

This eminently philosophical discussion is not pointless for Freire. There is a basic cognitive stance in the treatment of his better known educational problematics: the educator-educatee relationship; antagonistic cultural actions (domesticating cultural action versus liberating cultural action); and the political perspective proposed by Freire when he discusses the link between the masses and the avant-garde. The congruence of the subject-object, as Freire interprets it, embraces the possible dimensions of human action. Now, how can the subject-object dichotomy be overcome? From a dialectical standpoint, this overcoming occurs within the concept, which is a thought-out concrete thing (that is, if the concept is proper to subjectivity and at the same time includes and supposes objectivity). Yet this concept, by itself, is not merely a mental construction. Freire, remembering the learning experience of his youth, argues that texts, words, and letters were incarnated in the existential context of his homeland of Recife in Northeastern Brazil:

The texts, words, letters of that context were incarnated in the song of the birds—tanager, flycatcher, thrush—in the dance of the boughs blown by the strong winds announcing storms; in the thunder and lightening; in the rainwaters playing with geography, creating lakes, islands, rivers, streams. The texts, words and letters of that context were incarnated as well in the whistle of the wind, the clouds in the sky, the sky's color, its movement, in the color of foliage, the shape of leaves, the fragrance of flowers . . . part of the context of my immediate world was also the language universe of my elders, expressing their beliefs, tastes, fears, and values which linked my world to a wider one whose existence I could not even suspect. (Freire & Macedo, 1987, pp. 30–31)

The process of knowledge responds, therefore, to the movement of practicing on reality, recomposing on the plane of thought, the substantivation of reality by means of the reflexive turn, in order that, once a series of propositions concerning reality are formulated, such reflection will orient the subject in the transformation of that reality through praxis, which is also an instance of knowledge. Therefore, education is the act of knowing, as Freire has repeated over and over again, and thought, in this way, is converted into one step in the process of the structuring of objective reality. With regard to this process of knowing through the dialectics between reflection and praxis, or conscientization, Freire (1975b) indicates the following:

If conscientization cannot be produced without the revelation of objective reality, as an object of knowledge for those subjects involved in the process, then this revelation—even when it might be a clear perception of reality—is not sufficient for an authentic conscientization. In the same way that the epistemological cycle does not end in the stage of acquisition of already existing knowledge, but continues through to the stage of the creation of new knowledge, neither can conscientization be held back at the stage of the revelation of reality. It is authentic when the practice of revealing reality constitutes a dynamic and dialectic unity with the practice of transforming reality. (p. 28)

This awareness process is associated with a process that Freire (2005/1970), in one of his numerous witty phrases, defined as the *archaeology of consciousness*. Concerning this he says:

I think that through the problem of the relationship between men and the world, it is possible for man to again create, to be again part of the natural process through which conscientization appeared in the process of evolution precisely in the moment that Teilhard de Chardin calls "hominization" in the evolution of man. When conscientization appears, there is reflection, there is intentionality directed at the world. Man comes to be different, essentially different from animals. Man not only knows, but knows that he knows. (p. 7)

As has been reaffirmed many times, this situation in which consciousness and world constitute themselves mutually in an ongoing fashion,
in the Freirean vision, explains why consciousness and society are mutually dependent. Freire defines three distinct levels of consciousness:
critical-transitive consciousness, naïve-transitive consciousness, and
semi-intransitive consciousness. Each level of consciousness has its own
peculiarities and risks, and permits the articulating of a different passage
of consciential moments, which are, in turn, intimately linked (dialectical, as Freire would emphasize) with structural modifications through
which societies pass.

A liberating pedagogical theory, from this standpoint, only makes
sense in relation to a transformation of consciousnesses *and* societal
structures. From Freire's perspective, education would not be the only
suitable instrument for this transformation. On the educational front,
one can foresee the existence of a battlefield in relation to an effective
transformation of consciousness and structures. Political struggle, at its
most radical, is fundamental in such a transformation. For this reason,
the Freirean proposal is not restricted to the field of pedagogy, but rather
it is macrosocial, transgressing the limits (often self-imposed) of pedagogical practice. Throughout his lifetime, Freire has attempted a reading
and critique of pedagogy, educational practice, and culture itself on a
global level.

Therefore, to understand the "pedagogy of the question" in Freire as
only a form of critical education or method by which to promote critical
thinking (which seeks the transformation of consciousnesses or logically
articulated discourses) is to reduce the true dimensions of the project (see
Freire & Faúndez, 1989). Conscientization is not an individual, chronological phenomenon of conversion of a consciousness or of many consciousnesses as an unavoidable step in the transformation of structures.
Conscientization, in a genuinely Freirean perspective, enters into the dy-
namism of collective transformation (world consciousness), linking itself
to the collective consciousness of groups and classes. If then one recognizes the subjective factor in every process of social transformation (and,
from there, the efforts brought to reality by Freire in well-circumscribed
educational areas such as the nonformal education of adults), one accepts
that this transforming process can only come about when the subjective
and the objective begin to converge, opposing and uniting with one another, mutually constituting each other, in a single process and project of
societal transformation. This is the philosophical foundation of Freire's
methodology, which is commonly indicated as distinct moments that span
from descriptive investigation to pragmatic thematization and pragmatic
problematization.[7]

HEGEL ON FREIRE: AN INTERDIALECTIC COMPARISON

We can find the key to the relationship between Hegel and Freire in a paragraph of Hegel's *Phenomenology of Mind*:

> [The Master] is thus not assured of self-existence as his truth; he finds that his truth is rather the unessential consciousness, and the fortuitous unessential action of that consciousness. The truth of the independent consciousness is accordingly the consciousness of the bondsman. This doubtless appears in the first instance outside itself, and not as the truth of self-consciousness. But just as lordship showed its essential nature to be the reverse of what it wants to be, so too, bondage will, when completed, pass into the opposite of what it immediately is: being a consciousness repressed within itself, it will enter into itself, and change round into real and true independence. (*PM*, p. 237)

Let us contrast this paragraph with the central definition of "pedagogy of the oppressed": "The pedagogy of the oppressed, animated by authentic, humanist (not humanitarian) generosity, presents itself as a pedagogy of human beings" (Freire, 1975c, p. 53). Why is it that only the pedagogy of the oppressed can attain this objective? Because, as Freire asserts, the humanistic and historical duty of the oppressed consists of the following:

> As the oppressed, fighting to be human, take away the oppressors' power to dominate and suppress, they restore to the oppressors the humanity they had lost in the exercise of oppression. It is only the oppressed who, by freeing themselves, can free their oppressors. The latter, as an oppressive class, can free neither others nor themselves. (Freire, 1975c, p. 53)

For Freire, the historical process confronts human beings with tasks and challenges that, starting first from the proper existential reality of the oppressed, causes them to execute a giant, qualitative leap from a past of oppression to a present of conscientization. Conscientization, being not only intersubjective and causal knowledge or recognition, but also option and commitment, allows the oppressed to launch themselves forward toward a future of human beings seeking to share, unconditionally, the communal truth. Therefore, only one humanizing pedagogy exists: that of the oppressed, which restores at once the humanity of both the oppressed and the oppressor.

For this reason, Brazilian philosopher Ernani Maria Fiori (1975), in his preface to the Spanish edition of *Pedagogy of the Oppressed*, says that "The pedagogy of the oppressed is, then, liberator of both, of the oppressed and of the oppressor. In a Hegelian manner we would say: the truth of the oppressor resides in the consciousness of the oppressed" (p. 11). This double restoration, in the same liberating act, indicates the presence of the Hegelian assumption, by which consciousness in itself needs the consciousness of and for itself, while, in turn, the latter recognizes itself as such only through the former, which, in its relationship with nature, gives the possibility of being the proprietor (of the good that the nonessential consciousness toils over) and owner (of the Slave, in itself) that toils over nature.

Hence, just as Hegel indicated and Freire explicitly assumes, where the center of the Master's power should rightly appear to be (property-possession), one finds his greatest weakness: the immediate need of the Slave (consciousness in itself). Freire (1970a) asserts the following, corroborating this argument:

> In order for the oppressed to be able to wage the struggle for their liberation, they must perceive the reality of oppression not as a closed world from which there is no exit, but as a limiting situation which they can transform. This perception is a necessary but not a sufficient condition for liberation; it must become the motivating force for liberating action. Nor does the discovery by the oppressed that they exist in dialectical relationship to the oppressor, as his antithesis—that without them the oppressor could not exist—in itself constitute liberation. The oppressed can overcome the contradiction in which they are caught only when this perception enlists them in the struggle to free themselves. (p. 34)

Meanwhile, this weakness does not escape the Slave either, since servitude, according to Hegel, is self-consciousness, and that self-consciousness as such can lead to the road of class-consciousness—in Freire's more contemporary terms. The encounter between class-consciousness (and we should add consciousness of gender, race/ethnicity, and sexual preference), as embodied in a critical appraisal of cultural experiences that are never self-contained but crossed by and constituted through relationships of domination and exploitation, and critical consciousness, is the last step in conscientization. What are the moments of the pedagogy of the oppressed? Freire (1975c) writes that

> The pedagogy of the oppressed, as a humanist and libertarian pedagogy, has two distinct stages. In the first, the oppressed unveil the world of oppression and through praxis commit themselves to its transformation. In the second stage, in which the reality of oppression has already been transformed, this pedagogy ceases to belong to the oppressed and becomes a pedagogy of all men in the process of permanent liberation. In both stages, it is always through in-depth action that the culture of domination is culturally confronted. In the first stage this confrontation occurs through the change in the way the oppressed perceive the world of oppression; in the second stage, through the expulsion of the myths created and developed in the old order, which like specters haunt the new structure emerging from the revolutionary transformation. (p. 52)

In this moment, this pedagogy ceases to be the exclusive responsibility, or in a euphemistic way, the "property" of the oppressed, and comes to be the pedagogy of human beings in the process of permanent liberation. Freire characterizes the magical consciousness as a servile consciousness, borrowing the Hegelian expression, and all the dialectical development of conscientization shows us its similarity with the Hegelian view. Freire, in *Sobre la Accion Cultural [On Cultural Action]* (1971), argues that "This culture of silence, characteristic of our colonial past, a culture that remains in conditions favorable to feudal-like land ownership in Latin America, has constituted the peasant consciousness, historically and culturally as the 'servile consciousness' in the expression of Hegel" (p. 82).

For Freire conscientization is a rational outcome, pedagogic and political, of the mutual opposition between antagonistic cultural actions: a cultural action that reflects domination and a cultural action that reflects struggles for liberation. In the context of this struggle, Freire conceives the notion of a cultural revolution as the negation of the negation (cultural revolution as project and, at the same time, new affirmation). The notion of a cultural action for freedom, in Freire, embodies the history of struggles and historical dialectics. From an educational perspective, however, there is a pedagogy and pedagogical action which appears as specific negation, the pedagogy of the oppressed. This is not a generic pedagogy but a pedagogy with a specific political and epistemological characteristic. Yet, this is not the end of the process. Conscientization, incorporating the pedagogical, methodological, epistemological, and political foundations of a pedagogy of the oppressed, does not simply conclude in negative reason or a more complex language of critique. It goes beyond a critique and explanation of the conditions for social transformation, becoming part of the texture and dynamics of social change. That is the reason that in the Freirean vision, the implementation of a pedagogy of the oppressed constitutes a complex synthesis of a process that is in itself political and historical-educational, a complex interaction between structure and agency.

Freire's pedagogical view can be seen as revolutionary, and every revolution considered educational as well as political. In strictly educational terms, a pedagogy of the oppressed can only be implemented as a directive but antiauthoritarian pedagogy for liberation, both in form and content, and in substance and style. The teacher is at the same time a student, the student at the same time a teacher; the nature of their knowledge may differ, but as long as education is the act of knowing and not merely transmitting facts, students and teachers share a similar cognitive condition and are linked together through a pedagogical dialogue characterized by horizontal relationships. The educational agenda will not necessarily be carried out in a classroom but in a "culture circle."

Emphasis is placed on *sharing* and *reflecting critically* upon the learner's experience and knowledge, both as a source of rough material for analyzing the "existential themes" of critical pedagogy, and as an attempt to demystify existing forms of false consciousness. The transmission of ideas, values, and knowledge is secondary to the importance of the sharing of experience, of learning from experience, of making experience in and by itself problematic. This cannot be accomplished by resorting to experience as the only epistemological source of knowledge and praxis. As poet T. S. Eliot (1943/1971) claimed, we have the experience but we miss the meaning, and an approach to the meaning restores the experience.

The notion of experience thus cannot be essentialized. In educational praxis, experience needs to be captured and mediated through rational and emotional discourses. For Freire, a pedagogy of the oppressed should always confront the learnings from experience with broader social, philosophical, and scientific frameworks. Not only individual or group-specific experiences should be made problematic in problem-posing education, but also collective experiences representing historical struggles. These struggles, in turn, are not seen in terms of a pedagogy of heroes, or in terms of a pedagogy of social agencies free of structural constraints. Experience, identities, and struggles are themselves contradictory. Social agencies are seen constrained by structures but there is always a basis for hope: structures are a part of social regulations, routines, and practices that, because they are socially constituted, can be socially transformed. For such a pedagogy, the educational agenda does not necessarily take place in the classroom, but in cultural circles characterized by horizontal relationships, as part of collective and not just individual endeavors and struggles.

As I have shown here, the structure of the dialectic of the pedagogy of the oppressed is very similar to Hegel's. It could be said that Hegel and Freire start by considering the same phenomenon: the situation of Servitude. Nevertheless, there would not be a specific similarity here, unless we included the following: Both start from the phenomenon of the perception that the consciousness has of Servitude both as a social and concrete fact, and as a formation of the generic being.

In Hegel, it was manual servitude that provoked the feeling of the universal (that is, it provoked the recognition of Nature and its domain and, at the same time, the conviction that obedience to the Master was the nexus that united Nature to both Master and Slave). Hegel had shown us that, in synthesis, the cultural formation was given through fear, obedience, and work; that is, with culturally prescribed ends. Hegel laid the foundations of the dialectic of the Master and Slave when he described the confrontation (the intersubjective coming face-to-face) that he qualified as the struggle of opposed consciousnesses. Hegel saw himself compelled to disentangle its intersubjective and cultural genesis. Freire looks upon this struggle as a given in the phenomenon of oppression and, taking up this genetic analysis, tries to show the mechanism of oppression as the mechanism of social alienation, reproductive (for example, in education) through domesticating cultural action.

In Hegel, Freire finds the sources of an analysis of the situation of oppression, and elaborates it in relation to pedagogic practice. Hegel described the originating intersubjective genesis of oppression. Freire describes and analyzes the social development of the mechanisms of oppression as forms of the subordination of consciousnesses, namely, as social servitude or, simply put, as "thingification." The important difference here between Hegel and Freire will be, and rightly so, the overcoming of the positivity of the determinate Hegelian negation in the pedagogy of the oppressed.

Smith explains the notion of determinate negation:

> The logic of "determinate negation" is the principle of development which exhibits the movement from one category or form of consciousness to another. It constitutes a method for moving from one stage to another that is not externally imposed. . . . The logic of determinate negation has both a critical and a constructive aspect. It is critical because it does not merely accept what a body of thought, a philosophical system, or even an entire culture says about itself, but is concerned to confront that thought, system, or culture with its own internal tensions, incoherences, and anomalies. It is constructive because out of this negation or confrontation we are able to arrive at ever more complete, comprehensive, and coherent bodies of propositions and forms of life. (pp. 188–189)

This notion of "determinate negation" became a centerpiece of early critical theory. Certainly, Herbert Marcuse (1964/1991) draws from this notion when he speaks of the power of negative reason, and how that power is being obliterated in the context of authoritarian industrial societies.

Therefore, the rational nucleus of the Hegelian dialectic is the notion of positivity of the determinate negation, so brilliantly criticized by Julio De Zan (1973). For Hegel, self-consciousness tended to negate the actual forms that it would find along its way (as a notion and not the truth of thinghood), in search of the emergence of the immanent unfolding of the Mind (which is its *very* self), present in daily life. This negation is denominated as the positivity of the determinate negation.

History would thus be the road of the Mind, wholly self-conscious, which identifies with the totality of the historical process, whereas this historical process, in its logic, is nothing more than the manifestation—in itself already ahistorical—of immanent life at the historical unfolding of the Mind. The philosophizing consciousness (or the Mind), upon negating in a determinate fashion the objects that confront it, with the aim of clearing a path on the road of rationality, in reality will be constructing an infinite totality, which is nothing more than its own life.

Freire has shown in his work that, although accepting some of the logical premises of Hegel's dialectics, he could not accept the notion that the reconciliation or overcoming of contradictions is a logical process.[8] Nor could Freire accept the Hegelian notion that following a period of estrangement there will come one of reconciliation and synthesis. Conscientization is a contradictory individual and social process, embedded in concrete political and social conditions (tensions, contradictions, uncertainties), of a given society or community. The different forms of consciousness that Freire identifies, particularly in his works in the 1960s and 1970s, are not stages of development of an imaginary Reason searching for its own rationality. Clearly, for Freire, education cannot be reduced to constructing the premises for logical argumentation. If education is the act of knowing, it should go beyond reason and reach practice. It should move beyond the constraints of Enlightenment and idealism, beyond any transcendental *ding-an-sich*, even beyond lived experience, and reach for utopian emancipation and liberation. Yes, education is an act of reason (theoretical and practical), but a *political* act of reason. That is why Freire (1986) argues that

> As an educator I give much more emphasis to the comprehension of a rigorous method of knowing. Still we must ask ourselves, to know in favor of what, and therefore, against what to know; in whose favor to know, and against whom to know. Those questions which we pose to ourselves as educators, brings us to the confirmation of another obviousness which is the political nature of education. (p. 97)

Freire's theory of consciousness is based on a theory of domination. His project is a reconstructive integration of the pedagogy of the oppressed as a pedagogy for decolonization of the lifeworld. At the same time, following the tradition of Karl Mannheim, John Dewey, and Jürgen Habermas, he discusses some of the perils of democracy (for instance massification, the manipulation of the masses) in the context of populist societies. In his later work, the crucial elements of domination by virtue of class or race are complemented with clear antisexist positions, linking class, race, and gender in a complex synthesis. His intellectual roots have explored different directions and seem to be continually evolving. Not by chance, many proponents of theories of agency will find reverberations in Freire of the

works of Max Weber or Karl Mannheim. Similarly, proponents of theories of action will find, at times, some of his analysis and themes closer
to phenomenology or symbolic interactionism. Finally, others will find in
Freire's heuristic framework echoes of the works of Karl Marx and particularly Antonio Gramsci.

Freire has been able to put together a synthetic yet dialectical approach
to structures and social agency in education, and has done so at the level
of metatheory, that is to say, discussing basic ontological commitments
about the nature of social reality, human individuals, history, and society, and how they affect the relationships between knowledge, power, and
education.

If Freire imagined that his dialectic of the *Pedagogy of the Oppressed*
simply needed to negate the forms of consciousness that exist in Latin
America, in a systematic way (a determinate negation) with the conviction that, by virtue of an inescapable historical process, real consciousness
will then appear, hidden between the folds of this historical process, he
would never have assumed the notion of an education that collaborates
with the oppressed in the process of its social organization. Nor would he
ever have postulated a concept of intersubjective liberation, pedagogical
and political, in the context of a project of revolutionary utopia.

NOTES

1. I use the term epistemology for its convenience. Freire's approach, however,
is more a theory of knowledge in general than a theory of scientific knowledge
(thus epistemology) in particular.

2. The positivist or logical-empiricist approach to the human sciences is based
on several premises including the following: (1) theory and science can be defined
in a unitary manner; (2) human sciences are mostly based on a model of natural
science; (3) it is based mostly on experimentation (or quasi experimentation) and
measurement; and (4) it is based on causal explanations, often connected to math-
ematical models or manipulation of statistical analyses.

3. Hegel proposed the notion of *aufhebung*, the centerpiece of Hegelian dialectics. It implies three different moments linked in a complementary way: in the first
place "to suppress" *(wegraumen)*, in the second place "to retain" *(auf bewahren)*, and
in the third place "to sublate" *(hinaufnehmen)*. In other words, *aufhebung* implies a
triple act of negating, preserving, and superseding. See H. Marcuse (1967, 1968,
1970, 1987) and S. B. Smith (1989).

4. Hegel, G. W. F. (1949). *The phenomenology of mind* (2nd ed., rev. and corrected;
J. B. Baillie, Trans.). London: Allen & Unwin. This book will be referred to as *PM*
with page numbers in the text for all subsequent citations.

5. Here obviously Hegel proposes the notion of *aufhebung* which is central to
the notion of dialectics.

6. Here in Hegel we can also see the key idea that influenced Marx's view of the struggle between the working class or proletariat and the bourgeoisie.

7. For a discussion of these methodological questions in Paulo Freire and their association with participative methodologies, that is, methodologies of action research or participatory research, see P. Freire (1992b); M. Gajardo (1982); McLaren & Lankshear (1994); McLaren & Leonard (1992); and C. A. Torres (1992c).

8. Smith's (1989) criticisms of Hegel's logic are quite pertinent here (see pp. 191–192).

CHAPTER 6

From
The Pedagogy of the Oppressed
to *A Luta Continua*

The Political Pedagogy of Paulo Freire

Paulo Freire is perhaps the best-known educationalist of the Third World, whose work has inspired a whole generation of progressive and socialist teachers. His principle of education as cultural action, his method of "conscientization," his techniques for literacy teaching have all been adopted and adapted to fit a thousand projects where the learning situation forms part of a social conflict situation. But what is the political background to Freire's theory and practice? What is the political content of the method? How have Freire's ideas evolved over the last 3 decades? These are the questions this chapter sets out to answer. I trace Freire's development from the beginnings of his work in Brazil and Chile, to his attempts to apply his method in the very different cultural settings of Africa, and then back to the Brazil of the 1980s and early 1990s.

THE LATIN AMERICAN BACKGROUND

Since the publication of *Educacão e Atualidade Brasileira* in Recife, Brazil, in 1959 (afterwards reviewed and published with modifications as *Education as the Practice of Freedom*) the works of Paulo Freire have been influential in pedagogical practice in Latin America as well as in Africa (See bibliographies by Hartung & Ohliger, 1973; Gadotti, Freire, Ciseski, Torres et al., 1996). His main works have been translated into several languages and new generations of educators are looking at Freire as a classic in his field. Notwithstanding this, there has been a theoretical reassessment of Freire's initial works, which emphasizes their connection with the ISEB-developmentalist ideology[1] in Brazil in the early 1960s, and with the sociological theory of Karl Mannheim.[2]

Vanilda Paiva has attempted to show in detail the similarity between Freire's concept of the "critical consciousness process" with the "awareness process" proposed by the Hungarian sociologist. Similarly, Mannheim's major themes, such as the whole discussion about liberty, democratic planning, fundamental democratization of society, and the theory of democratic personality, are crucial issues in Freire's early writings. Paiva's "ex-post" evaluation is risky. It overly emphasizes formal similarities while omitting a substantive analysis of the differences between Mannheim and Freire. It is clear, however, that in his origins the Brazilian educator was ideologically a democratic-liberal thinker strongly influenced by the theory of Christian personalism (i.e., Tristan de Ataide in Brazil or Emmanuel Mounier in France). Over time, however, his thought and writings have evolved to incorporate critical theory, Gramsci's analysis, and concepts from radical Deweyism (Torres, 1980a).

There are several reasons why Freire's work has been so influential. First, Freire's earlier works have philosophical assumptions that reflect an innovative synthesis of most of the main advanced streams of philosophical thought, including existentialism, phenomenology, Hegelian dialectics, and historical materialism. This view of Freire as an innovative but firmly grounded philosophical thinker as well as his exceptional talent as a writer in the Spanish and Portuguese languages have given his early works, *Education, The Practice of Freedom* (1976) and *Pedagogy of the Oppressed* (1970b), a very large audience among educators, social scientists, theologians, and political militants alike.

Undoubtedly, English readers have to struggle with the translation of his work, rendering its understanding more difficult. However, I will contend that the difficulties that some English readers experience with Freire have less to do with the translation of his work—notwithstanding some serious flaws in some translations—than with the nature of Freire's dialectical thinking and strategy of explanation. This difficulty may be compounded because his most recent books have been "talked" or "dialogical" pieces with a distinct oral flavor. Freire's dialectical thinking evolves into a pattern of reasoning and logical analysis different from positivist explanations, thus lying outside mainstream writing in English-speaking countries.

Second, Freire's initial writings appeared during a period of intense political conflict with substantive phases of class struggle in Latin America; thus the "historical moment" is extremely important in understanding Freire's popularity in Latin America. The period extending from the beginning of the 1960s through the early 1970s was marked by several interrelated characteristics: among the most important are the triumph and consolidation of the Cuban Revolution (1959–61) and the installation of the first socialist government in the region (1962); the relative advance and consolidation of the position of popular forces (particularly working-class trade unions and left-wing political parties) under populist regimes;[3] and the project of the Alliance for Progress, designed and supported by the Kennedy administration as the U.S. response to the radical trends emerging from the Cuban Revolution, that brought a sizeable amount of financial support for economic, political, and educational programs in the region. Two aspects of this program of development should be highlighted: first, the support of mild agrarian reforms of bourgeois origin which were attempting to destabilize the power of the traditional agrarian bourgeoisie and to promote agribusiness in the region; and second, the diversification and expansion of the process of industrialization through import substitution during this period of consolidation of the penetration of multinational corporations of U.S. origin in the region. The implications that these trends had in altering the original economic and political structures are many.

This was also a period when the first symptoms of a "crisis of hegemony" among the bourgeoisie became clearly perceptible in some countries of the region. In particular, the Bonapartist (populist) experience (that of Peronismo, Vargismo) appeared only as an interlude between the crisis of the oligarchical state in the 1930s and the attempt to establish a capitalist-industrial bourgeois hegemony in South American societies in the 1960s. The failure of this attempt and the political activation of the masses prompted the bourgeois bloc to appeal for a coup d'état *and* the administrative control of the state by the military, seen as the last chance to restore the bourgeois order.

A major outcome of this process was the rise of the popular-revolutionary movements in Latin America with different expressions and strategies according to each country's historical experience. Therefore, Freire's proposal for education as a practice of freedom—in contrast to the educational positivism and pragmatism then prevailing in educational circles—and his proposal for a "pedagogy of the oppressed" were naturally listened to and tried out by progressive educators in the region.

In this period, given the Latin American societies' political and juridical democratic-bourgeois superstructure, these popular movements were able to organize political mass activities, sometimes confronting the capitalist state. Thus, extensive anticapitalist and anti-imperialist politics were played out in a context where human rights were moderately well respected, in contrast to the experience of the 1970s and early 1980s.[4] In this sense the 1960s represent a period during which a political pedagogy like Freire's could arise in Latin America and have an impact upon progressive educational settings worldwide.

Third, and probably one of the main reasons for Freire's success, was the close relation between Freire's early philosophy of education and Catholic thinking. At this time, after the Second Vatican Council (1965) the Catholic Church (as well as some other Christian churches), underwent a process of ideological transformation and a broadening of their sociocultural policy and strategy toward the civil society.

The most important document to support our contention regarding the ideological-political turnabout in the Catholic Church may be found in the Final Documents of Medellin, produced at the regional assembly of Bishops in Medellin, Colombia, in 1968. The influence of Freire's thought is clearly evidenced in the document on education:

> Without forgetting the existing differences among educational systems in Latin American countries our opinion is that the curriculum, in general, is too abstract and formalistic. The didactic method tries to transmit knowledge rather than, among other values, a critical approach to reality. From a "social" point of view, the educational system tries to support the social and economic structure rather than its change. When Latin Americans try to find their own being under the banner of rich cultural pluralism, they are confronted with a uniform educational system. Educational systems have an economic orientation toward possession of goods, while youth needs to augment his own being by the enjoyment of self-realization in service and love. Our thinking about this panorama seeks to promote one view of education that agrees with an integral development of our Continent. This education is called education for liberation; that is, education which permits the learner to be the subject of his own development. (Il Conferencia General del Episcopado Latinoamericano, 1968, pp. 70–72, my translation)

This language is similar to that of *Education as the Practice of Freedom* which achieved great resonance as a basic text for Christian educators. In the same way, in 1963, Freire's method of literacy was given official approval by the national Bishop's Conference in Brazil and was adopted by the Movimento de Educação de Base (MEB, Movement of Education from the Bases) as its own method of attaining literacy by means of the teleschool—distance education using television and monitors (see De Kadt, 1970; Sanders, 1968; Wanderley, 1984).

In summary, the development of Freire's thought reflects the new intellectual horizon in Latin America. Without unfolding a comprehensive history of ideas in Latin America, it may be said that this intellectual atmosphere has several key features—first of all, the rebirth of Marxist thought after the Stalinist closure. In this sense, the reverberations of the work of Louis Althusser and subsequently Antonio Gramsci in the Latin American scholarly environment, and the emblematic figures of Ernesto "Che" Guevara and Fidel Castro in the practical and political environment, were symptomatic of the new socialist and progressive groups. In addition to that, the revival of guerrilla and armed struggles whose predominant characteristic was the progressive and massive incorporation of petty-bourgeois militants—many of them from Catholic roots—raised new political issues,[5] and brought about a shift in the main front: from the countryside to the urban centers. In certain cases, these guerrilla movements (e.g., Uruguay with the *Frente Amplio* or Argentina with the Montoneros-Peronist experience) were strongly linked with political activation of the masses.

In this connection, the progressive incorporation of Catholic militants was highly significant, especially the symbolic importance of the priest Camilo Torres who died fighting alongside the Colombian guerrillas in the late 1960s. Other indicators of a new era for Catholic and Protestant churches in the region included the new theology and philosophy of liberation, the Christian for Socialism Movement, and the widespread new ecumenism supported by the World Council of Churches (see Torres, 1992a).

Meanwhile, in the philosophical scholarly environment, there was a renewed interest for national and indigenous issues, as well as a revaluation of the popular content of the national culture, in opposition to past and present emulation of European or North American lifestyles. Finally, in the social sciences, new approaches to the study of the development process such as the so-called Theory of Dependence acquired great relevance, transcending Latin American scholarship and being projected to the United States, the former Soviet Union, and even Africa through the writings of Fernando H. Cardoso and Enzo Faletto (1979), Andre Gunder-Frank (1969), Osvaldo Sunkel and Pedro Paz (1979), Theotonio dos Santos (1970), and others (see also Chilcote, 1974; Vogeler & de Souza, 1980). To this extent, Freire represents and reflects in his writings devoted to pedagogy a particular ideological momentum in Latin American societies.

After the Brazilian coup d'état of 1964, Freire left the country and lived and worked in Chile at the Institute for Training in Agrarian Reform (ICIRA), an organ of the Christian Democratic government with responsibility for educational extension within the agrarian reform (De Witt, 1971). There Freire had the opportunity of experiencing his methodology in a new intellectual, political, ideological, and sociological environment; working with the most progressive sectors of the Christian Democratic Party Youth (some of them afterwards incorporated into new parties inside the Unidad Popular coalition) and finding himself in contact with highly stimulating Marxist thought and powerful working-class organizations. This was at the dawn of triumph of the Unidad Popular in Chile which was the first successful electoral experience of transition to socialism in the region, which started in 1970 and ended in 1973 with the coup d'état that brought Pinochet to power.

In 1970 Freire left the region after accepting an invitation from the World Council of Churches in Geneva to work as principal consultant for its Department of Education. Meanwhile, the popularity of Freire's method and his problem-posing philosophy of education grew and embraced progressive educators in Latin America, being experienced almost everywhere, on a small scale or incorporated into national experiences of adult education, such as in Uruguay, Argentina, Mexico, Chile, Peru, and Ecuador (Torres, 1981).

Up to this point, almost without exception each progressive experience in pedagogy advocates to some extent the main Freirean themes and assumptions, and the word *concientizacao* ("conscientization" or "critical consciousness") acquires the strength of a political-cultural program for the socialist groups. Its popularity as a new educational perspective grew everywhere. Indeed, Freire had to explicitly warn against the fetishist use of this emblematic word (Freire, 1990; Kennedy et al., 1975) as a front for conservative programs whose educational principles were closer to "banking education" than to "problem-posing education" or "cultural action for freedom."[6]

Freire's thought can now be clearly perceived as an expression of socialist pedagogy, and the Freirean analysis has been, over time, worked into the historical-materialist framework, redefining to some extent its old existentialist-phenomenological themes without, however, ever adopting an orthodox stance.

This brief introduction leads me in the next section to point out the characterization of the process of education, cultural action, and critical consciousness in Freire's work and consider its contribution to radical social change.

PAULO FREIRE'S POLITICAL PHILOSOPHY

My perspective is dialectical and phenomenological. I believe that from here we have to look to overcome this opposed relationship between theory and praxis: surmounting that should not be done at an idealistic level. From a scientific diagnosis of this phenomenon, we can state the requirement for education as a cultural action. Cultural action for liberation is a process through which the oppressor consciousness "living" in the oppressed consciousness can be extracted. (Freire, 1980a, p. 85)

Thus, from Freire's perspective, education as a cultural action is related to the process of critical consciousness, and, as problem-posing education, aims to be an instrument of political organization of the oppressed:

The first level of apprehension of reality is the *prise de conscience*. This awareness exists because as human beings are "placed" and "dated," as Gabriel
Marcel used to say, men are *with* and *in* the world, looking on. This *prise de
conscience*, however, is not yet critical consciousness. There is the deepening of the *prise de conscience*. This is the critical development of the *prise de
conscience*. For this reason, critical consciousness implies the surpassing of
the spontaneous sphere of apprehension of reality by a criticist position.
Through this criticism, reality appears to be a cognoscible objectum within
which man assumes an epistemological position: man looking for knowing. Thus critical consciousness is a test of environment, a test of reality.
Inasmuch as we are conscientizing, so much are we unveiling reality, so
much are we penetrating the phenomenological essence of the object that
we are trying to analyze.

Critical consciousness does not mean to be confronting reality by assuming a falsely intellectual position, that is "intellectualist." Critical consciousness cannot exist outside the praxis, that is, outside the action-reflection
process. There is no critical consciousness without historical commitment.
Thus critical consciousness means historical consciousness.

In the last analysis, class consciousness is not psychological consciousness. Second, class consciousness does not mean class sensitiveness. Class
consciousness does not imply class practice and class knowledge. For this
reason the revolution is also an act of knowledge. It is for no other reason
that Lenin has emphasized the importance of revolutionary theory without
which—he asserted—there would not be a revolution.

Finally, class consciousness has a strong identity with class knowledge.
But as it happens, knowledge does not naturally exist as such. If we defined knowledge as a concluded fact in itself, we are losing the dialectical
vision that can explain the possibility of knowledge. Knowledge is a process resulting from the permanent praxis of human beings over reality. Indeed, individual existence, even though it will present singular features, is
a social existence. (Freire, 1980c, pp. 73–74, my translation; see also Freire,
1980d, pp. 158–159)

Thus education implies the act of knowing between knowledgeable
subjects, and conscientization is at the same time a logical possibility and
a historical process linking theory with praxis in an indissoluble unity.
At this point, it is important to summarize some of the major features of
Freire's analysis:

1. Freire's global purpose transcends a criticism of the current
    educative forms, and goes on to virtually become a criticism of
    culture and the construction of knowledge. In short, the basic
    assumptions of Freire's works lie in a dialectical epistemology
    for interpreting the development of human consciousness in its
    relationships with reality.

2. Nevertheless, for Freire the principal issues and problems of education are not pedagogical issues. Instead, they are political issues. In the last instance, the schooling system does not change society; instead, society can change the schooling system (Freire & Faúndez, 1985a, pp. 139–140). However, the educational system may play a crucial role in a cultural revolution. For Freire, revolution implies the conscious participation of the masses. Critical pedagogy, as a cultural praxis, contributes to lifting the ideological veil in people's consciousness. Moreover, revolution itself is a meaningful pedagogy for the masses—Freire has spoken of revolutions as a continuing political workshop.

3. But, what can be done before the revolution takes place? Freire's pedagogy of the oppressed is designed as an instrument of pedagogical and political collaboration in the organization of the subordinate social classes. In this sense, it is worthwhile to emphasize the distinction proposed by Freire (1970a) between "cultural action" and "cultural revolution":

> Cultural action is developed in opposition to the elite that con- trols the power; in contrast, the cultural revolution occurs in complete harmony with the revolutionary regime in spite of the fact that the cultural revolution should not be subordinate to the revolutionary power. The limits of cultural action are determined by the oppressed reality and by the "silence" imposed by the elite in power. The nature of the oppressed consequently determines the different tactics, necessarily different from the tactics used in the cultural revolution. While cultural action for liberation con- fronts the "silence" as an exterior fact and, at the same time, as an internal reality, the cultural revolution confronts the "silence" only as an internal reality (p. 51).

4. The specificity of Freire's proposal is the notion of critical consciousness as class knowledge and class praxis. Following Brazilian philosopher Alvaro Viera Pinto, Freire (1980b) considers the "heuristic activity of consciousness as the highest possible contribution of the process of thought" (p. 143). In this sense, he sees his contribution to the process of humanization of social beings as a constant reassessment of the "subjective" conditions for the revolutionary praxis.

5. It is a pedagogy of consciousness. Thus it emphasizes a fundamental aspect in the process of political organization of the subordinate social classes: the links between revolutionary

leadership and mass practices (particularly in *Pedagogy of the Oppressed*). These are mainly expressed in a generic plane, close to a political ethic, without discussing in detail the problems and characteristics of the state and the political revolutionary party—particularly in the early writings before the African experience.

6. Finally, in educational terms, its proposal is an antiauthoritarian though directivist pedagogy, where "teachers" and "students" are teaching and learning together. Since education is the act of knowing, "teacher-student" and "student-teacher" should engage in a permanent dialogue characterized by its "horizontal relationship," which, of course, does not preclude power imbalances or different everyday living experiences and knowledge. This is a process taking place not in a classroom, but in a cultural circle. There is not a "discursive" knowledge but a knowledge starring from the living everyday and contradictory experience of teachers-students/students-teachers. Certainly this set of notions dismantles the most important framework of authoritarian pedagogy and, to this extent, appears as a "counterhegemony" practice and ideology within teacher training institutions.

To this extent, the Freirean proposal in the 1960s does not deal with the formal schooling system before the revolution. On the contrary, from its inception this proposal avoided suggesting change within formal schooling which represents a concentration of bureaucratic machinery. Instead, it shifts the concern to the nonformal, less structured system. Another important characteristic of this strategy is that with few exceptions, its representatives have avoided working out this pedagogy within capitalist state institutions and are accustomed to working professionally in universities or private institutions, often closely connected with churches.[7]

There are some complementary arguments for this strategy:

1. Freire and liberation educators had originally developed their approach in this field in Brazil (1960–64), in Chile (1965–70), and in Africa.

2. The political implications of adult education vastly exceed those of formal schooling (e.g., using community needs for designing vocabulary for literacy programs).

3. Adult education programs from the point of view of this educational philosophy are better linked to community needs and more responsive to community pressures than the formal

schooling system. Thus this "popular education" should be understood more as a form of education developed *by* the oppressed than *for* the oppressed (Freire, Oliveira, Oliveira, & Ceccon, 1980; Torres, 1990b).

4. This education has the curricular and organizational flexibility that formal schooling lacks.
5. The results of adult education are more immediate than those of formal schooling. It is not necessary to wait 10–15 years, as in formal training of children, for the incorporation of the "graduate" into the labor market or into political activities.
6. The potential demanders of adult education in peripheral capitalist social formations are always the dispossessed. This testifies to their lack of power and, furthermore, shows that illiteracy, far from being a "social illness," is an outcome of a hierarchical class structure or violent historical processes such as colonization.
7. Finally, adult education has shown great importance as an instrument for political mobilization and critical consciousness in some processes of transition to socialism, such as in Cuba and Nicaragua.

It is worth adding that, as the Latin American experience shows, this pedagogical approach needs to be used at least in a liberal-democratic institutional and political context. Obviously, this restricts its applicability to some Third World countries under despotic-bourgeois regimes. Similarly, in its full expression, this pedagogy may be carried on by a revolutionary party as part of its educational strategy in a process of social transition, or could be supported by social movements based on nongovernment organizations.[8]

THE AFRICAN BACKGROUND

Paulo Freire's first contact with Africa came about through his peripheral involvement with the Tanzanian literacy campaign after 1970. He was invited to present his method of literacy teaching at the Institute of Adult Education of the University of Dar es Salaam, and to help in organizing new experimental projects as well as the curriculum in the Adult Education Diploma Course. Unfortunately, there are only scattered references in Freire's work on Tanzania, and there is little documentation on experiments with Freire's literacy method, which could help in evaluating his Tanzanian experience.

Nevertheless, Freire's introduction to African reality through the Tanzanian experience was an important step toward his more significant participation in Guinea-Bissau, Cape Verde, and São Tomé e Principe. Moreover, Freire has often expressed his concern with the experiences of Angola and Mozambique in adult education.

At this point, we can roughly summarize some of the more significant contrasts and similarities with the Latin American experience. In Africa educational development has been strongly influenced by the process of decolonization, particularly because the structure of colonial education was distinct from noncolonial education (Altbach & Kelly, 1978, pp. 1–53). It was an elitist form of education: for instance, between 1961 and 1965 enrollment in primary education in Guinea-Bissau included only 16.4% of the total population in the appropriate age cohort (Rudebeck, 1974, pp. 27–40). According to Erick Pessiot, enrollment at school for the year 1974, when the PAIGC came into power in Guinea-Bissau, was as shown in Table 6.1 (cited in Oliveira & Oliveira, 1976, p. 53).

For the people involved, colonial education was basically a means of cultural "de-Africanization," particularly in the more violent colonizing mode (such as the Portuguese style); a means of creating a selected corps of civil servants that usually, after graduating, became government employees in middle positions within the bureaucracy, under the leadership of colonial officials; a means of creating a selected group of

TABLE 6.1. School Enrollment in Guinea-Bissau, 1974

Level	Number of students
Preschool	28,500
Primary Level	
1st grade	23,500
2nd grade	10,500
3rd grade	6,500
4th grade	3,700
Secondary Level	
1st year	3,000
2nd year	2,000
3rd year	2,000
4th year	600
5th year	300
6th year	350
7th year	80

the urban elite who would support the colonizers' project: "a black-skin, white-mask petty bourgeoisie," in Frantz Fanon's words (1967). To this extent, Freire (1977) has perceived in the Guinea-Bissau case, following Amilcar Cabral's approach, that the petty-bourgeois intellectuals only have this alternative: "to betray the revolution or to commit class suicide constitutes the real option of the middle class in the general picture of the struggle for national liberation" (p. 16).

However, Freire argues that the new educational system not only has to help this class suicide of the intellectuals, but also must impede its evolution into an elite in the new society. Thus, to this extent, Freire in the Guinea-Bissau case argues that an important measure should be to link education with productive work, avoiding full-time students and combining study time with working hours in intimate relationship with peasants.

A second important difference is the level of development of the productive forces and social relations of production that has determined the class structure and dynamics of society. The African societies differ from the Latin American in a number of ways. For instance, there is no extensive agrarian bourgeoisie in the rural areas with "oligarchical" origins—conserving the ownership of the means of production—comparable to the *coronelismo* in the Brazilian case with its "patrimonialist" foundations and clientelist practices that have historically affected the configuration of the Brazilian bureaucratic state (see Rodrigues, 1982; Roniger, 1990; Uricoechea, 1980).

Similarly, there is no extensive industrialization process which to a certain extent can bring about a sort of national-indigenous industrial bourgeoisie with some objective (although secondary) differences in its economic and political interest from those of the agrarian bourgeoisie, multinational corporations, or the state bureaucracy—as might be, for instance, the case of Argentina, Brazil, or Mexico. These differences, expressed in the political struggle, would bring about broadly different political strategies as well as different levels of relative autonomy of the state in Latin America. Likewise, the petty bourgeoisie in African societies, although strongly linked to the postcolonial state, has not developed an extensive educational network as in the post-populist experiments in Latin America (Torres, 1990b, pp. 33–45). In other words, extended middle classes pushing for an expansion of secondary and higher education institutions are not present. This is compatible with Amilcar Cabral's (1969) views that "in colonial conditions it is the petty bourgeoisie which is the interior of state power" (p. 69). The military, although having a growing interventionist role in African societies, does not have the same historical importance in the constitution of the nation state as it has had, for instance, in Latin America. Neither has the Catholic Church—another major player in Latin American politics—secured the virtual religious monopoly and cultural influence that it has in Ibero- and Lusoamerica.

These differences notwithstanding, the capitalist social formations in Africa and Latin America share a number of similar characteristics, including the illiteracy of the peasantry. But the African postcolonial governments have already concentrated their educational efforts in the rural areas (e.g., see Carnoy & Samoff, 1990). In Latin America, by contrast, due to the process of accelerated urbanization, growing internal migrations, and agribusiness penetration—in short, the combined effects of uneven capitalist development—a progressive imbalance exists between the rural and the urban areas. The illiterates are concentrated, in equal measure, within the rural areas and within the periphery of metropolitan or major cities. Thus in Freire's Latin American experience, in addition to the peasantry, there has been an extensive urban marginality (with a recent peasant past, of course) that has represented a central constituency for his problem-posing education. Freire (1977) has emphasized the contrast between his Brazilian and Chilean experience and his experience in Guinea-Bissau (pp. 132–136).

Notwithstanding this, Freire (1980e) has claimed that adult literacy programs, understood as a political act and as an act of knowledge within the process of national reconstruction, will be successful only under conditions of radical and progressive alteration of the social relations of production in society. Freire (1986) argues:

> As an educator I give much more emphasis to the comprehension of a rigorous method of knowing. . . . My great preoccupation is method as a means to knowledge. Still we must ask ourselves, to know in favor of what and, therefore, against what to know; in whose favor to know? (p. 97, my translation)

Freire will argue that the successful conclusion of a literacy campaign and follow-up process (postliteracy) is strongly linked with the progressive attainment of the social transition to socialism in Guinea-Bissau.

To this extent, one of Freire's richest methodological suggestions in Guinea-Bissau and in São Tomé e Principe is to begin adult education programs in those areas in the process of transformation or having experienced key conflict (say, during the war of liberation, or through class tensions and conflicts). Freire would argue that adult education programs would help strengthen the revolutionary consciousness of the people who have been participating in the liberation struggle or are currently committed to the process of transition to socialism and to radical change in the social relations of production. However, there is a claim for linking, in a more coherent and systematic fashion, the process of literacy with the process of production and productive work (this was one of the more recognized theoretical weaknesses in Freire's early writings). This crucial methodological issue was pointed out by Rosiska and Miguel Darcy de Oliveira (1996) in an early evaluation of Freire's (and the IDAC team's) experience in Guinea-Bissau:

> It seems to us that priority areas in the countryside must be chosen in the light of political and technical considerations. Any given population will be more motivated for the literacy program if it has enthusiastically participated in the liberation struggle and accumulated the rich cultural and political experience which the program would hope to bring up to date and develop. However, the criterion of political receptivity growing out of the richness of a group's past experience is not sufficient. If the literacy campaign is to go beyond a celebration of the past and provide an opening towards the future, as mentioned above, the chosen region must be in the process of experiencing a socio-economic transformation. This point seems extremely important to us, for it is questionable whether learning to read and write corresponds to a real need for the peasant in a rural area who continues living and producing in traditional ways. On the other hand, literacy can take on much more meaning if it is related to new production techniques being introduced in a particular area or the creation of new production units, such as, for example, agricultural cooperatives. In other words, within the context of a transformation process, literacy could facilitate the peasant's acquisition of new technical understanding which is necessary to the project being carried out and could also contribute to the political mobilization of the community, enabling the peasant to take charge of the process of change rather than being simply passive "beneficiaries" of a plan worked out and applied from the outside. (Oliveira & Oliveira, 1976, p. 49)

In addition to this "economic determination," a third important difference from the Latin American background resides in specific political variables. First, the Tanzanian experience offered Freire the opportunity of working within a socialist experiment, with centralized planning, a revolutionary socialist party, and a substantive concern with adult education as a real methodological alternative to the formal schooling system. Adult education in Tanzania is far from being irrelevant: in a population of 17 million people, the rate of literacy in 1966–67 (when the functional literacy programs started) was 25–30%; when these programs were evaluated in 1975–76, the government claimed that the rate of literacy had grown to 75–80%, although other sources have declared that it was 55–60% (Torres et al., n.d.).

These issues were enriched with the PAIGC experience of revolutionary struggle in Guinea-Bissau when the literacy campaign appeared to be
an essential step forward in the process of national reconstruction after the
war of liberation, an experience comparable to that of Nicaragua during
its own literacy campaign (Arnove, 1986; Carnoy & Torres, 1990). Adult
education was clearly political education that, as Denis Goulet (1978)
has pointed out, embraced several politicized themes such as the political unity between Guinea-Bissau and Cape Verde, the proposal of linking
manual and intellectual work, the responsibility of all citizens to help the
PAIGC build a just society, and so forth.

In this respect, Freire has stressed the contrasting results of the first attempts in Guinea-Bissau: for while the literacy campaign was completely
successful among the militants of the Revolutionary Army in the urban
areas of Guinea-Bissau, adult basic education directed toward society in
general failed in its primary objectives (Freire et al., 1980).

Second, another feature of this African period is Freire's enthusiastic
appraisal of the significant role of charismatic leadership or revolutionary
political leaders in the process of social transition to socialism, particularly
in the effects of their writings, speeches, and practice on political mass-
consciousness and political culture (e.g., Amilcar Cabral in Guinea-Bissau,
President Julius Nyerere in Tanzania, or President Pinto de Acosta in São
Tomé e Principe). It is particularly true in the constant references given by
Freire to the writings of Amilcar Cabral as a Marxist revolutionary theore-
tician (see Cabral, 1975).

Third, Freire has raised the dilemma of choosing a language of
teaching for literacy programs, that is, should it be in the indigenous
language(s) or should it be done in Portuguese. This issue, even though
briefly analyzed, remains quite relevant—in Freire's approach—to the
process of national identity, particularly when "although precise figures
are unavailable, approximately 80% of the Guinea-Bissau total population does not speak Portuguese. The lingua franca of the country's varied ethnic groups is Creole, a hybrid of Portuguese and African dialects"
(Goulet, 1978, p. 31; see also Freire & Macedo, 1987, pp. 105–119). Furthermore, Creole is spoken by about 45% of the population and is not a
written language.

At a personal level, it is very understandable that Freire, a sensitive intellectual, demonstrates interest in the issues revolving around language,
having reencountered his own mother language in Guinea-Bissau, not too
far from Brazil, 10 years after his exile.

Lastly, and a very different feature in the Freirean African experience,
is the strong emphasis placed on the postliteracy process as indissolubly
linked with the literacy phase. In a letter to coordinators of cultural circles

in São Tomé e Principe, Freire (1980e) has emphasized the following goals for this postliteracy process:

1. To consolidate the knowledge acquired in the previous phase in the field of reading, writing, and mathematics.
2. To deepen this knowledge through a systematic introduction of basic rudiments of grammatic categories and arithmetic (fundamental operations).
3. To continue, in a more profound manner, "reading" reality through reading texts with more varied and rich themes.
4. To develop a capability for critical analysis of reality and oral expression of this reality.
5. To prepare the learners for a following stage, in which due to the needs imposed by the national reconstruction process, courses to technical training (never technicist training) have to be created in different sectors. That is to say, these human resource training courses will be developed specifically with a critical view and, through this, with a global view of their own activity, as opposed to a narrow and alienated view. (p. 188, my translation)

The work of Paulo Freire in Africa has been the focus of criticism and controversy. What follows is a brief presentation and analysis of literacy training in Guinea-Bissau.

The planning stage of the mass literacy campaign began in 1975, and the first literacy campaign was launched in 1976 with over 200 literacy animators organizing cultural circles in the villages. Literacy training inspired by Freire's method was held in the rural areas and in the capital city of Bissau. Linda Harasim claims that, by 1980, reports from Guinea-Bissau began to acknowledge that the goals of literacy for national reconstruction had failed to materialize: of the 26,000 students involved in literacy training practically none became functionally literate (Harasim, 1983, p. 6).

In her study, Harasim claims that the causes for this failure of literacy training are threefold:

1. The underdeveloped material conditions of Guinea-Bissau
2. The contradictory political conditions of the process of national reconstruction
3. Some unexamined assumptions of Freire's theory and method, particularly his ideological populism and idealism which seem to have been shared by the ruling revolutionary party (PAIGC) in Guinea-Bissau

On the one hand, there seems to be an endless list of material conditions undermining any effort of economic or educational development in one of the poorest 25 countries in the world. These include a low level of productivity, scattered and isolated self-subsisting villages—Harasim estimates that 88% of the total population in Guinea-Bissau is engaged in subsistence farming—cultural, linguistic, tribal, ethnic, and economic differences, and lack of political unity (Harasim, 1983, pp. 139, 107).

On the other hand, exacerbated by the low level of development of productive forces, the effort at national reconstruction in Guinea-Bissau confronted some of the proverbial problems of any transition to socialism in the Third World. Harasim notes as among the key problems of national reconstruction the following: an increasingly bureaucratized, centralized, and inefficient state apparatus; lack of trained cadres, and the need to rely on the colonial bureaucracy who have not supported the struggle of the PAIGC; the centralizing action in the capital city of Bissau, where 83% of all the civil servants work, and where 55% of total investment was channeled, thus deepening the urban-rural contradiction; the failure of a strategy of development based on establishing state farms and cooperatives; and the need to rely on external financing for literacy training (Harasim, 1983, pp. 148–152).

Finally, in addition to these contradictions resulting from the poor material conditions and problems of national reconstruction, Freire's theory and practice failed to offer an efficient approach to literacy. Freire is accused of imposing a Westernized worldview in the very different setting of Guinea-Bissau. Harasim claims that this may have led Freire to thinking idealistically that his method has universal validity and appropriateness in any Third World society—a problem that became compounded by his romantic perception of the level of political literacy of the Guinea-Bissau rural population. Due to these misleading assumptions, the planning and organization of the campaign, and the method implemented, did not take into account the lack of well-trained Guinea-Bissau militants capable of understanding and implementing the literacy strategy and method (Harasim, 1983, pp. 197–199).

According to Harasim, this political criterion was taken at face value: "The fundamental contradiction lay in the fact that Freire's concept of 'the political' was rooted in moral and philosophical notions and contained no implicit practical plan of action" (Harasim, 1983, p. 345).

In Harasim's evaluation, by assuming a utopian view of social reality and an idealist stance in education, Freire overestimated the ability of literacy animators to implement the process of literacy training, and the need to produce educational material in the appropriate amount, quality, and timing to be effective.

The introduction of the Freire method into the conditions of the Guinean reality led to mechanical, rote learning, based on memorization—exactly, in fact, what Freire professed to abhor. Students for the most part were unable to progress beyond the first five or six words in the manual; those who did were unable to "create" new words. Even where there was a high level of participation by the peasants, it was found that after six months the students were able to read and write, but when questioned about what they were reading and writing, the comprehension was found to be nil: they could understand nothing. (Harasim, 1983, pp. 377–379)

Freire has addressed the criticisms of his work in Guinea-Bissau in a number of places, including his conversations with Antonio Faúndez (Freire & Faúndez, 1985a) and Donaldo Macedo (Freire & Macedo, 1987). Freire does not address the issue of the political economy of Guinea-Bissau, but disputes the charge of ideological populism (see Freire & Macedo, 1987, pp. 100–102; Oliveira & Dominice, 1981, pp. 134–138), emphasizing also the constraints or political conditions imposed upon his practice in a society in social transformation, and how that has affected his work. He makes references to the communalities between his work in Africa and his previous experiences in Chile and Brazil, but the central question that he attributed to the failure of his work in Guinea-Bissau is the selection of language for literacy training.

Revisiting literacy in Guinea-Bissau, Freire argues that, as a militant intellectual, he is not a typical researcher working under the protection of an umbrella of "academic autonomy" or "scientific objectivity." As a militant intellectual, what he could not do in Guinea-Bissau was "overstep the political limitations of the moment. As a foreigner, I could not impose my proposals on the reality of Guinea-Bissau and on the needs as perceived by political leaders" (Freire & Macedo, 1987, p. 103).

Freire concludes that he wanted the PAIGC leadership to change their initial decision to conduct the literacy campaign in Portuguese, the language of the colonizers (Freire & Faúndez, 1985b, p. 124). But, as Freire soon discovered, his suggestion was out of the political boundaries imposed on his work, and he had to accept Portuguese as the language of instruction, even if his own method was not originally designed for second-language acquisition. He defends his experience in literacy training stating:

With or without Paulo Freire it was impossible in Guinea-Bissau to conduct a literacy campaign in a language that was not part of the social practice of the people. My method did not fail, as has been claimed. . . . The issue should be analyzed in terms of whether it is linguistically viable to conduct literacy campaigns in Portuguese[9] in any of these countries. My method is secondary to this analysis. If it is not viable to do so, my method or any other method will certainly fail. (Freire & Macedo, 1987, pp. 112–113)

THE LAST FREIRE: BRAZIL, 1980–91

After living in exile for 16 years, Freire returned to his country in 1980, Freire attempted to "relearn Brazil" (Freire, 1982), traveling incessantly throughout the country, lecturing, engaging in dialogues with students and teachers, and publishing.

This relearning Brazil was succinctly summarized by Freire himself when he told me in a torrid Californian summer in July 1983 at Stanford University that he believes in "reading Gramsci, but also listening to the *popular Gramsci* in the *favelas* [Brazilian shantytowns]. That is the reason why I spend at least two afternoons a week with people in the *favelas*."

Since 1980 Freire worked as professor in the Faculty of Education of the Catholic University of São Paulo, and as professor in the Faculty of Education in the University of Campinas—a research university sponsored by the state of São Paulo, located about 100 kilometers from the city of São Paulo.

In addition to his involvement in higher education, he created the Educational Center, "Vereda," that agglutinates many people who worked in the original projects of popular education in the 1960s. Politically, Freire collaborates with the Commission of Education of the Partido Trabalhista Party or Workers' Party (a socialist democratic party that he joined from Geneva when it was being formed in 1979), and accepted the honorary position of president of the Workers' University of São Paulo, an institution sponsored by the Workers' Party and mostly concerned with trade union and political education.

Perhaps what has most deeply marked Freire's everyday life experience in the last years has been the loss of his wife, Elza, who died of cardiac failure in October 1986. With Elza's heartbreaking death, Freire not only lost his lifelong companion, friend, and lover, but also his vital optimism and desire. Freire married again in 1988, to a longtime friend of the family and a former student, Ana Maria Araujo.

Most recently, with his appointment in January 1989 as Secretary of Education of the city of São Paulo, Freire took charge of 662 schools with 720,000 students from K–8, in addition to heading adult education and literacy training in the city of São Paulo, which, with 11.4 million people, is one of the largest cities in Latin America.

In his capacity as Secretary of Education, Freire found a unique opportunity to implement his educational philosophy in his own country, this time not as an academic adviser but as a policy maker in a municipality controlled by a socialist party. The socialist goals of the Workers' Party, however, should be considered in the framework of the new democracy and constitutional reform in Brazil. Freire formally resigned on May 22, 1991, as Secretary of Education, but one of his close collaborators has been appointed to replace him. Freire has agreed to remain as a kind of "honorary ambassador" of the Municipal Administration (Torres, 1991a).

Since returning to Brazil in 1980, Freire has produced a number of "talking" books and articles, which by and large have not been translated into English, including his dialogues with Sérgio Guimarães (Freire & Guimarães, 1982), Moacir Gadotti and Guimarães (Gadotti, Freire, & Guimarães, 1986), Frei Betto (Freire & Betto, 1985), and Adriano Nogueira and Debora Mazza (Freire, Nogueira, & Mazza, 1986), among others. However, his book with Faúndez (Freire & Faúndez, 1989) has been translated into English.

Paulo Freire's perspective on literacy work becomes relevant for industrial societies. In his book with Donaldo Macedo, Freire calls for a view of literacy as cultural politics. That is, literacy training should not only provide reading, writing, and numeracy but also be considered as

a set of practices that functions to either empower or disempower people. In the larger sense, literacy is analyzed according to whether it serves to reproduce existing social formations or serves as a set of cultural practices that promotes democratic and emancipatory change. (Freire & Macedo, 1987, p. viii)

Literacy as cultural politics is also related in Freire's work to emancipatory theory and critical theory of society. Hence, emancipatory literacy is

grounded in a critical reflection on the cultural capital of the oppressed. It becomes a vehicle by which the oppressed are equipped with the necessary tools to reappropriate their history, culture, and language practices. (Freire & Macedo, 1987, p. 157)

The reverberation of Freire's work in current pedagogical scholarship is impressive and cannot be restricted to literacy training. The Freirean approach has been implemented not only in social studies and curriculum studies in adult education, secondary education, and higher education, but also in such diverse subjects as the teaching of mathematics and physics, educational planning, feminist studies, romance languages, educational psychology, critical reading and writing, and so forth (e.g., see McLaren, 1986; Shor, 1987b). Freire's dialogues with Ira Shore (Shor & Freire, 1987) attempt to formulate a pedagogy of the oppressed, taking into account the *problematique* of social reproduction in the context of industrialized societies.

It can be argued that Freire's work has been simultaneously reinterpreted or "reinvented," as Freire would like to term it in industrially advanced societies by those who attempt to construct a new theoretical synthesis by bringing together Freire, Dewey, and Haberman. A noted representative of this agenda is Henry Giroux and his theory of resistance in pedagogy and curriculum (Giroux, 1983, 1984).

In addition, Freire's political philosophy has fared well with socialist democratic perspectives of schooling in the United States. In this respect, the work of Ira Shor is exemplary in trying to understand the reproductive power of schooling in spite of the "Culture Wars" that prevail in the U.S. mosaic, and the possibilities of linking North American struggles with pedagogy for liberation (Shor, 1986; Shor & Freire, 1987). Hence, the apparent paradox is that literacy political activism in industrialized societies is nurtured by notions of education and social change developed in the Third World (Wagner, 1989).

ARE THERE ANY DARK CLOUDS IN THE SKY? FINAL REMARKS

The Latin American and African background in Freire's pedagogy has shown a surprising unity of topics, themes, assumptions, and methodological requirements. This is possibly due to Freire's tendency to discuss his practical experience theoretically. That is, Freire's approach is a systematization of the political-pedagogical practice: "Without exception, every book that I have written has been a report of some phase of the political-pedagogical activity in which I have been engaged ever since my youth" (Freire, 1977, p. 176).

Nevertheless, a pedagogy as controversial as Freire's raises several issues regarding political-pedagogical praxis in peripheral capitalist social formations. In these final remarks, I would like to address myself to only two of the substantive questions: (1) Is it a pre- or postrevolutionary pedagogy? (2) In Gramscian terms, can the process opened up by critical consciousness be thought of as the process of counterhegemony in the historical bloc? There are, certainly, many other extremely relevant points that should be treated in a very extensive and theoretical discussion. Nonetheless, I shall confine myself, in this discussion, to offering only some insights in terms of the questioning of, rather than the answering of, both topics.

To begin with, what are the political factors that can give shape to an education for freedom? What are the minimum conditions for starting an education for freedom? Under what functional conditions can we foresee methodological, didactic, curricular, and even organizational or administrative changes that can help in developing this alternative educational proposal?

Moreover, given the strength of the educational bureaucracy—located particularly in the schooling system—and the state ownership of the principal means of production of knowledge, should this political-pedagogical space be abandoned within the schooling system and the concern shifted to the nonformal system? Or, given the priority of political struggle, is pedagogical practice meaningless?

Thus, assuming as Freire does that we cannot change society by changing the school (a liberal utopia), is it necessary also to abandon altogether educational reforms? In other words, if the schooling system is an arena of struggle in capitalist social formations, which are the real spaces of this struggle? That is, do spaces which will contribute to the process of political organization of the oppressed exist? Or, paradoxically, will they contribute to the process of political legitimation of the capitalist state, through an indulgent state policy sustaining an acceptable and necessary opposition within the schooling system, but systematically obstructing its organic links with the working class and social movements?

By the same token, even assuming the potential utility of this pedagogy in a process of social transition, is it possible to sustain this directivist, nonauthoritarian pedagogy in the long haul? Or, instead, is Freire's pedagogy some sort of "Jacobinism" that should be cleared up after the institutionalization of revolution?

Similarly, considering the strong emphasis placed by this pedagogy on the process of critical consciousness, how can we reconcile the process of political deliberation opened up by this pedagogy with the process of ideological consolidation of a triumphant revolutionary movement?

In the same line of reasoning, emphasizing the importance of critical consciousness, is it possible to underline and in the same way to support "spontaneist" practices in politics, to the detriment of the process of political organization, coordinated struggle, and centralized political leadership needed for a successful revolution?

The second question is of similar importance. Generally speaking, the majority of Marxist authors have been addressing the analysis of education, hierarchical class structure, and ideological domination; that is, focusing on education from the perspective of the hegemonic classes. Freire's works, instead, have shown another perspective: the need to redefine education from the perspective of the subordinate classes. To this extent, there is a very wide coincidence with the Gramscian formula of education contributing to the development of a new culture and new *Weltanschau-ung* (view of the world) of the subaltern classes.

This new culture—weltanschauung—has to be developed by the op-pressed class and, through its organic intellectuals, from the bosom of the capitalist society. In this sense Freire's premises are equally important:

1. It is crucial to study educational process from a dual perspective: using the lens of the hegemonic classes—reproduction of social relations of production—and using the lens of the subordinate classes—education as a means of constructing a new hegemony.
2. Education is important for reconstituting the culture of the oppressed, particularly through the notion of systematic elaboration of popular knowledge: knowledge understood as an instrument of counterhegemonic struggle.
3. Designing autonomous educational practices within urban and rural poor communities can help in enlarging the organization and power of the oppressed.
4. Finally, Freire's notion of a dialectical relationship between the revolutionary leadership and the masses has in educational practices a rich terrain, indeed—in Gramscian terms—a rich terrain for developing youth workers' leadership. To this extent, the relevance given by Freire to the epistemological and political "self-vigilance" of the militants' praxis in Guinea-Bissau raises a new important issue for political practice: How should this vigilance be achieved within a revolutionary process?

Nevertheless, some costly experiences of several experiments in popular education in Latin America (e.g., dismantled after a military *coup* d'état and the assassination of certain militants due to their "public exposure") have led some people to ask themselves, is this pedagogi-cal program a feasible project that can help in the process of building a counter-hegemony or, instead, might it be viewed only as a sympathetic but impossible dream? Or, indeed, should the aforementioned educa-tional process be evaluated in order to discover the political and peda-gogical variables that have to be controlled for a better performance of such educational programs? This may include linking educational prac-tices with a revolutionary party, or redefining the importance, scope, and means of the political struggle within the schooling system and within the capitalist state bureaucracy.

To respond to all these questions will demand a comprehensive study well beyond the limits and possibilities of this chapter. However, it is possible to conclude that there are good reasons why, in pedagogy today, we can stay with Freire or against Freire, but not without Freire.

NOTES

This is a revised and expanded version of an article originally published in *Education with Production Review*, 2 (Spring), pp. 76–97, Gaborone, Botswana. I want to thank Davis Elias, Joel Samoff, Maria Pilar O'Cadiz, and Peter McLaren for their advice in writing this article. A National Academy of Education Spencer Fellowship, as well as the Graduate School of Education and the Latin American Center at the University of California at Los Angeles provided the support for my current research on policy-making in São Paulo, Brazil. I am solely responsible, however, for what is being said.

1. The Higher Institute of Brazilian Studies (ISEB) was the most important experience in Brazil before the coup d'état of 1964 for developing a nationalist ideology that should contribute to the process of social modernization supported by the government of Joao Goulard. Paulo Freire as well as other intellectuals—Helio Jaguaribe, Roland Corbisier, Alvaro Vieira Pinto, Vicente Ferreira da Silva, Guerreiro Ramos, Durmeval Trigueiro Méndez—were participants in the intellectual atmosphere produced within the workshops of ISEB. Among the more influential authors for the ISEB theoreticians was Karl Mannheim, but also influential was the German anthropology of the 1930s—J. Spengler, Alfred Weber, and Max Scheller—the philosophy of existence—M. Ortega y Gasset, J. P. Sartre, M. Heidegger, and K. Jaspers—and historical-sociological sources—Max Weber, Alfredo Pareto, and Arnold Toynbee. For an analysis of ISEB, see C. N. de Toledo (1977); for an analysis of the intellectual traditions underpinning Freire's work, see the polemic work of Vanilda Pereira Paiva.

2. V. P. Paiva (1980) provides a documented essay on this subject arguing that Freire's perspective was eminently populist, and related to the developmentalist nationalism prevailing in Joao Goulart's administration. This argument, which has been considered the first academic criticism of Freire's work in Brazil, overlooked my own more sympathetic criticisms of Freire's work published earlier in Spanish and Portuguese. Paiva's analysis relies heavily on a limited understanding from a fairly orthodox Marxist perspective of the notion of Russian populism, and is coupled with a dissatisfaction with Freire's Christian philosophical and anthropological roots. As an alternative, see C. A. Torres (1979, 1981) and the later work of M. Gadotti (1989).

3. There is an extensive literature on the characterization of the populist or Bonapartist regimes in Latin America. Among the most compelling work is O. Ianni (1975). Nevertheless, as a very general and descriptive overview, I shall underline the following features of a populist regime:

   a. It claims to be a state above the class conflict not representing a
      particular class, neither the bourgeoisie nor the subordinate classes.
   b. As principal electorate it is supported by the popular sectors and the
      working class, as well as by broad sectors of the petty bourgeoisie.
   c. Generally it is associated with the figure of a charismatic leader
      who tries to appear as a "neutral" referee among the tensions of the
      multiclass coalition, and claims to rule independently of the internal
      scheme of forces (e.g. Perón in Argentina, Vargas in Brazil, Ibañez in
      Chile, Cárdenas in Mexico).
   d. It tends to develop an extensive state bureaucracy.
   e. Generally it stimulates the creation of a "national political
      movement" instead of a "classical" liberal-fashioned political party.
   f. Often the proclaimed ideology is nationalist, anti-imperialist, and
      linked with Western Christianity.

   4. For instance, the military dictatorship that ruled Argentina during 1976–83
annihilated the political opposition by kidnapping, torturing, killing, and disappearing thousands of Argentine citizens. See the evidence reported in CONADEP
(1984).
   5. Certainly, there is considerable experience of armed struggle in the region
during this century such as the Mexican Revolution (1910–17), Sandino's movement in Nicaragua during the 1930s, and the Nicaraguan Revolution in the 1970s
leading to the successful overthrow of the Somoza dictatorship in 1979, the popular insurrection in El Salvador (1932), the Bolivian Revolution (1952), the armed
struggle in Cuba (1957–59), and the multiple guerrilla experiences in Colombia or
Venezuela between 1940 and 1970, to cite only the most relevant cases. But one of
the distinct features of the new guerrilla experience of the 1960s was the adherence
of middle-class members instead of the traditional campesinos brigades.
   6. Freire (1970b) has defined *pedagogy* as a cultural action, distinguishing two
main cultural actions: "banking education" and "problem-posing education": "The
former attempts to maintain the submersion of consciousness; the latter strives for
the emergence of consciousness and critical intervention in reality" (Ch. 2).
   7. It is not surprising that, since Freire returned to Brazil in June 1980, he has
worked for the Catholic University of São Paulo (PUC) and the public universities
of UNICAMP and the University of São Paulo; while Rosiska and Miguel Darcy de
Oliveira—who were members of the Institute for Cultural Action (IDAC), founded
in Geneva by Freire, and principal collaborators of Freire in Guinea-Bissau—also
worked upon their return to Brazil in São Paulo in a project of popular education supported by the Archdiocese of São Paulo (see *Jornal da Educação*, Campinas,
April 1980, pp. 3–5, 8–9).
   8. The experience of the Workers' Party-controlled municipal administration in
São Paulo and the role of Paulo Freire as Secretary of Education of the City of São
Paulo, with its new initiatives of a democratic curricular reform, the School Coun-
cils, and the Movement of Literacy Training (MOVA–São Paulo), show the limits
and possibilities of a partnership between progressive state and social movements
in public policy.

9. It is well known that Amilcar Cabral dismissed as cultural opportunism any criticisms of his strong suggestion of adopting Portuguese as the official language. For Cabral, Portuguese was the only truly universal gift that the colonizers gave to Guinea-Bissau (see Cabral, 1979, pp. 102–105). Freire disagrees (Freire & Faúndez, 1985b, p. 126).

Afterword

Pedro Demo

Having completed 25 years as a university professor, Carlos Alberto Torres, an Argentinian sociologist now teaching at the University of California, Los Angeles (UCLA), presents us with a collection of his recent
work in commemoration of this singular event. First, the fact that a Latin
American has reached the highest peak of North American university
careers in one of the most prestigious universities should be duly celebrated. With notable determination and skill, this professor realized the
goal of receiving his doctorate in the United States and becoming part
of the academy in this challenging country. Second, it is said that he
achieved this objective in a brilliant and convincing manner, allying his
"latinity" to North American academic expectations. He never ceased
to be the "Latino" professor, having the most vibrant and engaged vision of the problems confronting his area of study, capable of radiant
and involving rhetoric, obviously passionate about what he does and
greatly cherished by undergraduate and graduate students alike. At the
same time, he has never failed to meet the expectations of the North
American academic community, in terms of his rate of production and
theoretical and methodological skill. Third, he won his own place in the
world of education, above all in educational sociology, drawing his pro-
file in its most critical and open tradition, sustaining an immense span
of work. Taking into account that he is in his early 50s, the scale and
creativity of his work is notable, especially in the frenetically productive atmosphere of the United States. Certainly, this pressure is in great
part market-created, as it must be in the land of what Aronowitz (2000)
calls "the knowledge factory," but Carlos Alberto Torres has never been
distracted by the mutability of a market on which he has always drawn
critical bead. Fourth, this professor consolidated the flattering image
of open critical capacity, knowing how to be a personally independent
Marxist, a nonbombastic critic of neoliberalism, an unaffiliated figure in
the landscape of current critical theory, a questioner of modernism and

postmodernism, politically engaged and methodologically astute. Fifth, he is probably one of the greatest living specialists in Paulo Freire, which is of particular interest to the Brazilian public. The political background of the work of Carlos Alberto Torres emanates from this link.

In this brief afterword, I intend only to highlight some achievements of this noteworthy professor, particularly his critical vision, his liberating aim, and his multicultural expectations.

CRITICAL VISION

Always current with the most up-to-date critical theory, Carlos Alberto Torres is renowned for his persistent and penetrating critique of neoliberalism. Living in the United States, principal homeland of neoliberalism, his stance is notable for two fundamentally interconnected facets: On one hand, he faces an in-house struggle; on the other, he runs the risk of criticizing his means of livelihood. Keeping in mind that the United States, among central nations, is the one least affected by the current economic crisis—there is talk of a decline in wages, but not so much of a loss of jobs, as Castells (1996, 1997, 1998) amply demonstrates—such criticism is generally taken as clamor in the wilderness. But there are many reasons for the insistence of his criticism, starting with this professor's Latin American origin. Argentina has felt the effects of a horse-sized dose of neoliberalism, as has Brazil. Both countries are in the same boat, each with the distinctive ballast of its own history. The ambiguous value of education is one of Carlos Alberto Torres's favorite themes. Neoliberalism attributes consummate importance to education, motivated by competitiveness, based, these days, largely on the profit motive. The better prepared a populace in terms of basic skills, or in knowing how to think, the better its production, since the comparative advantages among peoples are, in practice, reduced to only one: the ability to manage innovative knowledge and to continually learn. Moreover, this linkage tends to be restricted to market dictates, excluding the properly critical content of educational systems. In other words, while the worker's formal quality is sought, his political quality is avoided. Add to this the theme of privatization, powerfully impelled by the system's forward line, the "development banks." In truth, the public system fell on the seamy side of the web of social politics, stricken as well by mass market offerings: poor stuff for poor people. On this one-way street, poor products for the poor are often more costly than private offerings, due to the numerous facets of corporate character now evinced by the state. Because of this, the state is being stigmatized as a place of managerial ineptitude, while the private sector—sometimes also called "the third sector"—is seen as the redeemer of quality of whatever kind, for instance so-called total quality.

Privatization would bring order to the house, would diminish costs, and would have a qualified educational system as a result. It is with considerable irony that Carlos Alberto Torres points to the flagrant and odious contradictions in this position, particularly in light of the neo-liberal critique implicit in the debate about the free public universities, whose "indiscriminate charity" has the visible effect of concentrating wealth. Ironically, Left and Right discover they are partners in the same dance, defending indiscriminate charity. This is because, principally in capitalism, all public policies of good quality tend to be appropriated by the elite, while those of poor quality are reserved for the poor. To sanitize this perverse effect, however, the neoliberal remedy is to bury the patient alive while trying to avoid losses, make fiscal adjustments and diminish the concentrated wealth. The poor are left out in the cold since the relation to the market becomes the focal point. We give a half-hearted imitation of the welfare state in our countries: in the "glorious thirty," with more homogeneous populations and seemingly residual poverty, indiscriminate charity reaches the poor in a minimally adequate way, whereas in Latin America, where the majority are poor, indiscriminate charity discriminates against the poor and saves the rich. In its abusive ideological commitment, neoliberalism neglects poor people's need for free schools, ignoring that the concentration of wealth is less the effect of the market than of the political poverty of the populace, incapable of effective democratic control. The history of capitalism demonstrates, with crude severity, that the decentralization of wealth is not obtained by the "rules of the market," but through citizenship, as indicated by the "welfare state," at least initially. Privatization can avoid the loss of public resources, now and then, but it restores the perspective of a class society in exacerbated fashion. From the viewpoint of opportunities for those excluded, the free public school continues to be one of the bulwarks of their possible and always problematic emancipation. This vision has made Carlos Alberto Torres a fundamental name in the battle for universal public school.

Within this same approach, the critique of globalization is also part of his agenda, particularly its substantial incongruity: It is mainly the discriminatory effects that are "globalized" rather than the opportunities which should be ever more interconnected and available. Certainly the world is more interconnected, but any notion of solidarity lags far behind. Under the sign of capitalist competition, the abstract logic of commodities is restored with renewed cruelty, aligning countries in the process of the "dollarization" of almost everything. Not only are nations having increasing difficulty exercising their sovereignty, they are being forced to align themselves with prevailing powers. The homogenizing effect of a unique market whose "rules" stopped being common and began to suffer ostensive manipulations is obvious in giant mergers of businesses. As De Landa (1997) notes, following Braudel, such "takeovers," rather than speaking the language of the market, manipulate it and determine its outcomes without any external control. He uses the expression "antimarket," meaning they are beyond market dictates and can do whatever they want. For example, only small and medium-sized firms follow the market and are able to benefit the consumer through open competition and by creating jobs. The perspective of the lack of alternatives imposed by such a process of globalization is dramatic indeed, as if there were no salvation beyond capitalism. It is ironic that globalization, rather than instituting a more consensual and unanimous solidarity, reproduces much more rigid and discriminatory lines because its dynamic is not one of opening but of avaricious alignment.

The critical vision of Carlos Alberto Torres, however, is not nourished merely by public political engagement, but in equal part by his academic creativity, which has always been fed by critical theory. Akin to the Frankfurt School, he cultivates an epistemological posture based on critical argumentation because he understands that to think is to question. That is why his critical vision does not owe fealty to any author, because he understands that autonomy is both the product and the central process of the ability to be critical. It is interesting that, in a land as pragmatic as the United States and as tied to positivist tendencies, this professor won a place for himself, without owing anything to anyone—not even to critical theory, because he practices it at the proper pitch, that is, critically. Nor is he indebted to the American academy. He knows how to be methodologically correct. He does not confuse political involvement with activism, flaccid theory, or dilettante arguments. On the contrary, he makes science of the best quality so his criticism deserves to be heard and respected.

LIBERATING VISION

Carlos Alberto Torres is, possibly, the leading expert on Paulo Freire. Radically tied to the Freirean oeuvre and a founding member of the Paulo Freire Institute of São Paulo, he has been a central figure in the international movement of liberationist pedagogy. It should be observed from the start that his tie to Paulo Freire never translated into intellectual alignment, especially since, according to the master, it is better to be a master than a disciple. The idea of being a "disciple" of Paulo Freire's makes no sense, not just because it would contradict Freirean perspective but, above all, because it does not jibe with the liberationist point of view. Even a minimally coherent liberating vision rejects any kind of servitude. Thus, in practice, Carlos Alberto Torres engages in a constant and creative reconstruction of Paulo Freire's work.

The concept that interests him most is that of "politicity," teasing out the intrinsic political structure of education. This politicity, far from refuting education's formal quality, assumes and vivifies it because it is a kind of citizenship that knows how to handle innovative knowledge. The "pedagogy of the oppressed" does not refer merely to the political movement of liberation, but also to the need to apprehend reality in a critical way so as to be able to transform it. To handle knowledge critically and creatively is an essential part of this. The determinants of this position are, first, that politicity is something intrinsic to education as a phenomenon or to its profoundest quality, and, second, that such politicity is not restricted to political quality, but impinges on formal quality as well. In this sense, the epistemological link essential to the concept lends it consistent substance: Knowing and learning are not merely logical and technical phenomena, but they are based on human character which is always political because it creates "subjects" able to forge their own history. "Colonizing knowledge" is, certainly, a one-way street in the opposite direction, an extremely competent tactic in the "imbecilization" of the oppressed but, like all two-faced coins and dialectical contradictions, one that also includes the possibility of liberation. The link with power that knowledge always reveals in its "archeology" does not occur from the outside as if it were something invented and imposed, but lives within, maybe even more than the link with truth.

Seeing things in this manner, Carlos Alberto Torres adapts with rare felicity one of Paulo Freire's most creative and remarkable intuitions: the dramatic dialectic between liberation and imbecilization, proposing more realistic alternatives for the emancipation of the oppressed. Fundamentally, Freire understood that the oppressed are "politically" impoverished not just by material privation but, above all, by being kept an ignorant and maneuverable mass, unable to autonomously construct their path to freedom. Obviously, liberation cannot come from outside, nor can it be imposed or donated. But how can we break the cycle of ignorance if the ignorant are trapped inside it? Gramsci (1971) forged the concepts of "organic intellectual" and "counterideology" as perspectives in the construction of alternatives, running the natural risk of the averse. An internal risk marks this contradictory dynamic: The same knowing-how-to-think that underlies the possibility of rupturing ignorance also manufactures it. The oppressed need outside "help" but must also know how to dispense with it. As a rule, no one self-emancipates. But it is necessary to learn to walk on one's own. It all depends on the external agents and the extent to which they can be understood as supporters, motivators, and compass points rather than conductors of the process. For the oppressed to achieve their liberation, they need to be in command of this process because, in the final analysis, they also have to liberate themselves from their liberators. Paulo Freire was an edifying example: He did a lot for the oppressed, but never announced himself as their "general." Educational theories, however critical and involving, do not "liberate" the oppressed, although they can be a salutary instrument for the construction of theoretical and practical alternatives.

Today we can better understand this dialectic if we look at modern and postmodern learning theories, particularly those with a biological slant. The evolutionary process, aside from replication as in the classic orthodox vision, can also be seen as the saga of the emancipation of matter and of life by means of emerging processes capable of producing entities very different from their origin. Thus from matter came life—something the matter did not seem to hold. Possibly we are still using a limited and prejudicial concept of matter, as if life were not part of it. In the living world, complex and creative entities arise, like human beings with their inventive brains. It is always a risk to see in this something similar to politicity since it quickly provokes the modernists who continue to see the dialectic as restricted to social-historical phenomena. Nevertheless, it is evident that the evolutionary trajectory is replete with showy leaps whose dialectic we have yet to truly understand. In the scheme of human life, politicity is less questioned because history, with its innovative and deconstructive knowledge, can now be guided by human beings. Against this backdrop, many see learning as a politically reconstructive phenomenon, indicating, first, that we are dealing with something not merely reproductive and, second, with something capable of forging personal histories.

MULTICULTURAL VISION

The idea of multiculturalism is, in one way, a response to globalization: To counteract its excessive homogeneity we attempt to value diversity and local identities. Without going into greater detail about this conceptual polemic, it is fitting to emphasize that Carlos Alberto Torres has become a fundamental reference in multiculturalism as well. Among so many gradations of this notion, I would like to stress the pertinent idea of conceiving these identities as, at the same time, turned in upon themselves and needing permanent opening in order to learn. Certainly, cultural identities are reflexive, provoking closure to the extent that they protect themselves from external interference or reject attempts to make their respective historical patrimony seem commonplace. Without being self-defensive, it is natural to do this—to counteract the homogenizing propensities that, often in the guise of egalitarian language, preach colonizing processes. This is the crucial problem for ethnic minorities: They need to live together in different surroundings and adapt to them, but they do not want to lose their historical or cultural identity. In the United States the Latino minority grows nonstop and will soon become the most numerous minority in the nation, surpassing African Americans. This is particularly evident in Los Angeles, where the Mexican presence is massive. Carlos Alberto Torres can witness firsthand the drama of an identity being gradually diluted since he is also a participant. Latinos in the United States have an identity condemned to adaptation: first, because they are a minority; second, because their presence is usually the result of a painful immigration; third, because the shock between the dream of living in the world's richest country and having impoverished origins is inevitable.

The problem of cultural identities is their fundamentalist tendency, capable of generating drastic separatism and environments of irreconcilable misunderstanding. However, it is also necessary to understand that globalization reflects its European colonial roots which proclaims cultural homogeneity, generally through alignment with the market. The very idea of "university" cultivates this perspective when it indicates that knowledge does not have a homeland and its scientific methodology is strictly universal. Many critiques have been elaborated, generally under the sign of postmodernism, to show that the "universals" of science also possess their cultural reference, but the dominant perspective of cultural alignment persists: Outside "Europe" there is no salvation, intelligence, wealth, or development. Studies with an evolutionary biological basis show that the process of conquest was principally one of "infection." Europeans devastated other peoples by transmitting diseases as well as compulsory cultural patronage. Thus the notion of multiculturalism imposes itself as a counterpoint to the devastation of the dominant culture of the capitalist center, which leaves nothing standing which is not of interest to the market. Peoples' cultural patrimonies have been totally dilapidated by the "commodification" of life. In this sense, multiculturalism broadcasts a clear message of defense for local minority cultures at risk.

However, putting aside postmodernist excesses that bet on fragmentation and relativism, cultural identities need to be seen as dialectic or, rather, dynamic phenomena capable of producing and incorporating change. That which is "identical" cannot be reduced to a mere historic replica, but naturally reflects the nonlinear historic process as well. Summing up this more dynamic vision, we can say that cultural identities need to know how to learn. That is, they need to know how to join the natural desire for patrimonial survival in supervening, and sometimes more powerful, surroundings. To purely and simply shut down does not guarantee preservation; rather it risks inevitable decadence since we start to spend all our energy on self-defense. To preserve local culture is above all to know how to transform it in such a way that its identity is permanent however much it changes. Change may be reflected in a loss of character, but the identity that does not permit any kind of change is even more characterless because it is already petrified and condemned to stasis. The most coherent image in this complex process is human learning: Through it, we change utterly and that is the way we identify ourselves. Human beings do not have a static identity, evolutionarily impossible to forge, but one which is mobile, dynamic, partly contradictory, partly logical. To preserve it, we have to change. Cultural identity is metamorphosis, not mummification.

This manner of seeing posits great challenges because it attempts to combine two sometimes violent powers: on the one hand, the always necessary defense of cultural identities and, on the other, the need to change so as to remain the same. The consolation, as current linguistic studies show, is that no two peoples are able to have the same culture because we are all interpretive beings, "hermeneutically" cultivated. Even when a strange culture is imposed, it is acculturated naturally. Although syntactical elements may be commonly shared between languages, the semantics necessarily vary in accordance with the historical context of each people. We are, in this sense, naturally creative. Identity, for creative beings, is less a matter of fixing stereotypes than the constant reconstruction of our historical projects.

TO CONCLUDE

Carlos Alberto Torres is the image of cultural identity success in the United States, because he always knows the methodologically appropriate stance to succeed in the local academy. He is so far above the median in terms of scientific production that his mobility and initiative are often greeted with surprise. What is more, he has made himself an authentic "manager of

knowledge" because he knows, as well as or better than his American colleagues, how to successfully negotiate academic initiatives, manage funds
of various origins, organize seminars and meetings, cultivate convergen-
ces between various connected areas, and dynamically move his activities
at UCLA beyond local frontiers. It is worthy of note that his impressive
success in the American academy, far from turning him into just another
cog in the wheel, makes him a paragon of theoretical and practical freedom, sometimes bitterly critical but always surrounded by Latin charm.
The recognition of his intelligence and capacity for scientific production
seems to me fundamentally a question of merit.

English translation by Peter Lownds

References

Adorno, T. W., & Horkheimer, M. (1972). *Dialectic of enlightenment* (J. Cumming, Trans.). New York: Herder & Herder.

Aguilar, M. (Ed.). (1990). *Critica del sujeto.* Mexico City: Universidad Nacional Autónoma de México (UNAM), Facultad de Filosofia y Letras.

Altbach, P. G., & Kelly, G. P. (1978). *Education and colonialism.* New York: Longman.

Althusser, L. (1971). *Lenin and philosophy and other essays* (B. Brewster, Trans.). New York: Monthly Review Press.

Anzaldúa, G. (1987). *Borderlands/La frontera: The new Mestiza.* San Francisco: Spinsters/Aunt Lute.

Apple, M. W. (1982). *Education and power.* Boston: Routledge & Kegan Paul.

Apple, M. W. (1993). *Official knowledge: Democratic education in a conservative age.* New York: Routledge.

Apple, M. W. (1995). *Education and power* (2nd ed.). New York: Routledge.

Apple, M. W. (1996). *Cultural politics and education.* New York: Teachers College Press.

Apple, M. W. (1997). *Teoria critica y Educación.* Buenos Aires, Argentina: Miño y Davila Editores.

Apple, M. W. (1999). *Power, meaning, and identity.* New York: Peter Lang.

Apple, M. W. (Ed.). (2003). *The state and the politics of knowledge.* New York: Routledge Falmer.

Apple, M. W. (2004). *Ideology and curriculum* (3rd ed.). New York: Routledge.

Apple, M. W. (2006a). *Educating the "right" way: Markets, standards, God, and inequality* (2nd ed.). New York: Routledge.

Apple, M. W. (2006b). Rhetoric and reality in critical educational studies in the United States. *British Journal of Sociology of Education, 27,* 679–687.

Apple, M. W., & Beane, J. A. (Eds.). (2007). *Democratic schools: Lessons in powerful education.* Portsmouth, NH: Heinemann.

Apple, M. W., & Buras, K. L. (Eds.). (2006). *The subaltern speak: Curriculum, power, and educational struggles.* New York: Routledge.

Apple, M. W., & Weis, L. (Eds.). (1983). *Ideology and practice in schooling.* Philadelphia: Temple University Press.

Arnove, R. (1986). *Education and revolution in Nicaragua.* New York: Praeger.

Arnove, R. (1994). *Education as contested terrain: Nicaragua 1979–1992.* Boulder, CO: Westview.

Arnove, R., & Torres, C. A. (1996). Adult education and state policy in Latin America: The contrasting cases of Mexico and Nicaragua. *Comparative Education, 31*(3), 311–325.

Arnove, R., Torres, C. A., Franz, S., & Morse, K. (1996). A political sociology of education and development in Latin America: The conditioned state, neoliberalism, and educational policy. *International Journal of Sociology of Education, 36*(1/2), 140–158.

Aronowitz, S. (2000). *The knowledge factory: Dismantling the corporate university and creating true higher learning.* Boston: Beacon.

Aspen Institute. (1992). *Convergence and community: The Americas in 1993.* Washington, DC: Inter-American Dialogue of the Aspen Institute.

Au, W., & Apple, M. W. (2007). Freire, critical education, and the environmental crisis. *Educational Policy, 21*(3), 457–470.

Avalos, B. (1986). Moving where? Educational issues in Latin American contexts. *International Journal of Educational Development, 7*(3), 151–172.

Bakhtin, M. M. (1968). *Rabelais and his world* (H. Iswolsky, Trans.). Cambridge, MA: MIT Press.

Barnet, R., & Cavanagh, J. (1996a). Electronic money and the casino economy. In J. Mander & E. Goldsmith (Eds.), *The case against the global economy and for a turn toward the local* (pp. 360–371). San Francisco: Sierra Club Books.

Barnet, R., & Cavanagh, J. (1996b). Homogenization of global culture. In J. Mander & E. Goldsmith (Eds.), *The case against the global economy and for a turn toward the local* (pp. 71–77). San Francisco: Sierra Club Books.

Bell, D. (1995). Racial realism—after we're gone: Prudent speculations on America in a post-racial epoch. In R. Delgado (Ed.), *Critical race theory: The cutting edge* (pp. 2–8). Philadelphia: Temple University Press.

Bernetti, J. L., & Puiggrós, A. (1993). *Peronismo, cultura política y educación.* Buenos Aires, Argentina: Galerna.

Bernstein, R. (1985). *Habermas and modernity.* Cambridge, MA: MIT Press.

Bhabha, H. (1994). *The location of culture.* New York: Routledge.

Bitar, S. (1988). Neo-conservatism versus neo-structuralism in Latin America. *Comisión Económica para Latina (CEPAL) Review, 34,* 45–62.

Block, F. (1987). *Revising state theory: Essays in politics and postindustrialism.* Philadelphia: Temple University Press.

Boli, J., & Ramirez, F. O. (1992). Compulsory schooling in the Western cultural context. In R. Arnove, P. G. Altbach, & G. P. Kelly (Eds.), *Emergent issues in education: Comparative perspectives* (pp. 25–38). Albany: State University of New York Press.

Boron, A. A. (1976). *The formation and crisis of the oligarchical state in Argentina, 1880–1930.* Unpublished doctoral dissertation, Harvard University, Cambridge, MA.

Bourdieu, P. (1984). *Distinction.* Cambridge, MA: Harvard University Press.

Bourdieu, P. (1988). *Homo academicus.* Stanford, CA: Stanford University Press.

Bourdieu, P. (2003). *Firing back: Against the tyrany of the markets.* New York: New Press.

Bowles, S., & Gintis, H. (1977). *Schooling in capitalist America: Educational reform and the contradictions of economic life.* New York: Basic Books.

Bowles, S., & Gintis, H. (1981). Education as a site of contradictions in the reproduction of the capital-labor relationships: Second thoughts on the "correspondence principle." *Economic and Industrial Democracy,* 2(2), 223–242.

Bowles, S., & Gintis, H. (1986). *Democracy and capitalism: Property, community, and the contradictions of modern social thought.* New York: Basic.

Brown, C. (1975). *Literacy in thirty hours: Paulo Freire's literacy process in northeast Brazil.* London: Writers and Readers Publishing Cooperative.

Burawoy, M. (2005). For public sociology. *British Journal of Sociology of Education, 56,* 259–294.

Burbules, N., & Torres, C. A. (Eds.). (2000). *Education and globalization: Critical concepts.* New York: Routledge.

Butler, J., & Scott, J. W. (1992). *Feminists theorize the political.* New York: Routledge.

Cabral, A. (1969). *Revolution in Guinea.* New York: Monthly Review Press.

Cabral, A. (1975). *L'Arme de la theorie.* Paris: Maspero.

Cabral, A. (1979). *Analise de alguns tipos de resistencia.* Guinea-Bissau: Edição do PAIG.

Cardoso, F. H., & Faletto, E. (1979). *Dependency and development in Latin America.* Berkeley: University of California Press.

Carnoy, M. (1984). *The state and political theory.* Princeton, NJ: Princeton University Press.

Carnoy, M. (1992). Education and the state: From Adam Smith to perestroika. In R. F. Arnove, P. G. Altbach, & G. P. Kelly (Eds.), *Emergent issues in education: Comparative perspectives* (pp. 143–159). Albany: State University of New York Press.

Carnoy, M., & Samoff, J. (with Burris, A. M., Johnston, A., & Torres, C. A.). (1990). *Education and social transition in the Third World.* Princeton, NJ: Princeton University Press.

Carnoy, M., & Torres, C. A. (1990). Education and social transformation in Nicaragua (1979–1989). In M. Carnoy & J. Samoff (Eds.), *Education and social transition in the Third World* (pp. 315–357). Princeton NJ: Princeton University Press.

Carnoy, M., & Torres, C. A. (1992). *Educational change and structural adjustment: A case study of Costa Rica* (UNESCO Occasional Papers Series). Paris: International Labor Organization (ILO) Interagency Task Force on Austerity, Adjustment, and Human Resources.

Castells, M. (1996). *The rise of the network society* (The Information Age: Economy, Society and Culture, Vol. 1). Malden, MA: Blackwell.

Castells, M. (1997). *The power of identity* (The Information Age: Economy, Society and Culture, Vol. 2). Malden, MA: Blackwell.

Castells, M. (1998). *End of millennium* (The Information Age: Economy, Society and Culture, Vol. 3). Malden, MA: Blackwell.

CEPAL. (1990). *Transformación educativa con equidad*. Santiago de Chile: Author.

Cerroni, H. (1976). *Teoría política y socialismo*. Mexico City: ERA.

Cerroni, H. (1992). *Política: Método, procesos, sujetos, instituciones y categorias*. Mexico City: Siglo XXI Editores.

Chilcote, R. H. (1974). Dependency: A critical synthesis of the literature. *Latin American Perspectives, 1*(1), 4–29.

Collier, R., & Collier, D. (1991). *Shaping the political arena: Critical junctures, the labor movement, and regime dynamics in Latin America*. Princeton, NJ: Princeton University Press.

CONADEP. (1984). *Nunca mas: Informe de la Comisión Nacional sobre la Desaparición de Personas*. Buenos Aires, Argentina: EUDEBA.

Connell, R. W. (1983). *Which way is up? Essays on sex, class and culture*. Sydney, Australia: Allen & Unwin.

Connell, R. W. (1987). *Gender and power: Society, the person and sexual politics*. Stanford, CA: Stanford University Press.

Coombs, P. (1971). *La crisis mundial de la educación*. Barcelona, Spain: Peninsula.

Coraggio, L. (1993). *Economía y educación en América Latina: Notas para una agenda de los 90's* (ECLA Papers, No. 4). Santiago de Chile: ECLA.

Counts, G. (1932). *Dare the school build a new social order?* New York: John Day.

Darling-Hammond, L. (1993). Introduction. *Review of Research in Education, 19*, xi–xxiii.

Darnton, R. (1982). *The literary underground of the old regime*. Cambridge, MA: Harvard University Press.

Davis, M. (2006). *Planet of slums*. New York: Verso.

De Kadt, E. (1970). *Catholic radicals in Brazil*. London: Oxford University Press.

De Landa, M. (1997). *A thousand years of nonlinear history*. New York: Zone Books.

De Toledo, C. N. (1977). *ISEB: Fabrica de ideologies*. São Paulo, Brazil: Etica.

De Witt, J. (1971). *An exposition and analysis of Paulo Freire's radical psycho-social andragogy of development*. Boston: Boston University School of Education.

De Zan, J. (1973, January-June). La dialectica en el centro y en la perisferia. *Nuevo Mundo, 3*, 109–110.

Dérrida, J. (1989). *Cómo no hablar? Y otros textos*. Barcelona, Spain: Anthropos.

Diamond, J. (1999). *Guns, germs, and steel: The fates of human societies*. New York: W.W. Norton.

DiFazio, W. (1998). Why there is no movement of the poor. In S. Aronowitz & J. Cutler (Eds.), *Post-work: The wages of cybernation* (pp. 141–166). New York: Routledge.

Dimitriadis, G., & McCarthy, C. (2001). *Reading and teaching the postcolonial*. New York: Teachers College Press.

Dos Santos, T. (1970). La crisis de la teoria del desarrollo y las relaciones de dependencia en America Latina. In H. Jaguaribe, A. Ferrer, M. S. Wionczek, & T. Dos Santos, *La dependencia politico-económica de America Latina* (pp. 147–187). Mexico City: Siglo XXI Editores.

ECLA. (1993, May-August). Panorama social de América Latina. *Revista Iberoamericana, 2.*

Eliot, T. S. (1971). The dry salvages. In *The four quartets.* New York: Harcourt, Brace. (Original work published 1943)

Entwistle, H. (1979). *Antonio Gramsci: Conservative schooling for radical politics.* London: Routledge and Kegan Paul.

Evans, P. (1979). *Dependent development: The alliance of multinationals, state, and local capital in Brazil.* Princeton, NJ: Princeton University Press.

Eyerman, R., & Jamison, A. (1991). *Social movements: A cognitive approach.* Cambridge, MA: Polity.

Ezcurra, A. M. (1991). *El globalismo de la post-guerra fría: La administración Bush y la renovación del intervencionismo norteamericano.* Buenos Aires, Argentina: Instituto de Estudios y Acción Social/Red Latinoamericana del CPID.

Fanon, F. (1967). *Black skin, white mask* (C. L. Markman, trans.). New York: Grove.

Faure, E. (1974). *Aprender a ser.* Mexico City: Alianza Editorial.

Feinberg, W. (1996, Spring). Affirmative action and beyond: A case for backward-looking gender- and race-based policy. *Teachers College Record, 97*(3), 363–397.

Fiori, E. M. (1975). Aprender a decir su palabra. In P. Freire, *Pedagogia del oprimido* (pp. 11–28, 14th ed.). Buenos Aires, Argentina: Siglo XXI-Tierra Nueva.

First Sectorial Education Investment Project (Ministerio de Cultura y Educación/Provincia de Buenos Aires/Banco Interamericano de Reconstrucción y Fomento). (1993). *Argentina: Proyecto de educación secundaria* (Working Paper). Buenos Aires, Argentina: Author.

Fox, J. (1997, July 6). Chretien: No cover-up over Somalia mission. *Miami Herald,* p. 12A.

Fraser, N. (1989). *Unruly practices: Power, discourse, and gender in contemporary social theory.* Minneapolis: University of Minnesota Press.

Fraser, N. (1997). *Justice interruptus.* New York: Routledge.

Freire, P. (1970a). *Cultural action: A dialectic analysis* (Cuaderno, No. 1004). Cuernavaca, Mexico: CIDOC.

Freire, P. (1970b). *Pedagogy of the oppressed.* New York: Herder & Herder; Seabury.

Freire, P. (1971). *Sobre la accion cultural.* Santiago de Chile: ICIRA.

Freire, P. (1972). *Pedagogia del oprimido* (3rd ed.). Montevideo, Uruguay: Editorial Tierra Nueva.

Freire, P. (1973). *Education for critical consciousness.* New York: Seabury.

Freire, P. (1975a). Conversation con Paulo Freire. In *Concientizacion y liberation* (pp. 29–30) (Documentos, No. 1). Rosario, Argentina: Axis.

Freire, P. (1975b). *Diálogo: Paulo Freire–Iván Illich*. Buenos Aires, Argentina: Editorial Búsqueda-CELADEC.

Freire, P. (1975c). *Pedagogia del oprimido* (14th ed.). Buenos Aires, Argentina: Siglo XXI-Tierra Nueva.

Freire, P. (1976). *Education, the practice of freedom*. London: Writers and Readers Publishing Cooperative.

Freire, P. (1977). *Pedagogy in process: The letters to Guinea-Bissau*. New York: Seabury.

Freire, P. (1978a). *Educación como práctica de la libertad*. Buenos Aires, Argentina: Siglo XXI.

Freire, P. (1978b). *Pedagogía del oprimido*. Buenos Aires, Argentina: Siglo XXI.

Freire, P. (1980a). Accion cultural liberadora. In C. A. Torres (Ed.), *Paulo Freire. Educación y concientización*. Salamanca, Spain: Signeme

Freire, P. (1980b). La concientizacion desmitificada. In C. A. Torres (Ed.), *Paulo Freire: Educación y concientización*. Salamanca, Spain: Signeme

Freire, P. (1980c). Concientizar para liberar. In C. A. Torres (Ed.), *Paulo Freire: Educación y concientización*. Salamanca, Spain: Signeme.

Freire, P. (1980d). Entrevista. In C. A. Torres (Ed.), *Paulo Freire: Educación y concientización*. Salamanca, Spain: Signeme.

Freire, P. (1980e). Quatro cartas aos animadores de circulos de cultura de São Tomé Principe. In C. R. Brandao (Ed.), *A questao politica da educação popular* (pp. 136–197). São Paulo, Brazil: Livraria Brasiliense Editora.

Freire, P. (1982, April). Os planos de Paulo Freire. *Jornal da Educação*, CEDES, Campinas, Year 1, pp. 3–5.

Freire, P. (1986). Educação: O sonho possivel. In C. R. Brandão (Ed.), *O Educador: Vida e morte* (pp. 89–101). Rio de Janeiro, Brazil: Edições Graal.

Freire, P. (1990). *Reading the world: Paulo Freire in conversation with Dr. Carlos A. Torres* [videotape]. Alberta, Canada: ACCESS Network.

Freire, P. (1992a). Foreword. In P. McLaren & P. Leonard (Eds.), *Paulo Freire: A critical encounter* (pp. ix–xii). London: Routledge.

Freire, P. (1992b). *Pedagogia da esperança*. São Paulo, Brazil: Paz e Terra.

Freire, P. (1993). *Pedagogy of the city*. New York: Continuum.

Freire, P. (1998). *Politics and education* (P. L. Wong, Trans.). Los Angeles: UCLA Latin American Center Publications.

Freire, P. (2005). Educación para un despertar de la conciencia: Una charla con Paulo Freire. In C. A. Torres (Compilzador), *La praxis educativa y la acción cultura de Paula Freire* (pp. 215–224). Valencia, Spain: Editorial Denes. (Original work published 1970)

Freire, P., & Betto, F. (1985). *E esta escola da vida*. São Paulo, Brazil: Atica.

Freire, P., & Faúndez, A. (1985a). Freire in conversation with Chilean philosopher Antonio Faúndez. In *Por uma pedagogia da pergunta* (pp. 139–140). Rio de Janeiro, Brazil: Paz e Terra.

Freire, P., & Faúndez, A. (1985b). *Por uma pedagogia da pergunta*. Rio de Janeiro, Brazil: Paz e Terra.

Freire, P., & Faúndez, A. (1989). *Learning to question: A pedagogy of liberation.* New York: Continuum.

Freire, P., & Guimarães, S. (1982). *Sobre educação: Dialogos* (2 vols.). Rio de Janeiro, Brazil: Paz e Terra.

Freire, P., & Macedo, D. (1987). *Literacy: Reading the word and the world.* South Hadley, MA: Bergin & Garvey.

Freire, P., Nogueira, A., & Mazza, D. (1986). *Fazer escola conhecendo a vida.* Campinas, Brazil: Papirus.

Freire, P., Oliveira, R. D., Oliveira, M. D., & Ceccon, C. (1980). *Vivendo e aprendendo—Experiences do IDAC in educação popular* (3rd ed.). São Paulo, Brazil: Livraria Brasilense Editora.

Freire, P., & Torres, C. A. (1993). Lessons from a fascinating challenge. In P. Freire (Ed.), *Pedagogy of the city* (pp. 94–136). New York: Continuum.

Freire, P., & Torres, C. A. (1994). Learning to read the world: Paulo Freire in conversation with Carlos Alberto Torres. In C. A. Torres (Ed.), *Education and social change in Latin America* (pp. 175–182). Melbourne, Australia: James Nicholas.

Frieden, J. A. (1991). *Debt, development, and democracy: Modern political economy and Latin America, 1965–1985.* Princeton, NJ: Princeton University Press.

Gadotti, M. (1989). *Convite a leitura de Paulo Freire.* São Paulo, Brazil: Editora Scipione.

Gadotti, M. (1990). *Uma só escola para todos.* Petropolis, Rio de Janeiro, Brazil: Vozes.

Gadotti, M., Freire, A. M. A, Ciseski, A. A., Torres, C. A., et al. (1996). *Paulo Freire: Uma bio bibliógrafia.* São Paulo, Brazil: Institute Paulo Freire, UNESCO, and Cortez Editores.

Gadotti, M., Freire, P., & Guimarães, S. (1986). *Pedagogia: Diálogo e conflito.* São Paulo, Brazil: Cortez Editora–Editora Autores Associados.

Gadotti, M., & Manfio, A. J. (1993, November 17–19). *Unidos ou dominados: Pluriculturalismo, diversidade cultural e a integraçao no Mercosul* (Workshop on Education without Frontiers, Foz do Iguaçu, Parana, Brazil) [mimeographed].

Gadotti, M., & Torres, C. A. (1991). Paulo Freire, administrador público. In P. Freire (Ed.), *A educação na cidade* (pp. 11–17). São Paulo, Brazil: Cortez Editora.

Gadotti, M., & Torres, C. A. (1992). *Estado y educação popular na América Latina.* Campinas, São Paulo, Brazil: Papirus.

Gadotti, M., & Torres, C. A. (Eds.). (1993). *Educación popular: Crisis y perspectivas.* Buenos Aires, Argentina: Miño y Dávila Editores.

Gadotti, M., & Torres, C. A. (Eds.). (1994). *Educação popular: Utopia Latino Americana (ensaios).* São Paulo, Brazil: Cortez Editores and Editora da Universidade de São Paulo.

Gajardo, M. (Ed.). (1982). *Teoría y práctica de la educación popular.* Ottawa, Canada: International Development Research Centre.

Garcia, H. P., et al. (1981). *América Latina 80: Democracia y movimento popular.* Lima, Peru: Centro de Estudios y Promocion del Desarrollo.

García Canclini, N. (1982). *Las culturas populares en el capitalismo.* Mexico City, Nueva Imagen.

García Canclini, N. (1990). *Culturas híbridas.* Mexico City: Grijalbo.

Gasche, R. (1986). *The taint of the mirror: Dérrida and the philosophy of reflection.* Cambridge, MA: Harvard University Press.

Giroux, H. (1983). *Theory and resistance in education: A pedagogy for the opposition.* South Hadley, MA: Bergin & Garvey.

Giroux, H. (1984). Introduction. In P. Freire, *The politics of education, culture, power, and liberation* (pp. xi–xxv). South Hadley, MA: Bergin & Garvey.

Giroux, H. (Ed.). (1991). *Postmodernism, feminism, and cultural politics: Redrawing educational boundaries.* Albany: State University of New York Press.

Giroux, H. (1992). *Border crossings: Cultural workers and the politics of education.* New York: Routledge.

Giroux, H., & McLaren, P. (Eds.). (1994). *Between borders: Pedagogy and the politics of cultural studies.* New York: Routledge.

Gitlin, T. (1995). *The twilight of common dreams: Why America is wracked by culture wars.* New York: Henry Holt.

Goldsmith, E. (1996). The last word: Family, community, democracy. In J. Mander & E. Goldsmith (Eds.), *The case against the global economy and for a turn toward the local* (pp. 501–514). San Francisco: Sierra Club Books.

Gordon, L. (Ed.). (1990). *Women, the state and welfare.* Madison: University of Wisconsin Press.

Goulet, D. (1978, March). *Looking at Guinea-Bissau: A new nation's development strategy* (Occasional Papers No. 9). New York: Overseas Development Council.

Gramsci, A. (1971). *Selections from the prison notebooks of Antonio Gramsci* (Q. Hoare & G. N. Smith, Trans.). New York: International Publishers.

Gramsci, A. (1985). *La alternativa pedagógica.* Barcelona, Spain: Fontanara.

Gunder-Frank, A. (1969). *Capitalism and underdevelopment in Latin America.* New York: Monthly Review Press.

Habermas, J. (1975). *Legitimation crisis* (J. Shapiro, ed. & trans.). Boston: Beacon.

Habermas, J. (1981). Psychic thermidor and the rebirth of rebellious subjectivity. *Praxis International, 1,* 79–86.

Habermas, J. (1984). *Theory of communicative action.* Boston: Beacon.

Habermas, J. (1985). Neoconservative culture criticism in the United States and West Germany: An intellectual movement in two political cultures. In R. J. Bernstein (Ed.), *Habermas and modernity* (pp. 78–94). Cambridge, MA: MIT Press.

Habermas, J. (1992). Citizenship and national identity: Some reflections on the future of Europe. *Praxis International, 12,* 1–19.

Harasim, L. M. (1983). *Literacy and national reconstruction in Guinea-Bissau: A critique of the Freirean literacy campaign*. Unpublished doctoral dissertation, Ontario Institute for Studies in Education, University of Toronto, Canada.

Harding, S. (1986). *The science question in feminism*. Ithaca, NY: Cornell University Press.

Harding, S. (1987). *Feminism and methodology: Social science issues*. Bloomington: Indiana University Press.

Hartung, A., & Ohliger, J. (1973). Quotational bibliography. In S. Grabowski (Ed.), *Paulo Freire: A revolutionary dilemma for the adult educator* (pp. 96–136). Syracuse, NY: Syracuse University Publications in Continuing Education.

Hegel, G. W. F. (1949). *The phenomenology of mind* (2nd ed., J. B. Baillie, Trans.). London: Allen & Unwin. (Original work published 1910)

Hegel, G. W. F. (1967). *The phenomenology of mind* (J. B. Baillie, Trans.). New York: Harper & Row.

Held, D. (Ed.). (1991). *Political theory today*. Stanford, CA: Stanford University Press.

Held, D. (1995). Democracy and the new international order. In D. Archibugi & D. Held (Eds.), *Cosmopolitan democracy: An agenda for a new world* (pp. 96–120). Cambridge, MA: Polity.

Horkheimer, M. (1972). *Critical theory: Selected essays* (M. J. O'Connell et al., Trans.). New York: Herder & Herder. (Original work published 1937)

Ianni, O. (1975). *La formación del estado populista en América Latina*. Mexico City: ERA.

Il Conferencia General del Episcopado Latinoamericano. (1968). *Documento Finales de Medellin*. Buenos Aires, Argentina: Editorial Paulinas.

Instituto Interregional de las Naciones Unidas para las Investigaciones sobre la Delincuencia y la Justicia. (1991). *Ser niño en Latina*. Buenos Aires, Argentina: Galerna.

Jacoby, R. (2005). *Picture imperfect: Utopian thought for an anti-utopian age*. New York: Columbia University Press.

Jules, D. (1991). Building democracy. In M. W. Apple & L. Christian-Smith (Eds.), *The politics of the textbook* (pp. 259–287). New York: Routledge.

Kellner, D. (1984). *Herbert Marcuse and the crisis of Marxism*. Berkeley: University of California Press.

Kellner, D. (1989). *Critical theory, Marxism, and modernity*. Cambridge, MA: Polity.

Kellner, D. (1997). *Globalization and the postmodern turn*. Unpublished manuscript.

Kennedy, W. B., Bean, W., Freire, P., & Illich, I. (1975). Invitation to conscientization and deschooling: A continuing conversation. *Risk, 11*(1), 4–58.

Kubler, B. (1991). *A World Book country study. Argentina. Reallocating resources for the improvement of education*. Washington, DC: World Bank.

Laclau, E. (1985). New social movements and the plurality of the social. In D. Slater (Ed.), *New social movements and the state in Latin America* (pp. 27–42). Amsterdam, Netherlands: Centrum voor Studie en Documentatie van Latijns Amerika.

Laclau, E. (1991). *New reflections on the revolution of our times*. London: Verso.

Laclau, E., & Mouffe, C. (1985). *Hegemony and socialist strategy* (W. Moore & P. Cammack, Trans.). London: Verso.

Laclau, E., & Mouffe, C. (1987). *Hegemonía y estrategia socialista*. Madrid, Spain: Siglo XXI.

Ladson-Billings, G., & Tate, W. F. (1995, Fall). Toward a critical race theory of education. *Teachers College Record, 97*, 47–68.

Lechner, N. (Ed.). (1987). *Cultura politica y democratizacion*. Santiago: Facultad Latino-Americana de Ciencias Sociales and Instituto de Cooperacion Ibero Americana.

Lengermann, P. M., & Niebrugge-Brantley, J. (1990). Feminist sociological theory: The near-future prospects. In G. Ritzer (Ed.), *Frontiers of social theory: The new syntheses* (pp. 308–357). New York: Columbia University Press.

Lenin, V. I. (n.d.). *V. I. Lenin: Selected works. Vol. 11: The theoretical principles of Marxism*. New York: International Publishers.

Levin, H. (1980). The limits of educational planning. In H. N. Weller (Ed.), *Educational planning and social change*. Paris: UNESCO-IIEP.

Lewis, D. L. (1993). *W. E. B. Du Bois: Biography of a race, 1868–1919*. New York: Henry Holt.

Lewis, D. L. (2000). *W. E. B. Du Bois: The fight for equality and the American century*. New York: Henry Holt.

Livingston, G. (2003). *Chronic silencing and struggling without witness: Race, education and the production of political knowledge*. Unpublished doctoral dissertation, University of Wisconsin, Madison.

Lockheed, M. E., & Verspoor, A. (1991). *Improving primary education in developing countries: A review of policy options*. Washington, DC: World Bank and Oxford University Press.

Lomnitz, L., & Melnick, A. (1991). *Chile's middle class: A struggle for survival in the face of neoliberalism*. Boulder, CO: Lynne Rienner.

Luke, A., & Luke, C. (2000). A situated perspective on cultural globalization. In N. Burbules & C. A. Torres (Eds.), *Globalization and education: Critical perspectives*. New York: Routledge.

Macedo, D., & Freire, P. (1987). *Literacy: Reading the word and the world*. South Hadley, MA: Bergin & Garvey.

Mannheim, K. (1936). *Ideology and Utopia*. New York: Harvest Books.

Marcuse, H. (1967). *Razón y revolucion* (J. D. de Sucre, Trans.). Caracas, Venezuela: Instituto de Estudios Politicos.

Marcuse, H. (1968). *Reason and revolution: Hegel and the rise of social theory*. New York: Humanities Press. (Original work published 1941)

Marcuse, H. (1970). *Ontologia de Hegel*. Barcelona, Spain: Martinez Roca.

Marcuse, H. (1987). *Hegel's ontology and the theory of historicity* (S. Benhabib, Trans.). Cambridge, MA: MIT Press.

Marcuse, H. (1991). *One-dimensional man: Studies in the ideology of advanced industrial societies*. Boston: Beacon. (Original work published 1966)

Marshall, T. H. (1950). *Citizenship and social class and other essays*. Cambridge: Cambridge University Press.

Marshall, T. H. (1963). *Sociology at the crossroads*. London: Heinemann Educational Books.

Marshall, T. H. (1965). *Social policy in the twentieth century*. London: Hutchinson.

Marshall, T. H. (1981). *The right to welfare and other essays*. London: Heinemann.

Marshall, T. H. (1983). Citizenship and social class. In D. Held et al. (Eds.), *States and societies* (pp. 248–260). Oxford, UK: Robertson, in association with the Open University.

Martín-Barbero, J. (1987a). Comunicación, pueblo y cultura en el tiempo de las trasnacionales. In *Procesos de comunicación y culturas populares en Latinoamérica* (pp. 38–50). Mexico: Federación Latinomericana de Asociaciones de Facultades de Comunicación Social.

Martín-Barbero, J. (1987b). Comunicacion, pueblo y cultura en el tiempo de las trasnacionales. In *Procesos de comunicación y matrices de cultura: Itinerario para salir de la razón dualista* (pp. 124–136). Mexico City: Edicion G. Gili and Federación Latinoamericana de Facultades de Comunicación Social.

Marx, K. (1935). *Selected work* (Vol. 1; F. Engels, Ed.). New York: International Publishers.

Marx, K., & Engels, F. (1970). *The German ideology* (C. J. Arthur, Ed.). New York: International Publishers.

Mayo, P. (1999). *Gramsci, Freire, and adult education*. London: Zed Books.

McCarthy, C., & Apple, M. W. (1988). Race, class and gender in American educational research: Toward a nonsynchronous parallelist position. In L. Weiss (Ed.), *Class, race and gender in American education* (pp. 9–39). Albany: State University of New York Press.

McCarthy, T. (1979). *The critical theory of Jürgen Habermas*. Cambridge, MA: MIT Press.

McLaren, P. (1986). Postmodernity and the death of politics: A Brazilian reprieve. *Educational Theory, 36*(4), 389–401.

McLaren, P. (1993). *Hacia una pedagogía crítica de la formación postmoderna*. Entre Ríos, Argentina: Universidad Nacional de Entre Ríos.

McLaren, P. (1993). *Schooling as a ritual performance: Towards a political economy of educational symbols and gestures*. London: Routledge.

McLaren, P., & Lankshear, C. (Eds.). (1994). *Politics of liberation: Paths from Freire*. London: Routledge.

McLaren, P., & Leonard, P. (Eds.). (1992). *Paulo Freire: A critical encounter*. London: Routledge.

Meyer, J. (1977). The effects of education as an institution. *American Journal of Sociology, 83*(4), 55–57.

Mezirow, J. (1978). Perspective transformation. *Adult Education, 28*(2), 100–110.

Mezirow, J. (1979, September 27). Public lecture at the University of Northern Illinois. Sponsored by the Department of Leadership and Policy Studies, Graduate Colloquium Committee. [mimeographed]

Mezirow, J. (1981). A critical theory of adult learning and education. *Adult Education Quarterly, 32*(1), 3–24.

Mezirow, J. (1985, March). A critical theory of self-directed learning. *New Directions for Continuing Education, 25,* 17–30.

Mezirow, J. (1997). Transformative learning: Theory to practice. In P. Cranton (Ed.), *Transformative learning in action* (pp. 5–12). San Francisco: Jossey-Bass.

Mitchell, T. R. (1998). *The republic for which it stands: Public schools, the state, and the idea of citizenship in America.* Los Angeles: University of California.

Morales-Gómez, D. A., & Torres, C. A. (1990). *The state, corporatist politics, and educational policy making in Mexico.* New York: Praeger.

Morales-Gómez, D. A., & Torres, C. A. (Eds.). (1992). *Education, policy and change: Experiences from Latin America.* Westport, CT: Praeger.

Morrow, R. A. (1989, June). *Habermas on rationalization, reification and the colonization of the life-world.* Paper presented at the joint session of the Canadian Association of Sociology and Anthropology and the International Sociological Research Association Research Committee on Alienation: Theory and Research, Vancouver, Canada.

Morrow, R. A., & Brown, D. D. (1994). *Critical theory and methodology.* Thousand Oaks, CA: Sage.

Morrow, R. A., & Torres, C. A. (1994). Education and the reproduction of class, gender and race: Responding to the postmodernist challenge. *Educational Theory, 44*(1), 43–61

Morrow, R. A., & Torres, C. A. (1995). *Social theory and education: A critique of theories of social and cultural reproduction.* Albany: State University of New York Press.

Morrow, R. A., & Torres, C. A. (1999). Paulo Freire, Jürgen Habermas, and critical pedagogy: Implications for comparative education. *Melbourne Studies in Education, 39*(2), 1–20.

Morrow, R. A., & Torres, C. A. (2002). *Reading Freire and Habermas: Critical pedagogy and transformative social change.* New York: Teachers College Press.

Morrow, R. A., & Torres, C. A. (2007). The state, social movements, and educational reform. In R. Arnove & C. A. Torres (Eds.), *Comparative education: The dialectics of the global and the local* (3rd ed., pp. 79–100). Lanham, MD: Rowman & Littlefield.

Mouffe, C. (1993). *The return of the political.* London: Verso.

Naes, A., Christophersen, J. A., & Kvale, K. (1956). *Democracy, ideology and objectivity.* Oslo, Norway: Oslo University Press. Quotation corresponds to Destutt de Tracy, *Elements d'Ideologie,* 1801, 3: 4.

Nash, K. (2000). *Contemporary political sociology: Globalization, politics, and power.* London: Blackwell.

Nuhoglu Soysal, Y. (1994). *Limits of citizenship: Migrants and postnational membership in Europe.* Chicago: University of Chicago Press.

Nuñez, I. (1984a). *Actores y estrategias para el cambio educaciónal en Chile: Historias y propuestas.* Santiago de Chile: Proyecto Interdisciplinario de Investigaciones en Educación.

Nuñez, I. (1984b). La educación chilena en el periodo 1945–1990. In C. L. Seijas & A. Puiggrós (Eds.), *Historia de la educación en Ibero América* (Vol. 1, pp. 231–252). Mexico City: Garcia y Valdez.

O'Cadiz, M. P., & Torres, C. A. (1994). Literacy, social movements, and class consciousness: Paths from Freire and the São Paulo experience. *Anthropology and Education Quarterly, 25*(3), 208–225.

O'Cadiz, M. P., Wong, P. L., & Torres, C. A. (1998). *Education and democracy: Paulo Freire, social movements, and educational reform in São Paulo.* Boulder, CO: Westview Press.

O'Donnell, G. (1987). *Bureaucratic authoritarianism: Argentina, 1966–1973, in comparative perspective.* Berkeley: University of California Press.

O'Reilly, B. (1992). Your new global workforce. *Fortune, 126*(13), 52–66.

Oakes, J. (1995). *Keeping track.* New Haven, CT: Yale University Press.

Offe, C. (1975). The capitalist state and the problem of policy formation. In L. N. Lindberg, R. Alford, C. Crouch, & C. Offe (Eds.), *Stress and contradiction in modern capitalism* (pp. 125–144). Lexington, MA: Heath.

Ohmae, K. (1990). *The borderless world: Power and strategy in the interlinked world economy.* New York: Harper Business.

Ohmae, K. (1995). *The end of the nation state: The rise of regional economies.* New York: Free Press Paperbacks.

Oliveira, R. D., & Dominice, P. (1981). Pedagogía dos oprimidos: Opressão de pedagogia. O debate pedagógico. In C. A. Torres (Ed.), *Leitura crítica de Paulo Freire* (pp. 134–138). São Paulo, Brazil: Edicoes Loyola.

Oliveira, R. D., & Oliveira, M. D. (1976). *Guinea-Bissau: Reinventing education* (IDAC Document 11–12). Geneva, Switzerland: Institute of Cultural Action.

Paiva, V. P. (1980). *Paulo Freire e o Nacionalismo-Desenvolvimentista.* Rio de Janeiro, Brazil: Editora Civilizacao Brasileira.

Parker, W. C. (1997). Citizenship education. In C. A Grant & G. Ladson-Billings (Eds.), *Dictionary of multicultural education* (pp. 39–40). Phoeniz, AZ: Oryx.

Pateman, C. (1986). Introduction: The theoretical subversiveness of feminism. In C. Pateman & E. Gross (Eds.), *Feminist challenges: Social and political theory* (pp. 1–10). Boston: Northeastern University Press.

Pateman, C. (1992). Equality, difference, subordination: The politics of motherhood and women's citizenship. In G. Bock & S. James (Eds.), *Beyond equality and difference: Citizenship, feminist politics, and female subjectivity* (pp. 17–31). London: Routledge.

Pateman, C. (1996). *Democratization and citizenship in the 1990s: The legacy of T. H. Marshall* (Vilhelm Aubert Memorial Lecture). Oslo, Sweden: University of Oslo, Institute for Social Research and Department of Sociology.

Pereyra, C. (1988). *El sujeto de la historia.* Mexico City: Alianza Universidad Mexicana.

Plank, D. (1987). The expansion of education: A Brazilian case study. *Comparative Education Review, 31*(3), 361–376.

Popkewitz, T. S. (1988). Educational reform: Rhetoric, ritual, and social interest. *Educational Theory, 38*(1), 78–83.

Popkewitz, T. S. (1991). *A political sociology of educational reform: Power/knowledge in teaching, teacher education, and research.* New York: Teachers College Press.

Popkewitz, T. S., & Fendler, L. (Eds.). (1999). *Critical theories in education: Changing terrains of knowledge and politics.* New York: Routledge.

Portelli, H. (1972). *Gramsi et le bloc historique.* Paris: Presses Universitaires de France.

Poulantzas, N. (1978). *State, power, socialism.* London: Verso.

Prebisch, R. (1985, August). The Latin American periphery in the global crisis of capitalism. *CEPAL Review, 26,* 63–88.

Prieto, A. (1992, July 26). Los hispanos en Estados Unidos: Las ficciones que nadie esperaba. *Primera plana* (cultural suppl.), pp. 2–3. Buenos Aires, Argentina.

Przeworski, A. (1991). *Democracy and the market: Political economic reforms in Eastern Europe and Latin America.* New York: Cambridge University Press.

Puiggrós, A. (1986). *Democracia y autoritarismo en la pedagogía Argentina y Latinoamericana.* Buenos Aires, Argentina: Galerna.

Puiggrós, A. (1990a). *Imaginación y crisis en la educación Latinoamericana.* Mexico City: Alianza Editorial Mexicana.

Puiggrós, A. (1990b). *Sujetos, disciplina y curriculum en los orígenes del sistema educativo Argentine.* Buenos Aires, Argentina: Galerna.

Puiggrós, A. (1993). *Universidad, proyecto generacional, e imaginario pedagógico.* Buenos Aires, Argentina: Paidós.

Puiggrós, A., et al. (1992a). *Escuela, democracia y orden (1916–1943).* Buenos Aires, Argentina: Galerna.

Puiggrós, A., et al. (1992b). *Interviews with teachers.* Buenos Aires: Instituto de Ciencias de la Educación, Universidad de Buenos Aires (UBA). [mimeographed]

Raban, L., & Sturzenegger, F. (n.d.). *Fiscal conservatism as a response to the debt crisis.* Unpublished manuscript.

Reich, R. B. (1991). *The work of nations.* New York: Vintage.

Reimers, F. (1990, December 3–6). *Educación para todos en América Latina en el siglo XXI: Los desafíos de la estabilización, el ajuste y los mandatos de Jomtien.* Paper presented to the workshop on "Pobreza, ajuste y supervivencia infantil," organized by United Nations Educational, Scientific and Cultural Organization in Peru.

Reimers, F. (1991). The impact of economic stabilization and adjustment on education in Latin America. *Comparative Education Review, 35*(2), 325–238.

Reimers, F., & Tiburcio, L. (1993). *Education, adjustment and reconstruction: Options for change.* Paris: United Nations Educational, Scientific and Cultural Organization.

Rhoads, R., & Torres, C. A. (Eds.). (2006). *The university, state and markets: The political economy of globalization in the Americas.* Stanford, CA: Stanford University Press.

Ricoeur, P. (1981). *Hermeneutics and the human sciences: Essays on language, action, and interpretation* (J. B. Thompson, Ed. & Trans.). Cambridge: Cambridge University Press; Paris: Editions de la Maison des sciences de l'homme.

Rocco, R. A. (1997, April). *Reframing postmodernist constructions of difference: Subaltern spaces, power, and citizenship.* Paper presented at the Symposium on the Challenge of Postmodernism to the Social Sciences and the Humanities, University Complutense, Somosaguas campus, Madrid, Spain.

Rodrigues, N. (1982). *Estado, educação e desenvolvimento económico.* São Paulo, Brazil: Autores Associados e Cortez.

Roniger, L. (1990). *Hierarchy and trust in modern Mexico and Brazil.* New York: Praeger.

Rosenthal, G. (1989). Latin America and Caribbean development in the 1980s and the outlook for the future. *CEPAL Review, 39,* 7–18.

Rudebeck, L. (1974). *Guinea-Bissau: A study of political mobilization.* New York: African Publishing Company.

Saldivar-Hull, S. (1994). Feminism on the border: From gender politics to geopolitics. In H. Calderon & J. D. Saldivar (Eds.), *Criticism in the borderlands: Studies in Chicano literature, culture, and ideology* (pp. 203–220). Durham, NC: Duke University Press.

Samoff, J. (1990). *More, less, none? Human resource development: Responses to economic constraint.* Palo Alto, CA: Prepared for the Interagency Task Force on Austerity, Adjustment, and Human Resources of the International Labor Office and United Nations Educational, Scientific and Cultural Organization. [mimeographed]

Samoff, J. (Ed.). (1994). *Coping with crisis: Austerity, adjustment, and human resources.* London: Cassell, with United Nations Educational, Scientific and Cultural Organization.

Sanders, T. G. (1968). The Paulo Freire method: Literacy training and conscientization. *South American Series, XV*(1), 1–17.

Sarmiento, D. F. (1956). *Educar al soberano.* Buenos Aires, Argentina: Ediciones Luz del Dia.

Sarmiento, D. F. (1989). *La educación popular.* Buenos Aires, Argentina: Banco de la Provincia de Buenos Aires. (Original work published 1850)

Schiefelbein, E. (1991). *Financing education for democracy in Latin America.* Santiago de Chile: UNESCO-Organización Regional de los Estados de America Latina y el Caribe. [mimeographed]

Schmitter, P. C. (1974). Still the century of corporatism? In F. B. Pike & T. Stritch (Eds.), *The new corporatism: Social political structures in the Iberian world* (pp. 85–131). Notre Dame, IN: University of Notre Dame Press.

Scott, J. W. (1989). Multiculturalism and the politics of identity. In M. R. Malson, J. F. O' Barr, S. Westphal-Uhl, & M. Wyers (Eds.), *Feminist theory in practice and process*. Chicago: University of Chicago Press.

Shor, I. (1986). *Culture wars: School and society in the conservative restoration, 1969–1984*. Boston: Routledge and Kegan Paul.

Shor, I. (1987a). *Critical teaching and everyday life*. Chicago: University of Chicago Press.

Shor, I. (Ed.). (1987b). *Freire for the classroom: A sourcebook for liberatory teaching*. Portsmouth, NH: Boynton/Cook.

Shor, I. (1992). *Empowering education*. Chicago: University of Chicago Press.

Shor, I., & Freire, P. (1987). *A pedagogy for liberation: Dialogues on transforming education*. South Hadley, MA: Bergin & Garvey.

Smelser, N. (1994, Spring). Contested boundaries and shifting solidarities. *International Sociological Association (ISA) Bulletin, 60*(5), 1–2.

Smith, S. B. (1989). *Hegel's critique of liberalism*. Chicago: University of Chicago Press.

Solorzano, D. G., & Villalpando, O. (1998). Critical race theory, marginality and the experience of students of color in higher education. In C. A. Torres & T. Mitchell (Eds.), *Sociology of education: Comparative perspectives* (pp. 211–224). Albany: State University of New York Press.

Sombart, W. (1939). Weltanschauung, science and economics. *The Examiner, 2*(3), 224–240.

Sonntag, H. R., & Valecillos, O. (1977). *El estado en el capitalismo contemporáneo*. Mexico City: Siglo XXI Editores.

Spivak, G. (1988). Can the subaltern speak? In C. Nelson & L. Grossberg (Eds.), *Marxism and the interpretation of culture* (pp. 271–313). Urbana: University of Illinois Press.

Sunkel, O., & Paz, P. (1979). *El subdesarrallo Latinoamericano y la teoría del desarrollo*. Mexico: Siglo XXI.

Teitelbaum, K. (1993). *Schooling for good rebels*. Philadelphia: Temple University Press.

Therborn, G. (1980). *The ideology of power and the power of ideology*. London: Verso.

Thurow, L. C. (1992). *Head to head: The coming economic battle among Japan, Europe, and America*. New York: William Morrow.

Thurow, L. C. (1999). *Building wealth*. New York: HarperCollins.

Torres, C. A. (1976a, April-June). A dialetica Hegeliana e o pensamento Logico-estrutural de Paulo Freire: Notas para uma analise e confrontação dos pressupostos filosoficos vigentes na dialética da pedagogia dos oprimidos a do pensamento freireano em geral. *Sintese, 3*(7), 61–78.

Torres, C. A. (1976b, September-December). Servidumbre, autoconciencia, liberation: La solución dialectica Hegeliana y la filosofía de la alfabetización problematizadora de Paulo Freire. Notas provisorias para su confrontación. *Franciscanum, 18*(54), 405–478.

Torres, C. A. (Ed.). (1978a). *Entrevistas con Paulo Freire*. Mexico: Editorial Gernika.

Torres, C. A. (Ed.). (1978b). *La praxis educativa de Paulo Freire*. Mexico: Editorial Gernika.

Torres, C. A. (1979). *Consciencia e historia: A praxis educativa de Paulo Freire*. São Paulo, Brazil: Editoes Loyola.

Torres, C. A. (1980a). *Paulo Freire: Educación y concientización*. Salamanca, Spain: Ediciones Sígueme.

Torres, C. A. (Ed.). (1980b). *Paulo Freire en América Latina*. Mexico: Editorial Gernika.

Torres, C. A. (1981). *Leitura critica de Paulo Freire*. São Paulo, Brazil: Edicões Loyola.

Torres, C. A. (1985). State and education: Marxist theories. In T. Husen & T. N. Postlethwaite (Eds.), *International encyclopedia of education: Research and studies* (Vol. 8, pp. 4793–4798). Oxford, UK: Pergamon.

Torres, C. A. (1989a). Education under fire: Nicaragua 1979–1984 [Review of Robert Arnove's "Education and Revolution in Nicaragua"]. *Compare*, *19*(2), 127–135.

Torres, C. A. (1989b). Political culture and state bureaucracy in Mexico: The case of adult education. *International Journal of Educational Development*, *9*(1), 53–68.

Torres, C. A. (1990a). Adult education, popular education: Implications for a radical approach to comparative education. *International Journal of Lifelong Education*, *9*(4), 271–287.

Torres, C. A. (1990b). *The politics of nonformal education in Latin America*. New York: Praeger.

Torres, C. A. (1991a, April). *Educational policy and social change in Brazil: The work of Paulo Freire as secretary of education in the municipality of São Paulo*. Paper presented at the annual meeting of the American Educational Research Association, Chicago.

Torres, C. A. (1991b). *Report of the universitywide task force on faculty rewards*. Prepared for the Office of the President, University of California, Oakland, California.

Torres, C. A. (1991c). The state, nonformal education, and socialism in Cuba, Nicaragua, and Grenada. *Comparative Education Review*, *35*(1), 110–130.

Torres, C. A. (1992a). *The church, society and hegemony: A critical sociology of religion in Latin America* (R. A. Young, Trans.). Westport, CT: Praeger.

Torres, C. A. (1992b). From the "Pedagogy of the oppressed" to "A luta continua": The political pedagogy of Paulo Freire. In P. McLaren & P. Leonard (Eds.), *Paulo Freire: A critical encounter* (pp. 119–145). London: Routledge.

Torres, C. A. (1992c). Participatory action research and popular education in Latin America. *International Journal of Qualitative Studies in Education*, *5*(1), 51–62.

Torres, C. A. (1994a). Education and the archeology of consciousness: Hegel and Freire. *Educational Theory*, *44*(4), 429–445.

Torres, C. A. (1994b). Intellectuals and university life: Paulo Freire on higher education. In G. Guevara Niebla, A. L. Fernandez, & M. Escobar (Eds.), *Paulo Freire at the National University in Mexico. A dialogue* (pp. 1–27). Albany: State University of New York Press.

Torres, C. A. (1994c). Paulo Freire as secretary of education in the municipality of São Paulo. *Comparative Education Review, 38*(2), 181–224.

Torres, C. A. (1995a). *Estudios Freireanos.* Buenos Aires, Argentina: Ediciones del Quirquincho.

Torres, C. A. (1995b). Fictional dialogues on teachers, politics, and power in Latin America. In M. Ginsburg (Ed.), *The politics of teachers' work and lives* (pp. 133–168). New York: Garland.

Torres, C. A. (1995c). State and education revisited: Why educational researchers should think politically about education. *Review of Research in Education, 21,* 255–331.

Torres, C. A. (1996). Adult education and instrumental rationality: A critique. *International Journal of Educational Development, 16*(2), 195–206.

Torres, C. A. (1998a). *Democracy, education and multiculturalism: Dilemmas of citizenship in a global world.* Lanham, MD: Rowman & Littlefield.

Torres, C. A. (1998b). The political pedagogy of Paulo Freire. In P. Freire, *Politics and education* (pp. 1–15). Los Angeles: Latin American Center, University of California.

Torres, C. A. (1998c). *Sociology of literacy training in Mexico: Adult education and popular urban sectors in Mexico.* Unpublished manuscript.

Torres, C. A. (1999). Structural adjustment, teachers, and state practices in education: A focus on Latin America. In T. J. Popkewitz & A. Kazamias (Eds.), *Educational change and educational knowledge: Changing relationships between the state, civil society, and the educational community* (pp. 87–115). Albany: State University of New York Press.

Torres, C. A. (Ed.). (2000a). *La educación en América Latina* [Education in Latin America]. Buenos Aires, Argentina: Consejo Latino Americano de Ciencias Sociales.

Torres, C. A. (2000b). Education, social class, and dual citizenship: The travails of multiculturalism in Latin America. In C. A. Grant & J. L. Lei (Eds.), *Global constructions of multicultural education: Theories and realities* (pp. 337–354). Mahwah, NJ: Lawrence Erlbaum.

Torres, C. A. (2000c, May 24–26). Education in Latin America and the Caribbean: Citizenship, democracy, and multiculturalism. Paper presented at the joint international conference center for Bedouin studies and development, Ben-Gurion University of the Negev and Center for Comparative Education, University of California at Los Angeles. In the Framework of the BGU-UCLA Program of Academic Cooperation. The future of Indigenous peoples: Strategies for survival and development.

Torres, C. A. (2003). Education, power, and the state: Successes and failures of Latin American education in the twentieth century. In C. A. Torres & A.

Antikainen (Eds.), *The international handbook on the sociology of education: An international assessment of new research and theory* (pp. 256–284). Lanham, MD: Rowman & Littlefield.

Torres, C. A. (2004a, Spring). Educació, sindicats de mestres I estat: Les tesis de Lisboa. *Quaderns d' Educació Contínua, 10*, 177–184.

Torres, C. A. (2004b). *Poesía perdida al atardecer.*valencia, Spain: Set I Mid, Germania.

Torres, C. A. (2005a). *Cuentos de amor, de locura y de muerte.* Valencia, Spain: Deges, Colección Cantábrica.

Torres, C. A. (2005b). *O manuscrito de Sir Charles.* Lisbon, Portugal: Don Quixote.

Torres, C. A. (2005c). *La praxis educativa y la educación cultural liberadora de Paulo Freire.* Xátiva, Valencia, Spain: Institute Paulo Freire D'Espanya.

Torres, C. A. (2006). *Educación y neoliberalismo: Ensayos de oposición.* Madrid, Spain: Ediciones Popular.

Torres, C. A. (2007). The distorted worlds of Ivan Illich and Paulo Freire. In C. A. Torres & A. Teodoro (Eds.), *Critique and Utopia: New developments in the sociology of education.* Lanham, MD: Rowman & Littlefield.

Torres, C. A., & Antikainen, A. (Eds.). (2003). *The international handbook on the sociology of education: An international assessment of new research and theory.* Lanham, MD: Rowman & Littlefield.

Torres, C. A., & Boron, A. A. (1996). The impact of neoliberal restructuring on education and poverty in Latin America. *Alberta Journal of Educational Research, 42*(2), 102–114.

Torres, C. A., & Freire, P. (1994). Twenty years after "Pedagogy of the oppressed": Paulo Freire in conversation with Carlos Alberto Torres. In P. McLaren & C. Lankshear (Eds.), *The politics of liberation: Paths from Freire* (pp. 100–117). London: Routledge.

Torres, C. A., & Mitchell. T. R. (Eds.). (1998). *Sociology of education: Emerging perspectives.* Albany: State University of New York Press.

Torres, C. A., & Morrow, R. A. (2002a). Gramsci and popular education in Latin America: From revolution to democratic transition. In C. Borg, J. Buttigieg, & P. Mayo (Eds.), *Gramsci and education* (pp. 179–200). Lanham, MD: Rowman & Littlefield.

Torres, C. A., & Morrow, R. (2002b). Theory and methods of Paulo Freire: A discussion of forms and content of emancipatory learning and revolutionary pedagogy and its reception in the United States. In F. Telleri (Ed.), *Il metodo Paulo Freire: Nuove tecnologie e sviluppo sostenibile* (pp. 57–70). Bologna, Italy: Coperative Libraria Universitaria Editrice Bologna.

Torres, C. A., Pannu, R. S., & Kazim Bacchus, M. (1993). Capital accumulation, political legitimation and educational expansion. In J. Dronkers (Ed.), *Education and social change* (pp. 3–32). Greenwich, CT: JAI Press.

Torres, C. A., & Puiggrós, A. (Eds.). (1995). Education in Latin America [Special issue]. *Comparative Education Review, 39*(1).

Torres, C. A., & Puiggrós, A. (Eds.). (1996). *Education in Latin America: Comparative perspectives*. Boulder, CO: Westview Press.

Torres, C. A., & Schugurensky, D. (1993). A comparison of the political economy of adult education in Canada, Mexico, and Tanzania. *Canadian Journal for the Study of Adult Education/Revue Canadienne pour l'étude de l'éducation des adultes, 7*(1), 51–70.

Torres, C. A., & Schugurensky, D. (1994). The politics of adult education in comparative perspective: Models, rationalities, and adult education policy implementation in Canada, Mexico, and Tanzania. *Comparative Education 30*(2), 131–152.

Torres, C. A., & Schugurensky, D. (1995). Therapeutic model of adult education in Canada: Skills and academic upgrading programs in the province of Alberta. *International Journal of Lifelong Education, 14*(2), 144–161.

Torres, C. A., et al. (2001). Prefacio. In P. Freire, *Educación y Actualidad Brasileña* (pp. ix–xii). Mexico: Siglo XXI.

Torres, C. A., et al. (n.d.). *Comparative adult education in Canada, Tanzania and Mexico: Final report*. Edmonton, Canada: University of Alberta. [mimeographed]

Torres Santome, J. (1992). *El curriculum oculto*. Madrid, Spain: Morata.

Touraine, A. (1981). *The voice and the eye: An analysis of social movements* (A. Duff, Ed.). Cambridge: Cambridge University Press.

United Nations Development Program (UNDP). (n.d.a). *Desarrollo humano y gobernabilidad*. UNDP Project, RLA/92/030/1/01/31. Montevideo. [mimeographed]

United Nations Development Program (UNDP). (n.d.b). *Mitigación de la pobreza y desarrollo social*. UNDP Project, RLA/92/009/1/01/31. Montevideo. [mimeographed]

United Nations Educational, Scientific and Cultural Organization. (1971, December 6–15). *Conferencia de ministros de educación y ministros encargados de ciencia y tecnología en relación con el desarrollo de América Latina y el Caribe: Venezuela*. Caracas, Venezuela: Author. [mimeographed]

United Nations Educational, Scientific and Cultural Organization. (1974). *Evolución reciente de la educación en América Latina*. Santiago de Chile: Author. [mimeographed]

United Nations Educational, Scientific and Cultural Organization. (1988). *Anuario estadístico*. Paris: Author.

United Nations Educational, Scientific and Cultural Organization/CEPAL. (1981). *Desarrollo y educación en Latina: Síntesis general* (4 vols). Buenos Aires, Argentina: Proyecto Desarrollo de la Educación en América Latina y el Caribe.

Uricoechea, F. (1980). *The patrimonial foundations of the Brazilian bureaucratic state*. Berkeley: University of California Press.

Urry, J. (2000). Sociology of time and space. In B. Turner (Ed.), *The Blackwell companion to social theory* (2nd ed., pp. 3–15). Oxford, MA: Blackwell.

Vilches, L. (1987). *Teoría de la imágen periodística*. Barcelona, Spain: Paidós.

Vincent, A. (1987). *Theories of the state.* Oxford, UK: Blackwell.

Vogeler, I., & de Souza, A. (1980). *Dialectics of Third World development.* Montclair, NJ: Allanheld, Osmun.

Wagner, D. (1989). Literacy campaigns: Past, present, and future. *Comparative Education Review, 33*(2), 256–260.

Wallerstein, I. (1987). *The capitalist world economy.* London: Cambridge University Press.

Wallerstein, I. (1997). Social science and the quest for a just society. *American Journal of Sociology, 102*(5), 1241–1257.

Wanderley, L. E. W. (1984). *Educar pra transformar: Educação popular, igreja Católica e política no movimento de educação de base.* Petropolis, Brazil: R.T., Vozes.

Weinberg, G. (1984). *Modelos educativos en la historia de América Latina.* Buenos Aires, Argentina: Kapelusz.

Weiner, L. (1998). Schooling to work. In S. Aronowitz & J. Cutler (Eds.), *Post-work: The wages of cybernation* (pp. 185–201). New York: Routledge.

Welton, M. (1990). *Shaking the foundations: Critical perspectives on adult development and learning.* Unpublished manuscript, Delhausie University, Halifax, Canada.

West, C. (1993). *Prophetic thought in postmodern times.* Monroe, ME: Common Courage Press.

West, C. (1993). The new cultural politics of difference. In C. McCarthy & W. Crichlow (Eds.), *Race, identity and representation in education* (pp. 11–23). New York: Routledge. Reprinted in Darder, A., & Torres, R. D. (Eds.). (1998). *The Latino studies reader: Culture, economy and society* (pp. 180–189). Oxford: Blackwell.

West, C., de Alba, K., & Sheris, E. (1996, April). Colloquy: Our next race question: The uneasiness between Blacks and Latinos. *Harper's, 292*(4), 55–63.

Wilensky, H. L. (1975). *The welfare state and equality: Structural and ideological roots of public expenditures.* Berkeley: University of California Press.

Wilensky, H. L. (1976). *The new corporatism: Centralization and the welfare state.* Beverly Hills, CA: Sage.

Williams, R. (1961). *The long revolution.* London: Chatto & Windus.

Williams, R. (1977). *Marxism and literature.* New York: Oxford University Press.

Wittgenstein, L. (1963). *Philosophical investigations.* Oxford, UK: Blackwell.

Wong, T. H. (2002). *Hegemonies compared.* New York: Routledge.

World Development Report: The challenge of development. (1991). Oxford, UK: World Bank and Oxford University Press.

Young, R. (2003). *Postcolonialism.* New York: Oxford University Press.

Index

Adorno, Theodor W., 37, 46
Adult education. *See also* Education
  in Africa, 161–169
  citizenship education, 6, 18–19
  critical pedagogy and, 160–161
  forced modernization model (Tanzania),
    7–8, 15
  instrumental rationality in, 45–48
  literacy training and, 7–8, 63, 171
  policy concerning, 6–7, 47
  recruitment model (Mexico), 7–8, 15
  state and, 73
  technical guiding-knowledge interest
    and, 45–48
  therapeutical model (Canada), 7–8, 15
Affirmative action, 101–102, 104, 113 n. 5
Africa
  adult education in, 161–169
  Cape Verde, 162
  de-Africanization process and, 162–163
  Paulo Freire and, 152, 161–169
  Guinea-Bissau, 162–169
  lack of industrialization in, 163–164
  mass literacy campaign in, 167–168
  São Tomé e Principe, 162, 164, 166–167
  school enrollment in, 162
  Tanzania, 7–8, 15, 45, 162, 165, 166
African Americans
  affirmative action and, 102
  school segregation and, 94, 96
Agency, 3–4
Aguilar, M., 12–13, 82
Algeria, democratic elections and, 107
Alliance for Progress program, 74
Altbach, P. G., 162
Althusser, Louis, 42, 54–55, 100, 155
Antiauthoritarian thought, 160
Antiglobalization movement, 128
Antikainen, A., 10
Anzaldúa, Gloria, 92
Apple, Michael W., ix–xi, xiii, xv, xvii, 12,
  51, 85 n. 8, 100, 132

Araujo, Ana Maria, 170
Archeology of consciousness, 131–150
  critical pedagogies and, 131–134
  dialectic of master and slave (Hegel),
    134–140, 147–148
  dialectic of pedagogy of the oppressed
    (Freire), 140–144
  Freire on definition of, 142–143
  interdialectic comparison (Hegel &
    Freire), 144–150
  struggle of opposed consciousness in, 35,
    133, 136–137
Arnove, R., 6, 9–10, 44, 166
Aronowitz, S., 178
Aspen Institute, 67
Ataide, Tristan de, 153
Au, W., xiii
Aufhebung (Hegel), 58, 133–134, 150 n. 3
Authoritarianism
  antiauthoritarian thought, 160
  bureaucratic-authoritarian state, 65–66
  in Latin America, 9, 65–66, 67, 71, 78–79
  nature of, 12
Avalos, B., 68
Awareness process (Mannheim), 153

Bakhtin, M. M., xviii
Barnet, R., 119, 129 n. 3
Bean, W., 157
Beane, J. A., xvii
Bell, Daniel, 48
Bell, Derrick, 94
Benjamin, Walter, 37
Bernetti, J. L., 78
Bernstein, Edward, 53
Bernstein, R., 47
Betto, Frei, 171
Bhabha, H., xii
Bitar, S., 66
Block, F., 9
Boli, J., 84 n. 1, 123
Borderless World, The (Ohmae), 120–121

Borders in education, 14, 83–84
Boron, A. A., 20, 64
Bourdieu, P., xi, xviii
Bowles, Samuel, 37, 42, 54, 98, 127
Brazil, Freire in, 170–172
Brown, C., 15
Brown, D. D., 33, 38–39
Brown v. Board of Education, 94, 96
Buras, K. L., xiii
Burawoy, M., xvi–xvii
Burbules, Nicholas, 129
Bureaucratic-authoritarian state, 65–66
Burris, A. M., 65, 71, 164
Bush, George W., 128
Butler, J., 24

Cabral, Amilcar, 163, 166, 177 n. 9
Calderon, Felipe, 30 n. 6
California
    "Californization of taste," 119
    output of, 129 n. 2
Canada
    federal government versus provincial
        states, 129 n. 2
    technocratic focus of education policy
        makers, 45
    therapeutical model of education, 7–8,
        15
Cape Verde, 162
Capital accumulation, 71
Capitalism, 5, 14, 39
    democracy and, 98, 108–109, 127–128
    division of labor in, 72
    globalization of, 125–126
    history of, 180
    markets and, 180
    Westernization and, 116–117
Cardoso, Fernando H., 71, 156
Carnoy, M., 3, 37, 44, 65, 69, 71, 164, 166
Castells, Michael, 30–31 n. 11, 179
Castro, Fidel, 155–156
Catholic thought, 155–156, 164
Cavanagh, J., 119, 129 n. 3
Ceccon, C., 161
CEPAL, 74–75
Cerroni, Humberto, 97
Chicana feminism, 92
Chilcote, R. H., 156
Christianity
    Catholic thought, 155–156, 164
    as *weltanshauung*, 61–62 n. 2
Christophersen, J. A., 51–52
Ciseski, A. A., 15, 17, 152

Citizens
    as disciplined pedagogical subjects, 64
    markets and, 117–121
Citizenship
    civic virtues and, 18, 103
    civil rights and, 89, 94, 95, 101
    dilemmas of, 87–88
    economic, 101–102
    education and, 6, 18–19, 88–97
    formation of, 109–110
    globalization and, 117–121, 125, 128
    legal status and, 103
    limits of, 121–126
    postnational, 122–123
Citizenship education, 6, 18–19
Citizenship theories, 86–97
    critical race theory, 94–95
    Enlightenment as basis of, 89–90, 126–127
    feminism, 11, 90–92
    "good citizen" and, 88–89
    new social movements, 51, 95–97
    postcolonialism, 92–94
Civic knowledge, 18
Civic skills, 18
Civic virtues, 18, 103
Civil rights, citizenship and, 89, 94, 95, 101
Class-consciousness, 51, 145
Clinton, Bill, 30 n. 7
Clinton, DeWitt, 109
Collier, D., 64, 70
Collier, R. B., 64, 70
Colonialism, 92–93, 112 n. 2
Communicative action, Habermasian vision
    of, xvii
Comparative Education Review, 10–11
Compensatory legitimation, 9
Compulsory education, 123
CONADEP, 176 n. 4
Condillac, 51
Conditioned states, 13, 71–72, 82–83
Connell, Robert W., 30 n. 4, 85 n. 6
Conscientization approach, 13, 97, 142, 143,
    144, 146, 157
Consciousness. *See also* Archeology of
    consciousness; Self-consciousness
    ideology as false, 53, 55–56
    levels of, 143
    philosophizing, 35–36
    struggle of opposed, 35, 133, 136–137
Constructivist perspective, 58–59, 100,
    106–107
Coombs, Philip, 74
Coraggio, L., 75

Corbisier, Roland, 175 n. 1
Corporatism, 70–73
Correspondence principle, 3–4
Cosmopolitan democracies, 125
Counterhegemonic perspective, xiii
Counts, G., ix
Crisis of hegemony, 12, 81–82, 154
Crisis of schooling, in Latin America, 5,
    74–75, 76–80
Critical consciousness process (Freire),
    15–16, 153, 157, 158–161, 173
Critical feminist perspective, 92
Critical imagination, 39
Critical pedagogy. *See also* Freire, Paulo
    adult education and, 160–161
    archeology of consciousness and, 131–134
    Hegelism and, 133–140
    subjectivity and power in, 131
Critical race theory, 94–95
Critical sociology, xvi–xvii, 46–47
    connections of movements in, xviii–xix
    educational studies in, x
    Paulo Freire and, xiii–xv
    key questions in, xvi
    tasks of critical analysis in education,
        xvii–xviii
Critical theory, 33–40. *See also* Political
    sociology of education
    agonic perspective in knowledge
        production, 59
    boundaries between competing
        disciplines, 39
    constructivism and, 58–59
    "critical" in, 38–40
    critique of education and, 40–41, 59–61
    defined, 34
    determinate negation in, 34–35, 148–149
    dialectics of policy formation, 41–43
    instrumental rationality and. *See*
        Instrumental rationality
    modernism and, 97, 117
    multicentered notions of power, 50–51
    as negative philosophy, 34–37
    neo-Marxism and, 33, 37–38, 54
    persuasion and, 57–58
    politicity of education (Freire) and, 48–50,
        182
    relevance for education, 33
Critical-transitive consciousness, 143
Cultural capital, xi–xii
Cultural diversity, 103
Cultural liberalism, pedagogical subject
    and, 12–13, 73–80

Cultural politics of education, x
Culture
    in Hegelism, 139–140
    hybridization of cultures, 111
    in neo-Marxism, 37
    organic crisis of education in Latin
        America, 76–80
    of street children, 75–76, 79–80

Darling-Hammond, L., 22
Darnton, R., xi
Davis, M., xvi
De-Africanization process, 162–163
de Alba, K., 100, 102
Decentralization, 25, 51
Deconstructionism, 106–107
De Kadt, E., 155
De Landa, M., 181
Demo, Pedro, 178–186
Democracy, xvi
    capitalism and, 98, 108–109, 127–128
    challenges and tensions of, 108
    citizenship and, 96
    as content, 97–98, 108
    defined, 97
    education and, 97–98, 103–104
    Latin American progress toward, 68
    liberalism and, 118–119, 120
    as method, 97–98, 108
    multiculturalism and, 99–112
    patriarchal foundations of, 91
    social pact as basis of, 102–103
    survival of, 112
    theories of, 88
Democracy, Education, and Multiculturalism
    (Torres), 19
Democratization process, 13
Dependent state
    in comparative perspective, 80–84
    concept of, 11
    dependent development and, 29 n. 1,
        70–73, 80–81
    hybrid cultures and, 80–81
    nature of, 2, 8–14
    state corporatism and, 70–73
    Theory of Dependence and, 156
Depoliticization, 47–48
Dérrida, Jacques, 11, 81, 84–85 n. 4
Desire, in Hegelism, 134, 135
de Souza, A., 156
Determinate negation
    logic of, 34–35
    positivity of, 35, 148–149

Dewey, John, 15–17, 33, 149, 172
De Witt, J., 156
De Zan, Julio, 148
Dialectics
  in dialectical-historical philosophy, 35
  interdialectic comparison with (Hegel &
    Freire), 144–150
  between liberation and imbecilization,
    182
  of master and slave (Hegel), 134–140,
    147–148
  of pedagogy of the oppressed (Freire),
    140–144
  of policy formation, 41–43
Dialogue, functions of, 12
DiFazio, W., 117
Diférénce, concept of (Dérrida), 11, 14, 81
Dimitriadis, G., xii
Diversity, plurality and, 100
Dominance, xii
Dominant ideology, 55, 62 n. 3
Dominice, P., 169
Dominion, in Hegelism, 137–138
Dos Santos, Theotonio, 156

ECLA, 67, 75
Economic citizenship, 101–102
Economic Commission of Latin America
  (ECLA), 67, 75
Economy
  economic determination in Africa, 165
  economic issues in education, 14, 21, 69,
    70, 74, 79, 83
  economic stabilization in Latin America,
    67–68
  relationship with politics and education,
    1, 9–10
Education
  as act of knowing, 142
  adult. See Adult education
  for all children, 10, 123
  "children at risk," 128
  citizenship and, 6, 18–19, 88–97
  compulsory, 123
  crisis of, 5, 74–75, 76–80
  critical theory critique of, 40–41, 59–61
  democracy and, 97–98, 103–104
  fractures in, 14, 83–84
  globalization and, 126–129
  political sociology of. See Political
    sociology of education
  private, 25, 26, 79–80
  problems of Latin American, 11

public. See Public education in Latin
  America
  standard criticism of, 5–6
  tasks of critical analysis in, xvii–xviii
Educational policy
  dialectics of policy formation, 41–43
  ideology and, 51–56
  political sociology of education and, 2–8,
    41–43
  politicity of education (Freire) and, 48–50,
    182
  state and, 43–44
Education, The Practice of Freedom (Freire),
  152, 153, 155
Education for Critical Consciousness (Freire),
  15–16
Ego, in Hegelism, 135, 136
Elementary education
  for all children, 10, 123
  enrollment growth in Latin America,
    68–69
Eliot, T. S., 101, 147
Emancipation Proclamation, 94
Emancipatory guiding-knowledge interest,
  46, 48
Emotional discourse, Freire and, 147
End of the Nation State, The (Ohmae), 117–
  118, 121
Engels, F., 53
Enlightenment, xi
  citizenship theory and, 89–90, 126–127
  moving beyond constraints of, 149
Entfremdung, 139–140
Entwistle, H., 50
Epistemological approaches, 5
Equality of education, 10
Escola Nova movement, 15
Essentialism, x
Essentialization of cultural struggles, 111
Evans, P., 71
Existentialism, 100
Extensionism
  concept of, 11–12
  in Latin America, 81
Eyerman, R., 96
Ezeuna, A. M., 75

Faletto, Enzo, 71, 156
Fanon, Frantz, 16, 93, 163
Faúndez, Antonio, 143, 159, 169, 171, 177
  n. 9
Faure, Edgar, 74
Fear, in Hegelism, 138–139

Feinberg, Walter, 101, 102, 113 n. 5
Female teachers, 23–25, 81
Feminism, 11, 90–92
Ferreira da Silva, Vicenta, 175 n. 1
Fiori, Ernani Maria, 144–145
First Sectorial Education Investment Project
  (Ministerio de Cultura y Educación/
  Provincia de Buenos Aires/Banco
  Interamericano de Reconstrucción y
  Fomento)., 79
Forced modernization model of education
  (Tanzania), 7–8, 15
Foundational canons, 105
Fox, J., 124–125
Fractures in education, 14, 83–84
Frankfurt School, 33, 34, 37, 54, 181
Franz, S., 9–10
Fraser, N., xviii, 91
Freire, A. M. A., 15, 17, 152
Freire, Elza, 170
Freire, Paulo, 1, 2, 31 n. 12, 33, 45, 59, 81, 97,
  102, 109, 112, 121, 131–133, 140–150, 151
  n. 7, 152, 153–172, 175 n. 1, 175 n. 2, 176
  n. 6, 177 n. 9, 179, 182, 183
  African background and, 152, 161–169
  archeology of consciousness and, 142–143
  Catholic thought and, 155–156
  critical consciousness process and, 15–16,
    153, 157, 158–161, 173
  critical sociology and, xiii–xv
  dialectic of pedagogy of the oppressed,
    140–144
  interdialectic comparison with Hegel,
    144–150
  issues regarding political-pedagogical
    praxis, 172–175
  Latin American background and, 152–
    157, 170–172
  literacy as cultural politics and, 171
  pedagogy of consciousness, 159–160
  pedagogy of the question, 143
  political philosophy of education, 11–18,
    133, 157–161
  politicity of education and, 48–50, 182
  premises of, 174
  reception in the U.S., 131–132
  as Secretary of Education in Brazil, 170–
    171
  at the World Council of Churches, 157
Frieden, J. A., 29 n. 1, 71
Fromm, Erich, 16, 37, 133
Functionalist structuralism, 3–4
Fundamentalist education, 6

Gadotti, Moacir, 3, 15, 17, 75–76, 131–132,
  152, 171, 175 n. 2
Gajardo, M., 151 n. 7
Garcia, Charly, 76
Garcia, H. P., 96
García Canclini, Néstor, 11, 80–81
Gasche, R., 84–85 n. 4
Gender
  female teachers, 23–25, 81
  feminism and, 11, 90–92
  hegemonic masculinity, 81
German Ideology, The (Marx & Engels), 53
Giddens, A., 30–31 n. 11, 42, 43, 51, 61 n. 1
Gintis, Herbert, 37, 42, 54, 98, 127
Giroux, H., 11, 81, 132, 172
Gitlin, Todd, 101, 103, 105, 127
Globalization, xi–xiii, 19, 114–131
  antiglobalization movement, 128
  blurring of national boundaries in, 115–
    116, 126
  of capitalism, 125–126
  citizenship and, 117–121, 125, 128
  comparative studies of education and,
    25–28
  critique of, 180–181
  defined, 30–31 n. 11, 75, 84 n. 3, 112–113
    n. 4, 115
  development of, 112–113 n. 4
  education and, 126–129
  fluidity of global economy, 70
  heterogeneity of production in, 75–76
  human rights and, 117, 121–126, 127
  implications for multiculturalism, 103–
    104
  markets and, 117–126
  phenomenon of, 115–117
  postmodernism and, 116–121, 125
  sovereignty and, 117, 124–125
  street children and, 75–76, 79–80
Goldsmith, E., 129 n. 3
Gordillo, Elba Esther, 23
Gordon, L., 90
Goulart, Joao, 175 n. 1, 175 n. 2
Goulet, Denis, 166
Gramsci, Antonio, xviii, 33, 36–37, 50, 54, 57,
  59, 61–62 n. 2, 76, 150, 153, 155, 170, 182
Guevara, "Che," 155–156
Guimarães, Sérgio, 171
Guinea-Bissau, 162–169
Gunder-Frank, Andre, 156

Habermas, Jürgen, xvii, 29–30 n. 3, 33, 37,
  43–46, 48, 57, 59, 87, 149, 172

Harasim, Linda M., 167–170
Harding, S., 49
Hartung, A., 152
Hegel, G. W. F., 16, 34–36, 53, 133–150, 150
    n. 3, 150 n. 4
Hegelism
    Aufhebung, 58, 133–134, 150 n. 3
    cultural formation in, 139–140
    dialectic of master and slave, 134–140,
        147–148
    dominion in, 137–138
    ego and desire in, 134, 135, 136
    Entfremdung, 139–140
    fear in, 138–139
    interdialectic comparison with Freire,
        144–150
    life and, 134–135
    recognition of self-consciousness in,
        135–136
    self-consciousness in itself and, 134
    struggle of opposed consciousness in,
        133, 136–137
Hegemony, xiii
    crisis of, 12, 81–82, 154
    defined, 54
    masculinity and, 81
    nature of, 12, 54
    postrevolutionary state in Latin America
        and, 73
Heidegger, M., 175 n. 1
Held, David, 30–31 n. 11, 75, 84 n. 3, 97,
    112–113 n. 4, 115, 125–126
Hermeneutical analysis, 37
Heuristic knowledge, 48
Higher Institute of Brazilian Studies (ISEB),
    175 n. 1
Horkheimer, Max, 37, 46
Human capital formation, 6
Human capital theories, 68
Human rights, 27–28
    markets versus, 121–126
    national sovereignty versus, 124–125
    paradoxes of, 126–128
Hybridization of cultures, 111

Ianni, O., 175–176 n. 3
Identity
    construction of, 100
    formation of, 109–110
    multiculturalism and, 99
    national, 100, 106
    sense of, 87

Ideology
    defined, 52
    dominant, 55, 62 n. 3
    educational policy and, 51–56
    as false consciousness, 53, 55–56
    scientific knowledge versus, 52
    in social reproduction process, 55
    in structural Marxism, 54–55
    as system of thought, 55
    as Weltanshauung, 51–52, 61–62 n. 2,
        174
    as worldview, 54
Illich, I., 157
Imperialism, 92–93
Instituto Interregional de las Naciones
    Unidas para las Investigaciones sobre la
    Delincuencia y la Justicia, 80
Instrumental rationality, 44–48
    in adult education programs, 45–48
    as central to critical theory, 129–130 n. 5
    defined, 44
    instrumental action and (Habermas),
        44–45
    paradoxes of human rights and, 126–127
Inter-American Dialogue, 67
Internationalization, x
International Monetary Fund (IMF), 14, 21,
    66, 83

Jacoby, R., xviii
Jaguaribe, Helio, 175 n. 1
Jamison, A., 96
Jaspers, K., 175 n. 1
Jefferson, Thomas, 98
Johnston, A., 65, 71, 164
Jules, D., xiii

Das Kapital (Marx), 34
Kautsky, Karl, 53
Kazim Bacchus, M., 6
Kellner, Douglas, 35, 39, 116
Kelly, G. P., 162
Kennedy, W. B., 157
Knowledge
    acquisition, 6
    agonic perspective in production of, 59
    types of, 59
Korch, Karl, 54
Korsgaard, O., 115
Kosic, Karl, 33
Kubler, B., 79
Kvale, K., 51–52

Lacan, Jacques, 84–85 n. 4
Laclau, Ernesto, 30 n. 5, 38, 85 n. 7, 96
Ladson-Billings, Gloria, 94, 95, 110
Lankshear, C., 131, 132, 151 n. 7
Latin America, 63–84
    authoritarianism in, 9, 65–66, 67, 71, 78–79
    in background of Paulo Freire, 152–157,
        170–172
    educational spending in, 69, 74
    education crisis of the 1960s, 5, 74–75,
        76–80
    evolution of state in, 9, 64–67, 70–73
    Freire and, 152–157, 170–172
    models of popular education in, 17,
        78–84
    school enrollment in, 68–69, 74
    sociopolitical background of, 67–68,
        152–157
    state in, 64–67
Lechner, N., 96
Lengermann, P. M., 46
Lenin, V. I., 34, 92
Leonard, P., 132, 151 n. 7
Levin, H., 47
Lewis, D. L., xiii
Liberalism. See also Neoliberalism
    cultural, 12–13, 73–80
    democracy and, 118–119, 120
    liberal state and, 64
    required conditions for, 118–119
Liberation movements
    liberating pedagogical theory, 143
    postcolonialism and, 93
Life, in Hegelism, 134–135
Linguistic capital, xi–xii
Literacy, x–xi
    adult education and, 7, 63, 171
    in Africa, 167–168
    as cultural politics, 171
    generative word and, 15
Lives on the Boundary (Rose), 59–61
Livingston, G., xiii
Locke, John, 51, 98
Lockheed, M. E., 68
Logocentrism, 12, 81
Lomnitz, L., 22, 66
Lukacs, George, 33, 54
Luke, A., 30–31 n. 11
Luke, C., 30–31 n. 11

Macedo, Donaldo, 132, 142, 166, 169, 171
MacPherson, C. B., 19

Madison, James, 98
Magrath, C. Peter, 43
Manfio, A. J., 75–76
Mannheim, Karl, xviii, 37, 149–150, 152, 153,
    175 n. 1
Mao Zidong, 57
Marcel, Gabriel, 158
Marcuse, Herbert, 34–37, 48, 59, 129–130 n.
    5, 148, 150 n. 3
Markets
    capitalism and, 180
    citizens and, 117–121
    globalization and, 97, 117–126
    human rights versus, 121–126
    regional economic markets, 66–67, 70
Marshall, T. H., 19, 89–90, 92, 94
Martín-Barbero, J., 12, 81–82
Marx, Karl, 34–38, 53, 61 n. 1, 150, 151 n. 6
Marxism
    Freire and, 156–157, 173–174
    Second International, 53–54
    structural, 54–55
    vulgar, 53–54
Mayo, P., 115
Mazza, Debora, 171
McCarthy, C., xii, 51
McCarthy, T., 44, 48, 129–130 n. 5
McLaren, P., 81, 131, 132, 151 n. 7, 171
McPherson, C. B., 33
Melnick, A., 22, 66
Méndez, Durmeval Trigueiro, 175 n. 1
Metalearning, 45, 47
Metaphysical canons, 105
Metaphysical cultural canons, 105–106
Mexico
    consolidation of corporatist state in,
        72–73
    pachuco culture and, 78
    recruitment model of education, 7–8, 15
    technocratic focus of education policy
        makers, 45
    Zapatista movement in Chiapas, 96
Meyer, J., 123
Mezirow, J., 45
Mitchell, Theodore R., 5, 39, 40, 109
Modernism, 33, 39. See also Postmodernism
    critical, 97, 117
    globalization and, 116
    modernization and state corporatism,
        70–73
    political sociology of education and,
        40–41, 57

Morales-Gómez, D. A., 71, 72–73
Morrow, R. A., 3, 4, 9–10, 12–13, 17, 33, 37–
	39, 42–45, 51, 61 n. 1, 82, 89, 104, 117
Morse, K., 9–10
Mouffe, Chantal, 30 n. 5, 38, 85 n. 7, 90–91
Mounier, Emmanuel, 153
Multiculturalism
	critical, 110
	democracy and, 99–112
	in education, 18–20, 99–104
	literature on, 110–111
	theories of, 87, 88
	in the U.S., 99, 110–111
	vision of, 183–185

Naes, A., 51–52
Naïve-transitive consciousness, 143
Nash, K., 30–31 n. 11
National identity, 100, 106
Nation-state. *See also* State
	borderless economy versus, 120–121
	education situated within, 114
	end of, 117–121, 125
Neoconservatism, 56–57, 111
Neoliberalism, ix, xii, xix, xvi, 20, 111. *See
	also* Liberalism
	critical theory versus, 56–57
	critique of, 179–181
	defined, 66
	globalization and, 127–128
	in Latin America, 66–67, 79
Neo-Marxism, 33, 37–38, 54
Network of North American Popular
	Educators, 17
New institutionalists, 123–124
New Right, 6
New School movement, 78
New social movements, ix, 51, 95–97
New Social Order, ix
New World Order, 125–126
Niebrugge-Brantley, J., 46
Nihilism, 111
Nogueira, Adriano, 171
Northern Illinois University, 17
Nuhoglu Soysal, Yasemin, 122, 124–125,
	129 n. 4
Nuñez, I., 79, 80
Nyerere, Julius, 166

Oakes, J., 112 n. 3
O'Cadiz, M. P., 15, 17
O'Donnell, Guillermo, 65

Offe, Claus, 33, 37, 44
Official knowledge, x–xi
Ohliger, J., 152
Ohmae, Kenichi, 70, 117–122
Oligarchical state, 64
Oliveira, Miguel Darcy de, 161, 162, 165
Oliveira, Rosiska D., 161, 162, 165, 169
O'Reilly, B., 69
Organic public sociology (Burawoy),
	xvi–xvii
Ortega y Gasset, M., 175 n. 1
Otherness
	concept of, x, 11, 14, 81, 100
	literacy and, x–xi
	richness of, 106
	in self-consciousness, 134

Paiva, Vanilda Pereira, 153, 175 n. 1, 175 n. 2
Pannu, R. S., 6
Parallelist reproduction theory, 4–5
Pareto, Alfredo, 175 n. 1
Parker, W. C., 18–19
Pateman, Carole, 90, 91, 92, 112 n. 1
Patriarchy, 91
Paulo Freire Institutes, 31 n. 12, 181–182
Paz, Pedro, 156
Pedagogical subjects, 12–13, 73–80, 82, 85
	n. 5
Pedagogy
	of consciousness (Freire), 159–160
	defined, 176 n. 6
	positivist, 58, 131, 150 n. 2
	of the question (Freire), 143
Pedagogy in Process (Freire), 15–16
Pedagogy of the Oppressed (Freire), 11–12, 13,
	15–17, 81, 102, 133–134, 140–150, 153,
	159–160
Pereyra, C., 12–13, 82
Persuasion, critical theory and, 57–58
Pessiot, Erick, 162
Phenomenology of Mind, The (Hegel), 53,
	144–150
Philosophy of history (Marcuse), 36
Pinochet, Augusto, 156–157
Pinto de Acosta, Manuel, 166
Plank, D., 30 n. 9
Political rights, citizenship and, 89, 95–97
Political sociology of education, 1–31, 56–61
	basic question, 1–2
	comprehensive survey of, 3
	critical modernist perspective on, 40–41,
	57

dependent state and. *See* Dependent state
educational policy and, 2–8, 41–43
features of, 41
goal of, 39–40
ideology and, 55–56
key issues of, 2–18
Latin American alternatives, 2, 14–18
need for, 2–8
organic crisis of education in Latin
America, 76–80
politicity of education (Freire), 48–50, 182
state in, 43–44
Popkewitz, T. S., 30 n. 8, 47, 65, 132
Popular education. *See also* Public education
in Latin America
in critical pedagogies, 131–132
defined, 17
models in Latin America, 17, 83
nature of, 10, 13, 63
Portelli, Hugues, 54, 61–62 n. 2
Positivist pedagogy, 58, 131, 150 n. 2
Possessive individualism, 47
Possible Lives (Rose), 60–61
Postcolonialism, x, xi–xiii, 33, 92–94,
161–169
Postimperialism theories, 29 n. 1, 71
Postmodernism, 39, 184. *See also* Modernism
critiques of education policies, 3–4
decline of nation-states and, 117–121, 125
globalization and, 116–121, 125
multicentered notions of power and,
50–51
Postnational citizenship, 122–123
Postrevolutionary state, education in
legitimating, 73
Poststructuralism, 4–5
Poulantzas, N., 55
Poverty. *See also* Social class
in Latin America, 71, 79
nihilism and, 111
street children and, 75–76, 79–80
in the U.S., 74
Power
academy and, xvi
adult education policy and, 7
in critical pedagogies, 131
critical theory of state, 43–44
cultural canons and, 105–106
of curriculum experts, 132
of landowners in Latin America, 65
multicentered notions of, 50–51
multiculturalism and, 100

new social movements and, ix, 51, 95–97
postmodernism and, 50–51
science and, 108
in traditional Western philosophy, 49–50
Practical guiding-knowledge interest, 46
Prebisch, R., 71
Prieto, A., 78
Private education
in Latin America, 79–80
privatization of education, 25, 26
Privatization
in capitalism, 180
of education, 25, 26, 79–80
Prophetic Thought in Postmodern Times
(West), 111
Prophetism, 38
Przeworski, A., 70
Public education in Latin America, 17,
68–84
authoritarianism and, 9, 65–66, 67, 71,
78–79
in comparative perspective, 80–84
funding reductions, 79
pedagogical discourse and, 78–79
pedagogical subject and, 73–80
systems of, 64
Puiggrós, Adriana, 10, 11–12, 63, 64, 68, 73,
75, 76, 78

Quality of education, 10

Raban, L., 67
Racism, critical race theory and, 94–95, 96
Ramirez, F. O., 84 n. 1, 123
Ramos, Guerreiro, 175 n. 1
Rational discourse, Freire and, 147
Reality, as social construction, 106–107
Reciprocity, Habermasian vision of, xvii
Reconstructed educational processes, 84–85
n. 4
Recruitment model of education (Mexico),
7–8, 15
Reductionism, x
Reflecting critically, Freire and, 146–147
Reich, R. B., 70
Reimers, Fernando, 68, 69
Relevance of education, 10
Reproduction theories, 3–5, 55
Resistance, 3–4, 172
Rhoads, R., 28
Ricoeur, P., 37
Rocco, Ray A., 93

Rodrigues, N., 163
Roniger, L., 163
Rose, Mike, 59–61
Rosenthal, G., 67
Rudebeck, L., 162

Saldivar-Hull, S., 92
Samoff, J., 65, 66, 69, 71, 164
Sánchez, Mary, 23
Sanders, T. G., 155
São Tomé e Principe, 162, 164, 166–167
Sarmiento, Domingo Faustino, 13, 79, 82–83
Sartre, J. P., 175 n. 1
Scheller, Max, 175 n. 1
Schiefelbein, E., 68
Schmitter, Philippe C., 72
Schooling. See Education
School reform agendas, 22, 25–28
Schugurensky, D., 6–8, 45
Scott, Joan W., 24, 99, 100, 106, 110
Second Vatican Council, 155
Seeds of Fire (newsletter), 17
Self-actualization, 51
Self-consciousness
    class-consciousness and, 51, 145
    cultural formation and, 139–140
    in dialectic of pedagogy of the oppressed,
        140–144
    in Hegelism, 134–140
    recognition of, 135–136
    servitude as self-conscious, 138, 145
    struggle of opposed consciousness and,
        133, 136–137
Self-emancipation, 183
Semi-intransitive consciousness, 143
Sharing of experience, Freire and, 146–147
Sheris, E., 100, 102
Shor, Ira, 45, 132, 171, 172
Smelser, Neil, 115–116, 129 n. 1
Smith, S. B., 34, 148, 150 n. 3, 151 n. 8
Sobre la Accion Cultural (On Cultural Action)
    (Freire), 146
Social class. See also Poverty
    citizenship and, 89–90
    class-consciousness, 51, 145
    domination based on, 9
    power of landowners in Latin America,
        65
Social construction, 107
Social movements, power and, ix, 51, 95–97
Social rights, citizenship and, 89–90
Social subjects, 12–13, 85 n. 5

Solorzano, Daniel G., 94–95
Sombart, Werner, 52
Sonntag, H. R., 65
Sovereignty, globalization and, 117, 124–125
Spengler, J., 175 n. 1
Spivak, G., xii
Standard criticism of schooling, 5–6
State
    conditioned states, 13, 71–72, 82–83
    defined, 9
    dependent. See Dependent state
    domination between classes or factions,
        9
    educational policy formation and, 43–44
    evolution in Latin America, 9, 64–67,
        70–73
    in Latin America, 9, 64–67, 70–73
    limits of autonomy, 114–115
    as modernizer, 123
    nation-state. See Nation-state
    political authority in Latin America, 9,
        65–66, 67, 71, 78–79
    sociopolitical background of, 67–68
    terrorism and, 123–124
    welfare state. See Welfare state
Street children, 75–76, 79–80
Structuralist models, 3–5
    historical-structural approach to policy
        formation, 42–43
    poststructuralism, 4–5
    structural functionalist models, 42
    structural Marxism, 54–55
Structuration theory, 61 n. 1
Sturzenegger, F., 67
Subjectivity, in critical pedagogies, 131
Subjects
    concept of, 12–13
    pedagogical, 12–13, 73–80, 82, 85 n. 5
    social, 12–13, 85 n. 5
Subordination, xii, 90–91
Sunkel, Osvaldo, 156

Tanzania, 162, 165, 166
    forced modernization model of
        education, 7–8, 15
    technocratic focus of education policy
        makers, 45
Tate, William F., 94, 95, 110
Teachers
    female. See Female teachers
    role in welfare state, 22–23
    unions for. See Teachers unions

Teachers unions, 20–25
  in Latin America, 72
  in the U.S., 30 n. 6
Technology
  in globalization of information, 119–120
  technical guiding-knowledge interest,
    45–48
Teitelbaum, K., xviii
Terrorism, 123–124
Therapeutical model of education (Canada),
  7–8, 15
Therborn, G., 62 n. 3
Thingification, 148
Third World, conditioned states in, 71
Thurow, Lester C., 70, 126, 128
Tiburcio, L., 69
Toledo, C. N. de, 175 n. 1
Torres, Carlos Alberto, 1, 3–6, 8–13, 15, 17, 18,
  20, 25, 28, 29, 30 n. 10, 34, 37, 39–45, 47,
  50, 51, 54, 61 n. 1, 61–62 n. 2, 65, 69, 71–73,
  81–83, 89, 102, 104, 108, 112–113 n. 4, 117,
  121, 129, 132, 133, 151 n. 7, 152, 153, 156,
  157, 161, 163–166, 171, 175 n. 2, 178–186
Torres Santome, J., 132
Touraine, Alain, 30–31 n. 11
Toynbee, Arnold, 175 n. 1
Tracy, Destutt de, 51–52
Transnationalization, 93

Underdevelopment, dependent state and,
  29 n. 1, 70–73
United Nations Development Program
  (UNDF), 67
United Nations Educational, Scientific and
  Cultural Organization (UNESCO), 68, 74
United States
  colonialism and, 112 n. 2
  critical race theory and, 94–95
  demographic traits of educational
    institutions, 104
  multiculturalism in, 99, 110–111
  racism and, 94–95, 96
  reception of Paulo Freire in, 131–132
  teachers unions in, 30 n. 6
  War on Poverty, 74
Unity of difference, 110
Uricoechea, F., 163
Urry, J., 30–31 n. 11
Utopia, 38

Valecillos, O., 65
Verspoor, A., 68
Viera Pinto, Alvaro, 159, 175 n. 1
Vilches, L., 12, 81–82
Villalpando, O., 94–95
Vincent, A., 9
Vogeler, I., 156
Voltaire, xi
Vouchers, 6
Vulgar Marxism, 53–54

Wagner, D., 172
Wallerstein, Immanuel, 71, 105–107, 125
Wanderley, L. E. W., 155
War on Poverty, 74
Weber, Alfred, 175 n. 1
Weber, Max, 33, 44, 47, 52, 129–130 n. 5,
  149–150, 175 n. 1
Weinberg, G., 11, 81
Weiner, L., 127, 128
Weis, L., ix
Welfare policies
  defined, 30 n. 8
  in Latin America, 65
Welfare state
  capitalism and, 180
  defined, 30 n. 8
  in Latin America, 64, 65
  teacher role in, 22–23
Weltanschauung
  nature of, 52, 61–62 n. 2, 174
  political philosophy and, 51–52
Welton, M., 45
West, Cornel, 99–100, 102, 111
Westernization process
  capitalism and, 116–117
  nation-state and, 123
  worldview in, 168
White Eurocentric feminism, 92
Wilensky, H. L., 30 n. 8, 65
Williams, R., x
Wittgenstein, L., xi
Wong, P. L., 15, 17
Wong, T. H., xiii
World Bank, 14, 21, 66, 70, 83
World Council of Churches, 157
World-system analysis, 71, 125

Young, Robert, xii–xiii

About the Author

Carlos Alberto Torres is Professor of Social Sciences and Comparative Education, and Director of the Paulo Freire Institute at UCLA. From 1995 to 2005 he served as Director of the UCLA Latin American Center. He is also the Founding Director of the Paulo Freire Institute in São Paulo, Brazil (1991), UCLA (2002), and Buenos Aires, Argentina (2003). He served as *ad-honorem* advisor to Paulo Freire during his tenure as Secretary of Education of the City of São Paulo (1989–1991). Among his many honors, he received the National Academy of Education Spencer Postdoctoral Fellowship (1991–1992).

Dr. Torres has been a Visiting Professor in universities in North America, Latin America, Europe, Asia, the Middle East and Africa. Dr. Torres' major areas of inquiry include research on policy, educational reform, and comparative education. His policy research focuses on issues of equality, equity, and efficiency in elementary, secondary, and higher education. Likewise, he focuses on the impact of globalization in the life of teachers in several regions of the world. His past research focused on the cognitive, social, and political returns of literacy training and state policies as compensatory legitimation

Dr. Torres' theoretical and empirical research has resulted in the development of a political sociology of education highlighted in his much-heralded book with Raymond Morrow, *Social Theory and Education*. He is considered one of the world's leading authorities on Latin American education, and, jointly with Moacir Gadotti, the principal biographers of Paulo Freire, Brazilian philosopher and critical social theorist.

Dr. Torres has authored more than 60 books, and more than 200 research articles, chapters in books, and entries in encyclopedias, in several languages. Most recently he has published several works of fiction, including a novel in Portuguese, and in Spanish a book of short stories and a book of poetry.